# QUEER HEROES

## OF THE NORTH SHORE

1977

## FOUR CENTURIES OF LOVE, REBELLION AND SURVIVAL

### (BLACK + WHITE EDITION)

2011

# Jim Moser

**QUEER HEROES OF THE NORTH SHORE**
**Four Centuries of Love, Rebellion and Survival**
**(Black & White Edition)**



Published by Deer Hill Press
Lynn, Massachusetts

Publisher's Cataloging-in-Publication data is available.
ISBN: 979-8-9948169-3-6 (Paperback, Black & White)
ISBN: 979-8-9948169-0-5 (Paperback,  Color)
ISBN: 979-8-9948169-2-9 (Hardcover, Premium Color)
ISBN: 979-8-9948169-1-2 (E-book)

Library of Congress Control Number: 2026903264

Cover design by the Author, Rev. Donna Spencer Collins and Gemini AI.
Interior design by the Author.

First Edition
Printed in the United States of America.

To every person

who has taken the risk to live authentically,

and to my husband Billy.

Of all the histories I could tell, ours is my favorite.

# CONTENTS

# Preface

You may know the feeling. It sits in the pit of your stomach in a crowded school cafeteria or keeps you awake in a silent bedroom while the rest of the house sleeps. It is the gnawing sense that you are a mistake, a glitch in the design. *I'm different. I don't belong. No one else feels like this.*

Let me stop you right there. You are not a glitch. You are part of a lineage.

You belong to a queer family with a deep, defiant, and exciting ancestry. We have lived in every era, walked every cobblestone street, and sailed every harbor of the North Shore. We have always been here—more numerous, more resilient, and more extraordinary than the history books have allowed us to know. For centuries, our stories have been erased, sanitized, or locked in the closet. But if you listen closely to the whispers of our past, you will hear us. We are the inventors who built castles on the rocks; we are the "spinsters" who wove lives of radical independence; we are the drag queens who sashayed through the grit of industrial cities in six-inch heels.

I am flipping the script. For too long, historians have operated under the presumption of "straight until proven queer," demanding irrefutable proof before allowing someone to be named as one of us. I refuse to play by those rules. I am interpreting history through a rainbow lens. While I acknowledge that gender and sexuality are concepts that shift over time, and that labeling the past is a contentious act, I lean into these stories because the alternative is silence.

This book is narrative history—it is the story of the human heart. To bring these lives to life, I have sometimes placed myself in the room, imagining the details that historical documents omit. You will see these moments marked by the phrase, "You can imagine...." Some may call it fiction; I call it a refusal to let the archives bury the truth.

Each chapter stands alone. They can be read in any order. This approach causes some repetition. The "North Shore" refers to all of Essex County, Massachusetts and not just the coast.

In these pages, you will meet "heroes." A hero is simply anyone who lived authentically in the face of adversity—anyone who took the risk to be their true self in a world that demanded conformity. You will see them gathered under the word "Queer." Once a slur used to wound us, we have reclaimed it as a badge of honor. It is a broad umbrella that loosens the rigid labels of the alphabet soup, making room for anyone whose spirit was too large for the constraints of a patriarchal society. When I call an ancestor queer, I am using my language, not theirs, but I use it as a compliment. It means they refused to fit into a box that was too small.

I write this as a cisgender gay white male, fully aware of the privilege that allows me to hold the pen. The archives are biased toward the wealthy and the artistic. While we can learn much from the "Lavender Aristocracy" who built mansions in Gloucester, we must never forget the countless queer people of color, working-class individuals and enslaved people who lived, loved, and left no record. The North Shore has no shortage of queer heroes.

Many amazing people are missing from this book. That is necessary, and I apologize. History is a kaleidoscope, not a monologue. In these pages, I offer snapshots—single stories told from specific perspectives—fully aware that every event contains a multitude of voices. Think of this book as a trailhead rather than a map; it is an invitation to dig deeper. Though I sometimes step back to reveal broader context, this book makes no claim to be exhaustive. It is not a catalog of names and dates, but an homage to individuals and the singular lives they lived.

Our story on the North Shore is a movement from silence to rebellion, and finally to the building of a brave new world. It begins in the severe cold of the Puritan colonies, where deviation was punished by the stocks or the gallows. It moves to the "Glass Closet" of the Gilded Age, where America's preeminent scientists and artists—titans like John Hays Hammond Jr. and Henry Davis Sleeper—used their immense wealth to build private sanctuaries like Hammond Castle and Beauport, hiding their loves in plain sight.

And then, the explosion. The story moves to Lynn, a city of grit and glory that became the unlikely capital of queer life. Long before the term "sanctuary city" existed, Lynn was one, supporting 19 queer bars, including The Light House Café (later Fran's Place). For 79 years, it stood as the oldest queer bar in Massachusetts, surviving police raids and the Great Lynn Fire to remain a beacon in the night.

This region has produced giants. We claim America's first same-sex marriage license, granted to Lynn union activists Marcia Hams and Susan Shepherd. We claim world champions like boxer Rashida Ellis and Tony Award-winners like Alex Newell. We claim political trailblazers like Coco Alinsug and Tiffany Magnolia, who proved that queer people belong in the seats of power. And we proudly claim our Governor, Maura Healey, who traces her roots to this rocky coast.

But this history isn't just a victory lap. It is a warning.

Progress is never guaranteed. Today, the rights our ancestors fought for are being clawed back. Books are being banned. Political language is sharpening into violence. Our enemies are attempting to build a new closet to contain us. That is why I wrote this book. I want every queer young person to know that they belong. I wish I had a book like this when I was growing up.

History teaches us that we have survived worse than this. We have survived plagues, violence and the silent smothering of the 1950s. We have never stopped fighting back, and we have never stopped dancing.

So, here is the call. The baton is being passed to you.

Become your own queer hero. Live your truest, bravest self. Stand up to adversity when you see it in your school, your workplace, or your town square. Protect your community. Register to vote. Run for office. Make history.

You are not alone. You are the latest chapter in a story that has been underway for 400 years. Now, turn the page and meet your family.

Jim Moser
Deer Hill
Lynn, MA
March 15, 2026


Contact me: https://queerheroesnorthshore.my.canva.site/

See new stories or add your own: https://www.facebook.com/
  groups/queerhistorynorthshore

# ONE

## Spirits & Secrets

1600 - 1800

In the beginning, history books offer only a cold silence, depicting the North Shore as the exclusive domain of the rigid, straight Puritan. But this silence is deliberate erasure. Long before colonizers, Indigenous peoples viewed gender not as a wall, but as a river, honoring those who walked between genders with reverence where settlers saw only sin.

When the settlers arrived, that reverence was replaced by scorn. The "queer" spirit was forced underground, surviving in the shadows of barns and in intense "romantic friendships" that defied platonic boundaries.

Yet, some silences are deeper. We must acknowledge unnamed women whose intimacies were doubly erased—first by a society ignoring female agency, then by historians deeming them unworthy of record. Similarly, the lives of enslaved people remain largely unwritten.

To find these ancestors, we must become detectives of the heart. We must read between the lines of court documents and decipher the coded language of letters. We were here, surviving in the silence, waiting for us to find them.

# Two Spirit

SHERRY SMILING OTTER GAGNE & JESSIE LITTLE FEATHER PENN

The scent of burning sage is ancient, a sharp, cleansing earthiness that cuts through time as easily as it cuts through the salt air of the North Shore. In a photograph that captures a moment of profound reclamation, Jessie Little Feather Penn places a ring on the finger of her beloved, Sherry Smiling Otter Gagne, surrounded by the sacred smoke. They are not merely getting married in the modern sense of a civil union; they are enacting a ceremony of balance that predates the very concept of "Massachusetts." They are Two-Spirit. To look at them is to see the survival of a worldview that the earliest European settlers tried to burn out of existence, a living testament that the Spirit, once silenced, has found its voice again.

> *In the eyes of their ancestors, this was not a confusion of biology, but a surplus of power.*

To understand the ground upon which we walk, we must first unlearn the myth of the empty wilderness. Open an early map of Gloucester harbor, drawn by the hands of European explorers like Samuel de Champlain. It does not show a desolate, lonely coastline waiting for civilization. Instead, it reveals a bustling, populated network of settlements ringing the water, smoke rising from hundreds of wigwams and cornfields stretching toward the sun. This was the home of the Pawtucket people. They were the stewards of Agawam, the "place across the marsh," now Ipswich, and

Naumkeag, the "fishing place," now Salem. For thousands of years, they lived in a society where everything had a Spirit, and everything had a place—including those who walked between the worlds of men and women.

> *Because they embodied this duality, Two Spirit people were trusted to bridge the divide between the sexes and bring balance to the community.*

The term "Two Spirit" is a modern English placeholder, adopted in 1990 to describe an ancient reality documented among more than 130 tribes across North America. It is not simply a synonym for 'gay' or 'transgender'—to name just two of many identities. As Sherry and Jessie explain, it is a spiritual distinction as much as a gendered one. It describes a person whose body houses both a masculine and

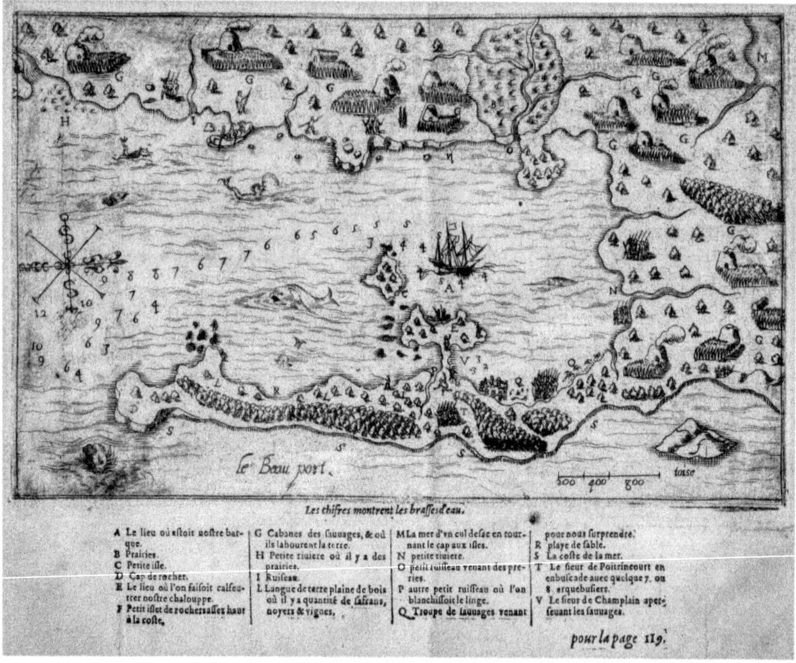


Samuel de Champlain's 1606 map depicts numerous Pawtucket settlements thriving around modern-day Gloucester Harbor.

a feminine Spirit. In the eyes of their ancestors, this was not a confusion of biology, but a surplus of power. Because they possessed this duality, Two Spirit people were viewed as the "social workers" of their time. They were the distinct, honored weavers of the social fabric, trusted to bridge the divide between the sexes and restore balance in the community.

However, a catastrophic silence fell upon this land in the early 17th century. Between 1616 and 1633, "virgin soil epidemics" of smallpox and influenza tore through the Pawtucket villages like a wildfire, claiming up to 90% of the population. The thriving harbor settlements turned into graveyards. The survivors were scattered, forced to move or live on the margins of a new, severe colonial order—an order that brought with it a strict, unforgiving gender binary. The Puritan world had no room for fluidity, no patience for the sacredness of ambiguity. In the collision of this apocalyptic loss and colonial intolerance, the specific rituals of the Pawtucket Two Spirit traditions were largely lost to history.

*The binary world is an invention. Fluidity is the natural state of this land.*

But silence is not the same as absence. The bloodlines endured, and so did the Spirits. Today, Sherry and Jessie embody that resilience. Sherry, who traces her roots to the Mohawk, Abenaki and Choctaw Nations, as well as French Canadian settlers, grew up feeling she never fit the boxes of "male" or "female." It wasn't until she attended a powwow and learned the term Two Spirit that she finally felt she could breathe. Jessie, who is White Mountain Apache and Navajo, comes from a long line of medicine people. In their lives and in their union, they are bringing the Two Spirit concept back to the North Shore. They remind us that the "queer" history of this region does not begin with the first queer bar or the first Pride parade. It begins here, in the wigwams that once dotted the coastline, where gender was not a wall, but a river.

When Sherry speaks of her identity, she describes a sensation of wholeness rather than fragmentation. To be Two Spirit is to be a vessel of mediation. In Indigenous cultures, these individuals were often healers, psychics, and seers, and were revered as highly as chiefs. They were the ones who could look at a problem from all angles, the ones who could stitch together the torn edges of a community. By reclaiming this title and living it openly, Sherry and Jessie are performing a modern act of healing. They are telling the Indigenous and queer youth of today that their feelings of being "different" are actually a connection to a sacred lineage of power.

Some tribes and nations have a place for Two Spirit folks to move into the gender roles of the opposite gender.  For the Diné of the

Jesse Little Feather Penn, right, places a wedding ring on Sherry Smiling Otter's finger.

Navajo Nation, for example, someone can identify as Two Spirit, which we might call bi, or as Two Spirit, which we might call trans.

We begin our journey here, with the First People, because to understand the queer history of the North Shore, we must understand that the binary world is an invention. Fluidity is the natural state of this land. Before the church bells rang in the steeples of Salem or Lynn, drums beat a rhythm that honored the masculine and the feminine in equal measure. As we move forward through centuries of secrecy and eventual rebellion, remember the image of Sherry and Jessie standing in the sage smoke. They are the bridge. They are proof that no matter how hard history tries to enforce a single story, the human spirit is vast enough to contain multitudes. The Pawtucket may have been silenced by plague and prejudice, but the land remembers. Today, through the continuing lives of Two Spirit people, the circle is finally beginning to mend.

https://historicipswich.net/native-americans-of-the-massachusetts-north-shore/

https://www.capeannmuseum.org/about/history-of-the-museum/history-of-cape-ann/

# Passionate Brotherhood

On a freezing dock in 1630, moments before boarding the *Arbella* to found a new nation, the man who would become the stern face of Puritan authority was weeping. John Winthrop (1588 - 1649) held his friend Sir William Springe in a final, desperate embrace, and later confessed in a letter that his soul was "knit" to Springe's, like the biblical Jonathan to David. He wrote of wanting to "bedew that sweet bosom with the tears of affection," a raw, physical declaration of male love that shatters our modern image of the stiff-collared patriarch. While history has painted Winthrop as the ultimate heteronormative authority figure, a closer examination of his private letters reveals a man deeply immersed in a culture of "romantic friendship," where the love between men was expressed with a physical and spiritual fervor that challenges our modern definitions of straight and queer.

Winthrop led the fleet that landed in Salem in 1630, and his vision shaped the lives of every settler from Ipswich to

John Winthrop.

Lynn. Yet, the emotional blueprint for this colony was drafted in the arms of his male friends.

> *I love thee such as I can not express... my soul is knit to yours.*

This language—of souls knitting and weeping upon bosoms—was not merely poetic; it was a radical expression of intimacy. As historian Richard Godbeer argues, Winthrop was a practitioner of a "passionate brotherhood" where men's love for men was considered a holy virtue, second only to the love of God. By invoking the biblical couple David and Jonathan, Winthrop legitimized a form of same-sex desire that prioritized male companionship above the "weaker" bonds of marriage. In his famous sermon "A Model of Christian Charity," he argued that the colonists must be "knit together" in love, effectively prescribing this homoeroticized spiritual bond as the glue that holds the state together. To include Winthrop in a queer history is to reclaim the "overflowing" male heart from the rigidity of the past, acknowledging a time when a man could build a nation while weeping for the touch of his beloved friend.

Godbeer, Richard. The overflowing of friendship : love between men and the creation of the American republic

# A Quarrelsome Witch

The carpenter William Osgood was terrified, but John Godfrey (c. 1622–1675) was laughing. Skipping around the frame of the unfinished barn in Newbury, the rugged herdsman taunted his neighbor with wild, dangerous claims, shouting, "I profess! I profess!" when asked if he had made a deal with the Devil. He also boasted that the Devil would drain the beer from every cellar in town. In a 1640s society that demanded rigid order, Godfrey was a chaotic storm of aggression, fighting over boys and cattle with equal fervor and using the fear of witchcraft as a shield for his own defiant bachelorhood. In a Puritan society that demanded rigid conformity, marriage and family, Godfrey stood apart—a "masterless man" who

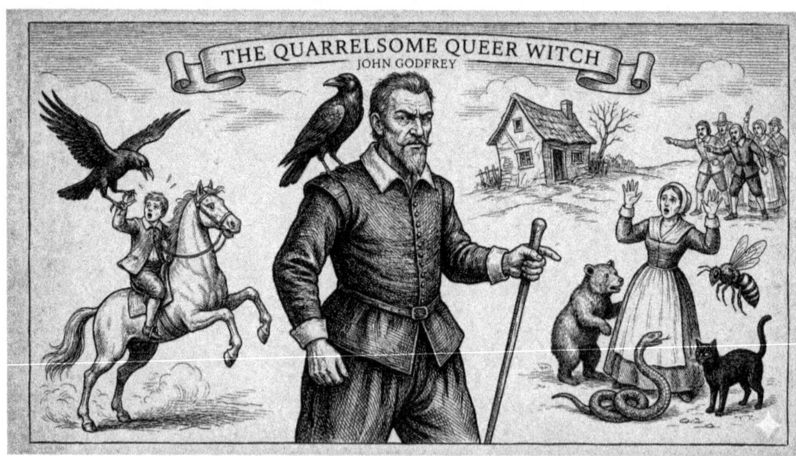



John Godfrey was tried for witchcraft four times and was probably gay.

never married, never settled and seemingly thrived on conflict. If, as historian John Demos suggests, Godfrey was gay—or the 17th-century equivalent—his survival strategy was not to hide in the corner, but to hide in plain sight behind a mask of aggressiveness .

*I profess! I profess! ... The Devil will drain every cellar in town!*


Godfrey chose the life of a herdsman, a profession that offered him the safety of solitude in the fields and woods. This itinerant existence took him on a restless tour of Essex County—from Newbury to Rowley, Ipswich, Andover, Salem and Haverhill. But he could not avoid human contact forever. When he did interact, it was often explosive. He was involved in no fewer than 130 court cases during his life, appearing as both plaintiff and defendant. He sued neighbors for slander and uncollected debts, while facing charges ranging from cursing and drunkenness to witchcraft. As one weary contemporary noted, Godfrey sought "peace with no man."

To the pious families of the North Shore, this wandering bachelor was terrifyingly "other." In the 17th century, difference was easily rebranded as witchcraft, and Godfrey, perhaps sensing that fear was a form of power, seemed to lean into the role. He tormented his neighbors with dark boasts, claiming that a witch could kill a creature just by looking "steadfastly" upon it.

The terror he inspired hallucinated its way into the court records. Witnesses swore that when he yawned in church, they saw a teat hidden under his tongue to suckle spirits. Neighbors accused him of causing their cattle and other animals to sicken and die mysteriously. Isabelle Holdred of Haverhill testified that after arguing with Godfrey, she was besieged by a nightmare menagerie: first a bumblebee, then a growling bear, then a snake that stole her voice, then a spectral horse and finally a large black cat that lay on her chest, stroking her face while she slept.

But the most searing incident—the one that rips the veil off his "queer" identity—involved a fifteen-year-old boy named John Remington Jr. After Godfrey was refused a job herding the Remington cattle, the boy was attacked by a great crow with a "very great bill" that knocked his horse to the ground. When Godfrey confronted the terrified teenager later, he didn't just threaten him with magic; he used a specific, sexually charged insult, sneering, "Every c#ck-eating boy must ride."

This wasn't just a curse; it was a window into a hidden life. As Demos speculates, this phrase hints at a man familiar with the rough, underground language of forbidden desire. Godfrey's compulsive conflicts with men, often fighting over the affection or control of boys and cattle, suggest a "reaction formation"—a desperate psychological defense where he attacked the very connections he craved but could never openly have.

Godfrey was tried for witchcraft four times—in 1658, 1659, 1666 and 1669, decades before the 1692 Salem Witch Trials. In a world that hanged people for far less, he was never convicted. Perhaps his sheer audacity saved him, or perhaps his legal maneuvering baffled the magistrates. He died in 1675, likely in Boston. He left his estate, which included 100 acres in Haverhill, to two men who had cared for him in his final days.

Walk down Essex Street in Salem today, and you will see a world Godfrey could only have dreamed of in his fevered, lonely wanderings. Witches and rainbow flags are everywhere. The word "witch" has been reclaimed as a badge of power, "queer" has been reclaimed as a badge of pride, and some Salem residents identify as both. John Godfrey, the queer, quarrelsome, outcast herdsman of the North Shore, was a pioneer of this defiance. He refused to be erased. He fought, he sued and he "professed," proving that even in the darkest times, the marginalized could find a way to make their presence felt.

Demos, John. Entertaining Satan: Witchcraft and the Culture of Early New England.

Witches frrom the Cabot Kent Hermetic Temple march at North Shore Pride.

# Matelotage

ROBERT CULLIFORD & JOHN SWANN

The gold ring splintered the sunlight, flashing against the granite backdrop of the Cape Ann coast. Taking the band in his calloused hand, the seasoned pirate looked into the eyes of his beloved and echoed the solemn vow: "I take you for my consort and my brother. From this day, we share one purse and one fate. If I fall, my share is yours. If you fall, your share is mine. We stand together against the world, for all time." The contract was formally sealed with ink and a draught of rum, followed by a fierce embrace as the deck gently pitched beneath their boots. Around them, the crew raised their cutlasses and roared a huzzah, their cheers carried away by the salt breeze.

*Together for all time.*

Matelotage was a formal partnership between sailors or pirates, similar in many ways to modern same-sex marriage.

In the cramped, swaying world of the fo'c'sle, privacy was a rare treasure. Yet, in the months prior, the two men had found themselves drawn together in the dark. What began as accidental brushes in the rigging turned into stolen glances across the mess deck. One night, in the stifling heat below, the tension broke, and passion overtook them. Since that moment, their trust had been forged into iron. Now, they were officially joined in matelotage—a binding brotherhood for high-seas outlaws. They would pool their plunder, inherit the other's share should death come calling and fight back-to-back against any merchant ship that dared cross their bow. The English slang "mate" (friend) originated from the Middle Dutch word mattenoot (bed partner/bunk companion).

*"Mate" comes from "matelotage," a bed partner.*

The best-documented instance of matelotage, one that likely brushed these very shores, was between Robert Culliford and John Swann. Court records from 1699 explicitly describe "John Swann, a great consort of Culliford's, who lives with him." Forged in the fires of a prisoner-of-war camp in India, their bond survived escape and the high seas, eventually leading them to establish a domestic household on St. Mary's Island, a pirate haven off Madagascar. However, Culliford's wake likely washed against the North Shore. Around 1690, before his Indian Ocean infamy, Culliford held a privateer's commission out of New York to hunt the French. To reach his targets in Acadia, he would have tacked his ship past the North Shore. Though no logbook records them dropping anchor for a tankard in Salem, unconfirmed rumors persist that Culliford eventually retired to Boston, hiding in plain sight just miles from the rocky hills of Lynn.

While the Puritan magistrates of Massachusetts would have hanged men for such a union, the waters of the North Shore were no stranger to pirates.

- Captain John Quelch (1703): The "Marblehead Mutineer" who boldly walked the streets of Marblehead before his capture,

- Thomas Veal (1658): The fugitive of Dungeon Rock in Lynn, buried alive with his treasure by an earthquake,

- John Phillips (1723): The "Newburyport Menace," whose reign of terror ended when his own men turned on him,

- Edward Low (1722): The "Psychopath of the Seas," known for his brutality in the waters off Marblehead.

Not all tales of love and the sea involved two men. Local lore tells the gender-bending story of Fanny Campbell and William Lovell, neighbors near High Rock in Lynn. William, dreaming of command, signed aboard a merchantman bound for the West Indies, only to be captured by pirates and later imprisoned in Cuba. Fanny waited two long years until a bedraggled sailor named Jack Herbert arrived with a letter from Lovell. Fanny didn't weep; she plotted. She grilled Herbert about the prison's defenses and made him swear to wait for a man named Channing, who would lead a rescue mission.

Fanny Campbell, female pirate captain, 1844.

True to her word, "Channing"—Fanny herself, disguised in breeches and a tricorne hat—signed onto a ship with Herbert. Channing was made second mate, and when he learned that the captain planned to sail to England and press the crew into the Royal Navy, Channing incited a mutiny. Seizing the helm, Channing sailed for Cuba. The loyal crew stormed the prison and liberated William. Once safe aboard the ship, Captain Channing summoned the bewildered William to the captain's cabin. There, the "Captain" threw off the heavy coat, embraced him and showered him with kisses. It took a moment for the shock to fade before William realized the dashing officer was his own beloved Fanny. They sailed the prize home, docked in Marblehead and returned to Lynn to raise a family—a testament that on the high seas, love is the only true captain.

Fanny is the protagonist of a 1844 swashbuckling adventure novel titled *Fanny Campbell: The Female Pirate Captain*. In 1844, women in fiction were usually damsels in distress. Fanny was a cross-dressing captain, a sword-fighter and the rescuer of her boyfriend— a very progressive character for the time.

Burg, B.R. Sodomy and the Pirate Tradition: English Sea Rovers in the Seventeenth-Century Caribbean.

# Severely Whipped

Dorothie Hoyt loved to wear trousers — and those trousers got her into a great deal of trouble.

One imagines that since she was a little girl, Dorothie preferred boys' clothing. No amount of scolding from her parents could dissuade her. The neighbors whispered, the ministers warned, but still she refused to stop. Something deep within her insisted on living differently, even in a place and time where conformity was demanded at the point of the whip.

By the autumn of 1677, the elders of the Puritan colony in Essex County had had enough. They convened a court in Salem, and on October 9, they sentenced Dorothie "to be severely whipped" for wearing men's clothing. Dorothie, however, left the county before judgment could be carried out. Her father, John Hoyt, who sat on the very jury that condemned her, declared that she had repented. The court spared her the whip, provided he pay a fine "in corn or money."

Dorothie Hoyt was convicted of wearing men's clothing in 1677.

Whether Dorothie ever returned to Essex County, we do not know. What we do know is that she refused to bow quietly to a world that demanded she be someone else.

Transgender and gender-nonconforming people have existed throughout human history. We can't know whether Dorothie would have called herself a trans man by today's language, but we should not assume she was not. The persistence with which she wore trousers, despite public shaming and threat of violence, suggests that this was far more than a matter of convenience.

*Whipped... for unseemly practices betwixt her and another maid.*

Dorothie was not alone. In seventeenth-century Essex County, others were punished for bending gender and sexual norms. In 1652, Joseph Davis of Haverhill was convicted "for putting on women's apparel and going from house to house in the nighttime with a female." A few years earlier, in 1642, Elizabeth Johnson was sentenced "to be severely whipped and fined 5 li. for unseemly practices betwixt her and another maid." By 1695, the Massachusetts colony had passed a law explicitly banning cross-dressing—evidence, perhaps, of how many people were defying the rigid gender codes of the time. But crossdressing did not stop. A century later, in the Dogtown section of Gloucester, which was once an Indigenous settlement, a freed mulatto enslaved person named Old Ruth, who dressed as a man and called herself John Woodman, built some of the town's stone walls. Also in Dogtown, Sammy Stanley was raised wearing girls' clothing and later took traditionally female roles, becoming a washerwoman in Rockport.

We may never know what became of Dorothie after her flight from Essex County. Her story vanishes into the archival silence that so often swallows the lives of those who defy the rules. Yet, 350 years later, the echoes of her defiance remain. Trans people are still punished, still misunderstood, still fighting to live authentically— just as Dorothie once did, in her forbidden trousers.

https://npshistory.com/publications/nhl/theme-studies/lgbtq-america.pdf

Sammy Stanley—who beat women! (at their own game)

Sammy Stanley was raised wearing girls' clothing and later took traditionally female roles, becoming a washerwoman in Rockport.

# A Man of Secrets

Night after night, by the flickering light of a candle in his Salem study, the Reverend William Bentley (1759 - 1819) poured his true self into the pages of his massive diary. While the town knew him as the busy, charitable pastor of the East Church, the ink on his private pages told a different story—chronicling his "watchful anxiety" over handsome young captains and his fascination with a "well-proportioned" male servant from India. Here, in the safety of his journals, the bachelor minister documented the "curious habits" of

Rev. William Bentley chronicled Captain John Gibaut's life.

a male-centered world that history has largely ignored. He was the town's intellectual engine, a polymath whose accomplishments were staggering. He possessed the second-best private library in the United States, surpassed only by that of Thomas Jefferson's, and he pioneered American journalism through his widely read columns in the *Salem*

*Gazette*. He was a man of immense public virtue, famously giving away half his salary to the poor and prioritizing good works over rigid doctrine.

> *In the flickering light of his study, the ink told a different story than the pulpit.*

But to the discerning eye, Bentley was also a man of secrets. A lifelong bachelor in a profession that almost mandated marriage, he built a life that was quietly, defiantly non-conforming. He created a domestic sphere that excluded women almost entirely, filling his home instead with books, specimens and a succession of young men whose "curious habits" he noted with a protective, coded affection. His massive diaries reveal a heart far more involved than that of a mere mentor. He formed a profound, life-altering attachment to a young man named Captain John Gibaut, a protégé he described as having an aversion to the "labours of society."

Bentley chronicled Gibaut's life with a watchful anxiety, documenting Gibaut's "greatest intimacy" with Captain George Girdler Smith. When the two captains separated in a "family dispute," Bentley inserted himself as the mediator. His diary is filled with "artfully revealing references" to the queer undercurrents of this male-centric world, including accounts of Gibaut hosting a "curious female adventurer" with a masculine name and bringing home a "well-proportioned" male servant from India whose beauty Bentley described in striking detail. Bentley lived in what historians describe as a "homosocial" world, navigating the "don't ask, don't tell" waters of the Federal period with remarkable skill. His legacy is his diary itself: a monument to a life lived on one's own terms, finding fulfillment not in the conventional family, but in the quiet, shared intimacies of a male-centered world in the heart of historic Salem.

Sargent, William R.,"Rev. Bentley's Man of Curious Habits"

# TWO

## Spinsters & Bachelors

1800 - 1900

The 19th century brought a shifting wind to the North Shore. As the rigid theology of the Puritans began to wane, it was replaced by a radical new idea: the divinity of the individual self. In this era, the "queer" spirit moved from the shadows of the barn to the parlors of high society and the pages of classic literature. It was the age of the "romantic friendship" and the "Boston marriage," a time when men

and women carved out domestic sanctuaries that defied the strict expectations of nineteenth-century life.

Here, "spinsters" were not lonely outcasts, but independent women like Sarah Orne Jewett and Annie Adams Fields who built lives of "absorbing affectionate intimacy" by the sea. "Bachelors" were not merely unmarried men, but souls like Henry Wadsworth Longfellow and Charles Sumner, whose profound emotional bonds sustained them through the tumult of the Civil War. They did not have our modern vocabulary—they didn't say "gay" or "lesbian"— but they spoke the language of the soul, penning letters of burning devotion and living in unions as absolute as any marriage.

Sparse records do not indicate absence. Amidst suffragists and Black abolitionists, queer lives were undoubtedly woven into the struggle for liberation on multiple fronts.

This section celebrates the pioneers who used their art, their wealth and their sheer brilliance to live authentically in a world that had no sanctioned place for them. From the transcendentalists who found God in their own desires to the industrial city that paused to gawk at the velvet-clad Oscar Wilde, these heroes proved that love, when true, creates its own legitimacy.

# Transcendentalism

RALPH WALDO EMERSON

In the noisy, chaotic commons of Harvard College, the young Ralph Waldo Emerson (1803–1882) sat frozen, his fork hovering over his plate. He wasn't looking at his books; he was staring, transfixed, at a freshman named Martin Gay. He later confessed to his journal that he felt "singular sensations" and "vivid pleasure" just from watching the younger man move across the room.

To the world, Emerson would become the "Sage of Concord," a marble bust of a man known for his cool, detached wisdom. But in the private fever of his youth, he was trembling. He wrote of Gay with a frantic, breathless intensity: "I have a strange passion for him. .. I cannot help it." He didn't speak to Gay; he stalked him with his eyes, exchanging "ocular conversations" that left him breathless. When the feelings became too dangerous to hold, he tried to erase them—literally crossing out the frantic entries in his journals with heavy ink, attempting to bury the evidence of a heart that beat wildly for other men.

This act of censorship reveals the true architecture of his philosophy. Emerson didn't just write about "Self-Reliance" and "Friendship" as abstract concepts; he forged them as armor. He seems to have sublimated his terrifying, forbidden desires into a high-minded spiritual code, transforming the specific ache for a male body into a universal ache for the "Over-Soul."

The North Shore became a sanctuary for this divided soul. Emerson was a frequent visitor to Pigeon Cove in Rockport, a place where the granite coastline was as rugged and guarded as he was. Here, away from Cambridge and Concord, he could breathe. The ocean offered a vast, safe companion for his solitude. He also lectured frequently at the Gloucester Lyceum, feeding the intellectual hunger of a maritime community that understood the power of storms. The Emerson Inn in Rockport stands today as a physical testament to his time there, named in his honor after he vacationed there with his family and fellow Transcendentalist (and queer icon) Henry David Thoreau.

His accomplishments are the bedrock of American identity; his essays, such as *Nature* and *The American Scholar,* championed the inherent divinity of the individual. But viewed through a queer lens, his most famous commands take on a heartbreaking resonance. When Emerson urges us to "trust thyself" and to reject the "names and customs" of society, he is not just speaking to the pioneer or the poet. He is speaking to the boy in the Harvard Commons, paralyzed by a love he cannot name, urging him—and us—to be true to our nature, no matter how unconventional it may be.

Ralph Waldo Emerson was captivated by Martin Gay.

Crain, Caleb. American Sympathy: Men, Friendship, and Literature in the New Nation

http://www.elisarolle.com/queerplaces/pqrst/Ralph%20Waldo%20Emerson.html

# Flagon of Life

Nathaniel Hawthorne & Herman Melville

The letter arrived from the Berkshires like a lightning bolt, carrying an offer of love so intense it threatened to burn Nathaniel Hawthorne's (1804–1864) carefully constructed walls to the ground. Herman Melville (1819–1891), wild and desperate for connection, had written to him of an "infinite fraternity of feeling," declaring, "Whence come you, Hawthorne? By what right do you drink from my flagon of life?" Panic set in. For a man raised in the guilt-ridden shadow of the Salem Witch Trials, this invitation to merge souls was not a gift, but a terrifying danger that would send

Nathaniel Hawthorne.

him fleeing back into silence. To understand why Nathaniel Hawthorne, one of the greatest fiction writers of 19th-century American literature." and author of *The Scarlet Letter* and *The House of the Seven Gables*, ultimately fled from the intense love offered by Herman Melville, one must look to the gray, salt-crusted streets of Salem. It was here, in the grim shadow of the

Witch City, that Hawthorne's psyche was forged in a kiln of guilt and silence.

He was born Nathaniel Hathorne, the great-great-grandson of John Hathorne, the only judge in the Salem Witch Trials who never repented for his role in the executions. The weight of this blood legacy was so heavy that Nathaniel added the "w" to his surname, a linguistic shield to distance himself from the "hanging judge." But Salem taught him a lesson that would define his queer life: that "secret sin" is the deadliest force on earth and that safety lies only in concealment.

*By what right do you drink from my flagon of life?*

This instinct for hiding was cemented during his "twelve dark years" in the attic of his mother's house on Herbert Street. After graduating from Bowdoin, while his classmates went on to become senators and naval commanders, Hawthorne returned to Salem and locked himself away. For over a decade, he lived as a ghost in his own home, eating meals left outside his door and walking the streets only at night. He later wrote that he was "the obscurest man of letters in America," a prisoner in a "haunted chamber" where he waited for the world to learn his name. These years of solitary confinement warped him; he learned to observe life through a windowpane, craving intimacy but terrified of the exposure that came with it. Although Hawthorne later married and raised a family, part of him must have remained locked up.

That wall of reserve was nearly battered down in 1850, when Hawthorne escaped the North Shore for the Berkshires and met Herman Melville. Melville was the anti-Salem: wild, oceanic and desperate for connection. He saw in Hawthorne a soulmate, a "dark brother" who understood the shadows. Melville pursued Hawthorne with a ferocity that shattered Victorian conventions. He wrote letters that sweat with intellectual and romantic desperation, declaring: "Whence come you, Hawthorne? By what right do you drink from my flagon of life? And when I put it to my lips—lo, they are yours and not mine. I feel that the Godhead is broken up like the bread at the Supper, that we are the pieces."

Melville dedicated the first edition of *Moby Dick* to Hawthorne: "In token of my admiration for his genius this book is inscribed to Nathaniel Hawthorne."

For a brief window, the ice of the North Shore melted. Hawthorne allowed Melville into his life, the two of them spending hours in the barn smoking cigars and lying in the hay, discussing eternity. Melville pushed further, writing of an "infinite fraternity of feeling" that was a "partnership of three persons, you and me and God." It was an offer of spiritual marriage. But the "Salem" in Hawthorne— the part of him raised on the logic of witch hunts and the safety of the attic—panicked.

The biographer James R. Mellow, in his definitive analysis *Nathaniel Hawthorne in His Times*, argues that this panic was inevitable. Mellow suggests that Hawthorne was a man who required the "haunted chamber" to survive; his identity was built on isolation. Melville's offer was not just of love, but of "engulfment"—a total merging of souls that threatened to dissolve Hawthorne's carefully constructed self. Mellow posits that Hawthorne

Herman Melville 1870 portrait.

recognized the "dark necessity" of Melville's attraction but simply did not dare to meet it. To accept Melville's "flagon of life" would mean stepping out of the shadows and into a blinding, dangerous light that Hawthorne had spent forty years avoiding.

Hawthorne retreated. He left the Berkshires, effectively ghosting the greatest genius of his age. The tragedy was sealed by Hawthorne's own hand in his final years. Reverting to the secrecy of his "Castle Dismal" days, he became a compulsive destroyer of his own archives. He burned vast amounts of his correspondence, including almost all of his letters to Melville. He told his publisher, "I wish God had not given me the faculty of writing... I want to have no memory." By burning the evidence, he ensured that the full extent of his reciprocal feelings would remain a mystery, protecting his reputation with the same ruthless efficiency his ancestor used to condemn witches. He died a man who had been offered a "flagon of life," but whose Salem-born fear forced him to pour it into the dust.

Katz, Jonathan Ned. Love Stories: Sex between Men before Homosexuality.

Illustration from an early edition of *Moby Dick*.

# The Bells of Lynn

HENRY WADSWORTH LONGFELLOW, CHARLES SUMNER & SAMUEL GRIDLEY HOWE

In the annals of 19th-century America, few figures loom as large—or as differently—as Henry Wadsworth Longfellow (1807–1882) and Charles Sumner (1811–1874). To the public eye, they were the twin pillars of New England's intellectual and political dominance: Longfellow, the bearded, benevolent bard whose verses were memorized by schoolchildren across the nation, and Sumner, the "Iron Senator," the thundering voice of abolition who viewed the Constitution as a mechanism for radical equality. Yet, beneath the marble veneer of their public monuments, these two men shared a private world defined by a profound "romantic friendship" that sustained them both. Their bond, physically affectionate and emotionally absolute, defies the rigid binaries of modern sexuality, existing in a queer historical spectrum that allows for a love as deep as any marriage.

*Sumner ought to have been a woman.*

Their sanctuary was Nahant. For over twenty-five years, Longfellow retreated to this rocky peninsula to escape the heat of Cambridge and the pressures of fame. It was here, in the atmosphere of salt air and crashing waves, that the poet found the rhythm for his work. The North Shore inspired his dark, atmospheric ballad *The Wreck of the Hesperus*, immortalizing the treacherous beauty of Norman's

Woe. But it was also here that he penned *The Bells of Lynn*. In this poem, Longfellow captured the haunting resonance of church bells drifting over the water from the industrial city to his seaside retreat. For Longfellow, those bells were a call to the heart, a melancholic and beautiful sound that echoed the deep, resonant connection he felt for the men who anchored his life.

Foremost among them was Sumner. Every summer, the senator would flee the toxic, sweltering atmosphere of Washington to join Longfellow in Nahant. He arrived not merely as a guest, but as a soul in desperate need of a harbor. Sumner's life in the capital was a battleground. In 1856, the passion of his rhetoric was met with the violence of the cane. After delivering his blistering "Crime Against Kansas" speech, Sumner was beaten bloody and unconscious on the Senate floor by a pro-slavery congressman. The assault left him physically shattered and psychologically scarred, transforming him into abolition's most visible martyr.

Yet, the man who lay on the Senate floorboards was far more complex than the rigid moralist his enemies described. Sumner

Charles Sumner, left, and Henry Wadsworth Longfellow in 1863.

coined the phrase "equality before the law" and fought for the Civil Rights Act of 1875, but his private life was marked by a "cage of celibacy" and a yearning for intimacy. Before cementing his bond with Longfellow, Sumner had shared an intense, almost marital bond with Samuel Gridley Howe (1801-1876). They were "bachelors both," spending evenings in such "free and warm communion" that Howe's wife, Julia Ward Howe, famously remarked that "Sumner ought to have been a woman" and that her husband should have married him instead. The tragedy of that relationship is lost to the silence of the archives—Howe burned their letters to protect them from "unfriendly eyes"—but the emotional void it left was filled by Longfellow.

This destruction of their correspondence was a deliberate, painful act of preservation through erasure. Howe understood the stakes of their intimacy in a way few others could, recognizing that the written evidence of their affection posed a threat in a society that rigidly policed male relationships. In a letter that survived the flames to offer a glimpse of what was lost, Howe articulated the heavy

Senator Charles Sumner was beaten on the floor of the Senate in 1856.

weight of this sacrifice to Sumner: "I have made a rule lately to put in the only safe place such notes of yours as might be disagreeable to you to have seen by unfriendly eyes—on the grate. It costs me something to burn a piece of paper that has been hallowed to my eye by the impress of your hand, but I do it." The use of the word "hallowed" elevates their connection to something sacred, while the reference to "unfriendly eyes" betrays the vigilance required to maintain it. By feeding their words to the fire, Howe ensured that while their bond might be whispered about, the most visceral proofs of it would vanish into smoke, protecting Sumner's public armor at the cost of their private history.

At Nahant, the "Iron Senator" and the gentle poet formed a "parallel relationship" that coexisted alongside Longfellow's marriages. They spent countless Sundays walking the cliffs, debating literature and sharing their deepest anxieties. Longfellow provided the softness Sumner lacked; Sumner provided the fiery idealism that Longfellow admired. Their relationship was not a secret, but it was intimate in a way that Victorian society permitted, yet modern observers recognize as queer. They traveled together and spoke of each other with a language of devotion that transcended friendship.

Samuel Gridley Howe.

To view Longfellow solely as the translator of Dante and the author of *Paul Revere's Ride*, or to view Sumner solely as the battered titan of Abolition, is to miss the heart of their story. They were each other's refuge. When the bells of Lynn rang out across the water, they signaled not just the time of day but the enduring presence of a love that healed the wounds of the Senate floor and quieted the storms of a literary life. In the crash of the Nahant waves, two of America's greatest men found a quiet, longing peace in each other's company.

Katz, Jonathan Ned. Love Stories: Sex between Men before Homosexuality.

Statue of Charles Sumner in Harvard Square, Cambridge, MA.

# To Live Deliberately

HENRY DAVID THOREAU

In September 1858, Henry David Thoreau (1817–1862) stood paralyzed in the middle of a river of rocks, staring up at a landscape that looked as if the sky had rained boulders upon the earth. He was wandering through Dogtown, the abandoned settlement in the heart of Cape Ann, and he was ecstatic. While most visitors found the jagged, glacial erratics eerie or desolate, Thoreau saw a rugged, chaotic beauty that mirrored his own soul. "It is the most peculiar scenery I have ever seen," he scribbled in his journal, feeling a profound kinship with this wild, unwanted land that refused to be tamed by the town below.

This attraction to the wild and the unconventional was the current that ran beneath his entire life. Thoreau is remembered as the solitary philosopher of Walden Pond, but, according to biographer Walter Harding, his journals reveal a man wrestling with a "pronounced vein of homoeroticism"—a deep, often tortured attraction to men that he sublimated into his worship of nature. He never married, finding his most intense emotional connections in the "romantic friendships" of his time.

He wrote with aching tenderness of Edmund Sewall, a young student who inspired the poem "Sympathy," in which Thoreau masked his desire as a spiritual connection, confessing, "I have no feature so fair as my love for him." His journals are filled with reverent descriptions of male beauty, from the "statuesque" forms of swimmers in the river to his complex bond with the poet William Ellery Channing, the friend who urged him to "devour himself alive" and became his most constant walking companion.

Thoreau brought this radical authenticity to the North Shore not just as a tourist, but as a provocateur. During his visit, he lectured at the Gloucester Lyceum, challenging the maritime community with his ideas on economy and civil resistance. Today, *Walden* and *Civil Disobedience* stand as pillars of American thought. Still, through a queer lens, they become something even more personal: the manifesto of a man striving to live deliberately in a world that had no place for his true nature. When he famously wrote of marching to the beat of a "different drummer," he was defending the right to love, live and exist outside the rigid laws of his time.

Harding, Walter. "Thoreau's Sexuality." Journal of Homosexuality, vol. 21, no. 3, p. 23. 1991.

Henry David Thoreau statue at the Topsfield Library.

# Bachelor Poet

While his poetry celebrated the cozy, snowbound families of New England, John Greenleaf Whittier (1807–1892) went to bed alone, night after night, in a silence that was both a burden and a choice. But his letters reveal that this solitude was punctuated by intense bursts of "romantic friendship," in which he poured his devotion not into a wife but into men like Bayard Taylor. In an era obsessed with lineage, Whittier's radical act was his refusal to procreate, choosing instead to channel his passion into the fight for abolition and the deep, non-sexual intimacies of brotherhood. Born in Haverhill and living much of his life in Amesbury, Whittier was the defining voice of rural New England. Yet, this lifelong Quaker lived entirely outside the domestic structures he poeticized. He never married. While history has often "straight-washed" this as the result of a lost early love or poor health, a closer look reveals a man who

John Greenleaf Whittier.

consciously chose a life of male companionship and political activism over the traditional family unit.

Whittier's poetry turned the Merrimack River and the hills of Essex County into sacred ground. However, his authentic life was one of "romantic friendship." He maintained intense, emotionally intimate relationships with other men. In the 19th century, men were permitted a physical and emotional closeness that modern standards might deem queer; they shared beds, declared deep love in letters and prioritized these bonds above all else. Whittier thrived in this space. He was a fierce abolitionist, channeling the passion that other men put into marriage into the fight for human liberty.

His contribution to society was monumental—he was a celebrity who used his fame to fight slavery—but his personal legacy is one of non-compliance. By refusing to marry, he rejected the patriarchal imperative to head a household and breed. He modeled a form of masculinity that was gentle, pacifist and communal rather than dominant. To the queer history of the North Shore, Whittier represents the dignity of the "odd" man, the one who builds a chosen family of friends and causes. He dared to live a life of the mind and spirit, proving that a man's worth was not determined by his ability to propagate, but by the fire he kindled in the hearts of his fellow citizens.

The John Greenleaf Whittier
Bridge in Amesbury, MA.

# Mill Girl

LUCY LARCOM

The suitor offered her a home, a husband and a traditional life, but he made one mistake: he demanded she stop writing. Lucy Larcom (1824–1893) didn't hesitate. She looked at the prospect of domestic servitude, and she chose the "slavery" of the cotton mills over the slavery of marriage, famously declaring she would not be a captive to any man. Long before she became a celebrated poet, this moment of refusal defined her—a "mill girl" who bought her own freedom and built a life centered on female friendship and professional ambition. Long before the modern feminist movement, Lucy was carving out a space for female independence that was radical for its time. Born in Beverly, she was swept up in the industrial revolution, working as a "doffer" in the cotton mills of Lowell as a child. Most "mill girls" worked to save a dowry for marriage; Larcom worked to buy her freedom. She became one of the most celebrated

Lucy Larcom in 1899.

voices of the working class, a poet and editor who proved that a woman's intellect was not determined by her station. But her most significant rebellion was her lifelong refusal to submit to the institution of marriage, choosing a life of professional ambition and intense female friendship instead.

> *I would rather be a slave in the mill than a slave in marriage.*

Larcom's heart remained in the North Shore, the landscape of her childhood, which she immortalized in her memoir, *A New England Girlhood, Outlined from Memory*. Her queerness is framed by the concept of the "Boston marriage"—a socially accepted arrangement where two wealthy or professional women lived together, independent of men. While Larcom was often on the move, her emotional world was centered on women. She formed deep, sustaining bonds with figures like Annie Adams Fields and John

Mills in Lowell, MA.

Greenleaf Whittier's sister, Elizabeth, establishing a network of "spinsters" who supported each other's careers and emotional needs.

Her contribution to culture was two-fold: she gave a voice to the industrial laborer, and she modeled a life where a woman could be a complete citizen without a husband. She dared to prioritize her own mind and her own pen over the expectations. In the coastal town of Beverly and the factory floors of Lowell, Larcom stands as a pioneer of the single life, a woman who lived authentically by recognizing that her greatest romance was with the world of ideas and the community of women who shared her hunger for something more than a household to manage.

Faderman, Lillian. Surpassing the Love of Men: Romantic Friendship and Love between Women from the Renaissance to the Present.

# Little Women

Louisa May Alcott

"I have fallen in love in my life with so many pretty girls and never once the least bit with any man." With those words, Louisa May Alcott (1832–1888) dismantled the myth of the dutiful spinster. Though she gave the world the ultimate story of American girlhood, she moved through the world with what she called a "boy's spirit" trapped in a woman's body, preferring to be called "Lou" or "gentleman" by her inner circle. Her life was a constant negotiation between the Victorian woman she was expected to be and the masculine protector she felt herself to be. This internal conflict fueled a life defined not by domestic submission but by a ferocious drive to support her family and challenge the rigid gender norms of the 19th century.

A vital but often overlooked episode of her life played out on the rocky shores of the

Louisa May Alcott circa 1870.

North Shore. Between 1839 and 1876, the Alcott family frequently retreated to Swampscott, Massachusetts, to escape the inland heat of Concord. These vacations were not merely leisure; they were periods of profound emotional weight that seeped directly into her fiction. In 1854, her youngest sister, Abbie May (the inspiration for Amy in *Little Women*), spent a month vacationing at King's Beach. Three years later, in 1857, Alcott's mother brought the ailing Elizabeth (Beth) to Swampscott, hoping the salt air would cure her. This heartbreaking trip—where the family desperately sought health by the sea—became the direct inspiration for the poignant chapters in *Little Women,* where Jo takes the dying Beth to the seashore. The granite cliffs and rolling waves of Swampscott provided the backdrop for Jo's fiercest protectiveness, mirroring Alcott's own devotion to her sister.

Alcott's accomplishments were vast. She served as a Civil War nurse, an experience she chronicled in *Hospital Sketches*, and was a dedicated abolitionist and suffragist, becoming the first woman to

Illustration for 1880 edition of Louisa May Alcott's *Little Women*.

register to vote in Concord. Yet, her most personal battle was with her identity. In creating Jo March, she gave the world a tomboy heroine who rejected marriage and femininity, a reflection of her own "boy's spirit" that refused to be tamed.

For many modern readers, however, Jo March represents something far more profound than a simple rejection of skirts and societal expectations. She embodies the complex reality of holding a masculine spirit while navigating a world that insists on perceiving her as a woman. This resonance goes beyond breaking from one's assigned gender; it is about the necessary reframing of life's most intimate relationships. Jo operates as a brotherly protector to her sisters, maintaining deep, loving ties to the female dynamic she was raised in while asserting an internal truth that defies it. In this light, Alcott did not just write a story about a girl who wanted to do "boy things"; she validated the nuanced experience of being masculine in a female space, offering a mirror to those who must reconcile their inner self with the world's expectations.

Bedell, Madelon. The Alcotts: Biography of a Family.

# Woman's Wrongs

Mary Abigail Dodge (1833–1896) didn't just write essays; she threw grenades. Under the pen name Gail Hamilton, she looked at the institution of marriage and called it a "steel trap," a mechanism designed to crush a woman's autonomy in exchange for room and board. While her contemporaries strove to be the "Angel in the House," Dodge built a triangular household with a married couple where she could find emotional and romantic intimacy without ever submitting to a husband. She didn't just reject the Victorian script of womanhood; she burned it, scattering the ashes across the quiet town of Hamilton, Massachusetts, and the halls of power in Washington, D.C.

Mary Abigail Dodge in 1866.

While history often remembers her merely as a recluse or an "odd woman," this erasure ignores the sheer scale of her industry. Dodge was a literary powerhouse, the author of numerous scorching essays and more than 25 books on religion, politics, travel, rural life, and women's rights. She was not a dabbler; she was a combatant who famously sued her own publisher for fair pay and won, setting a precedent for female laborers everywhere.

*Marriage is a steel trap.*

Her "queerness" was defined by her radical refusal to participate in the institution of heterosexual marriage, which she viewed not as a romance, but as a form of legal erasure. She built her life instead around a fierce devotion to Harriet Stanwood Blaine, living in a triangular household where she served as the intellectual equal to the powerful politician James G. Blaine and the emotional partner to his wife. She secured the domestic intimacy of a family without ever submitting to the legal domination of a husband.

Dodge reserved her most venomous ink for the concept of female subservience. In her seminal manifesto, *Woman's Wrongs: A Counter-Irritant,* she dismantled the idea that a woman's highest calling was to serve a man. With characteristic bite, she wrote: "I have seen the time when I would have married a man... for the sake of having a house of my own; but I never saw the time when I would have married a man for the sake of having a husband."

To Dodge, the "old maid" was not a failure, but a victor—a woman who had kept her soul intact. She died in 1896, not as a property of a husband, but as Gail Hamilton: independent, spouseless and fiercely, gloriously free.

http://www.elisarolle.com/queerplaces/klmno/Mary%20Abigail%20Dodge.html

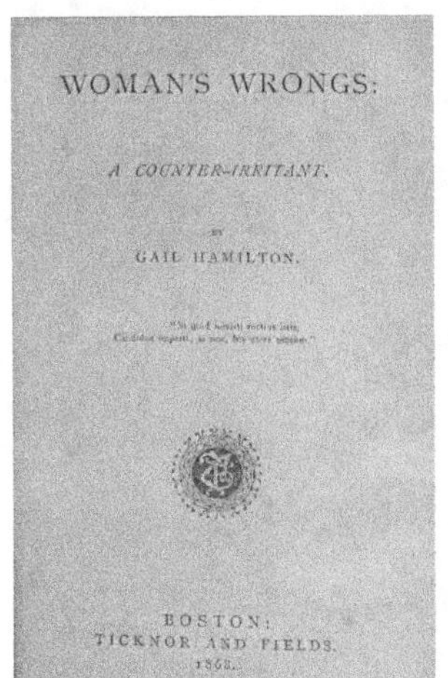

Woman's Wrongs 1868.

# A Boston Marriage

SARAH ORNE JEWETT & ANNIE ADAMS FIELDS


From the porch of Gambrel Cottage in Manchester-by-the-Sea, Annie Adams Fields (1834 – 1915) looked out at the crashing Atlantic, but her heart was focused on the woman standing beside her. After her husband's death, Annie did not fade into the quiet background of Gilded Age widowhood. Instead, she stepped into a vibrant, romantic partnership with the author Sarah Orne Jewett (1849 - 1909), a union lived in plain sight of the Boston elite. Here, atop the Thunderbolt Hill estate overlooking the waves of Singing Beach, they created a world where the term "Boston marriage" was never a mere euphemism for spinsterhood. It was a daily reality of

Annie Adams Fields in 1890.

Sarah Orne Jewett in 1894.

shared beds, shared literary triumphs and a love that Fields described as an "absorbing, affectionate intimacy."

Their relationship was the defining example of a Boston marriage—a committed, long-term cohabiting relationship between two independent women. While their home on Charles Street served as a hub of high society, the true heart of their world beat at Gambrel Cottage. In this coastal haven, away from the city's gaze, their bond deepened beyond friendship into a profound romantic connection. The intensity of their attachment was absolute; Jewett once confessed to Fields during a brief separation, "I feel as if I had left half of myself behind," while on another occasion declaring simply, "I am so quite yours."

The partnership was a meeting of two formidable intellectual forces. Fields was a prolific author and social reformer, publishing poetry like *Under the Olive* and chronicling literary history in *Authors and Friends*. She possessed a sharp, critical mind, as evidenced by her fearless biography of Harriet Beecher Stowe, while simultaneously

Annie Adams Fields (L) in her Charles Street home's library with companion Sarah Orne Jewett (R).

founding charitable organizations such as the Holly Tree Inns to feed people experiencing poverty.

Into this polished world, Sarah Orne Jewett brought the salt air of the Maine coast. She was not just a regional writer documenting the decline of maritime towns; she was living a radical emotional truth. In masterpieces like *The Country of the Pointed Firs* and the feminist ecological anthem *A White Heron*, Jewett rejected the dramatic marriage plots of the Victorian era. She instead championed narratives in which women found strength in nature, solitude, and female community rather than in dependence on men.

Together, Fields and Jewett navigated the 19th century with polished public personas while quietly subverting its norms. They proved that a woman's life could be defined by professional success and same-sex love, carving out a space where female intellect was the center of gravity. Their influence extended to the next generation, as they hosted and mentored a young Willa Cather at Gambrel Cottage, helping to spark the rise of queer modernist writers. Ultimately, their life together was a union as absolute as any marriage, a sanctuary where they found their strength in nature and in each other.

http://www.elisarolle.com/queerplaces/pqrst/
Sarah%20Orne%20Jewett.html

Eaglehead at Singing Beach, Manchester-by-the-Sea.

# Sculptor

Louisa Lander (1826 - 1923) was never meant to be a footnote. Raised in a wealthy Danvers mansion decorated with carvings by Samuel McIntire, she showed a precocious talent for sculpture, carving figures from alabaster and sealing wax before she was even an adult. At nineteen, she rejected the domestic script written for women of her class. She sailed for Rome, joining a vibrant, rebellious circle of American female sculptors led by Harriet Hosmer and Charlotte Cushman.

Henry James later dismissed this group as a "white marmorean flock." Still, in reality, they were a radical sisterhood of women living independently, wearing "mannish" clothes and forging careers in the dust of marble quarries. Lander thrived here, becoming the only pupil of the great American sculptor Thomas Crawford. When fellow Salemite Nathaniel Hawthorne arrived in Rome, he was captivated by her, sitting for a bust and marveling at her "perfect independence."

Louisa Lander in 1861.

But Rome was also a cage of gossip. When Lander returned from a trip to Boston to promote her work, she found herself the target of a vicious whispering campaign. Rumors swirled that she had posed nude or had an illicit affair—charges she refused to dignify with a response. The "scandal" terrified Hawthorne, who abruptly cut ties, and the community she had loved ostracized her. Despite her immense talent—demonstrated in works like her daring, semi-nude statue, *Virginia Dare*—Lander was effectively erased from the canon, her career suffocated by the very independence she had cherished. She died in 1923, a pioneer who snapped her fingers at Rome's patriarchy, only to pay the price with her temporarily lost legacy.

http://www.elisarolle.com/queerplaces/klmno/Louisa%20Lander.html

Louisa Lander - Evangeline.

# 100 Single Women

HARRIET S. PURINTON

Harriet was almost dizzy with delight. She had taken a reckless, breathtaking social gamble—and every moment proved it was worth it. It was June 1896, and the air around 831 Western Avenue in Lynn shimmered with possibility. Standing on her porch, Harriet S. Purinton (c. 1824–after 1896) didn't just survey her manicured lawn; she stood at the helm of a quiet revolution. Before her stretched a sea of confident, self-possessed women who had finally been given a space that belonged only to them.

One can imagine the atmosphere was intoxicating—grass crushed under light shoes, the mingled perfume of hundreds of dresses and flowers so abundant their fragrance seemed to rise like a hymn. But the real scent in the air was freedom. A deep, collective exhale. The feeling of corsets not yet loosened, but no longer cinched by expectation. Harriet had drawn an invisible velvet boundary around her home, and within it she had carved out something radical: a world where women answered to no one but themselves. Her invitation was more than etiquette—it was rebellion. No gentlemen allowed. And even bolder: no married women.

This was a gathering not for the "leftover" women society pitied, but for those who had refused to be consumed by it. Lynn's powerful families—the Breeds, the Newhalls—mingled with independent teachers, bookkeepers, nurses and shoeworkers, all shimmering in "gay" pale gowns and hats so extravagant they looked like spring gardens brought to life. Color flooded the grounds: ribbons, flowers, bunting "of all the colors of the rainbow," a riot of brightness that felt less like decoration and more like a declaration. A promise. A precursor to Pride, decades before the word would have the meaning it has today.

Here, women who lived in quiet companionship—some in tender "Boston marriages," others simply in fiercely chosen solitude—could walk arm-in-arm without disguise or apology. Laughter rang out in delighted bursts. Hands clasped freely. Cheeks were kissed openly, affection blooming without fear. For a few stolen hours,

Women dressed in Victorian era attire such as that worn to Mrs. Puirinton's Spinster's Party.

they inhabited a future that had not yet been written: one where their choices were not tragedies but triumphs.

Just beyond the glow of it all, married women lingered at the edges—curious, wistful, excluded. They watched the "spinsters," those supposedly pitiful figures, revel in a joy untethered to husbands, housekeeping, or duty. And for once, it was the married women who looked incomplete.

The climax came when Miss E. Josephine Roach rose to read the anthem of the day. A hush rippled through the crowd, followed by an eruption of cheers—sharp, unrestrained, glorious. It was the sound of women committing a beautiful act of defiance.

> *"The married folk have had their holiday,*
> *For bachelors and maids let all make way.*
> *The rulers of the world the spinsters shall be,*
> *The spinsters calm, serene, of spirit free."*

A Victorian house in Lynn, perhaps similar to Mrs. Harriet Purinton's.

As the sun sank low and shadows stretched across the grass, Harriet looked out over the lawn—over the bright eyes, the lifted chins, the women who stood tall in their own right. No shame. No apologies. No waiting.

Just pride.

Just independence.

Just hope.

Just freedom.

In a world that insisted they were missing something essential, Harriet and her guests showed the truth: they had claimed their lives fully, boldly, entirely for themselves.

"Spinsters' Party." The Daily Evening Item, 5 June 1896, p. 4.

# Bedridden

ALICE JAMES

To the outside world, Alice James (1848–1892) was a tragedy—the invalid sister of famous brothers, confined to her bed. But inside that sickroom, she was building a fortress of resistance. With Katharine Peabody Loring by her side as her "divine stabilizer," Alice turned her confinement into a space of intense, exclusive intimacy that baffled and terrified her family. In a life stripped of physical agency, her greatest act of rebellion was loving Katharine, proving that a "Boston marriage" could flourish even in the shadow of death. In a family of titans—her brothers were the novelist Henry James and the philosopher William James—Alice James was often dismissed as the hysterical younger sister, a professional invalid confined to her bed. While history often reads her illness as a tragedy, modern scholars view her diary and her life as a savage critique of the limitations placed on women and her relationship with Loring as a triumph of queer survival.

The North Shore was the backdrop for the blossoming of this union. The James

Alice James in 1891.

family summered in Manchester-by-the-Sea. It was here that the bond with Loring, a scion of North Shore society, solidified. Loring was not merely a nurse; she was Alice's intellectual equal, her protector and her primary emotional partner. Their relationship was a "Boston marriage" in its most potent form. Henry James, fascinated and repelled by the intimacy between the two women, used it as the basis for the lesbian dynamic in his novel *The Bostonians*, inadvertently immortalizing the very bond he sought to pathologize.

*Inside the sickroom, she built a fortress of resistance.*

Alice dared to live authentically by refusing to be silenced by her neurasthenia (chronic fatigue) diagnosis. Her diary, written in her final years, is a masterpiece of wit and observation, biting in its assessment of the British and American patriarchy. But her greatest act of defiance was loving Katharine. In a world that offered her nothing but pity, she found a passionate, sustaining love that saw her through to the end. She turned her sickbed into a space of resistance, proving that even a life restricted by illness could be expansive through the power of a chosen, queer devotion.

http://www.elisarolle.com/queerplaces/a-b-ce/Alice%20James.html

# A Wilde Visit

When Oscar Wilde (1854–1900) sauntered down Central Avenue, Lynn, in September 1882, you can imagine he was a peacock parading through a city of pigeons. The rough-hewn industrial city paused to gawk at this impeccably mannered dandy who treated the sidewalk like a runway. As factory workers bustled past, Wilde's gaze lingered, offering appreciative, stolen glances at the handsome young men of the shoe city—a subtle hint of the desires that would define his private life and eventually bring public scorn and imprisonment.

That evening at the Lynn Music Hall, the spectacle continued. Wilde appeared on stage in his full "court costume," a striking ensemble of black velvet coat and small clothes, accentuated by a jabot with ruffles of duchesse lace and tight black silk stockings that showed off his calves. He was there to lecture on "The Decorative Arts," bringing a message of beauty to a crowd of 500, easily outdrawing the mere 300 souls who had gathered in Salem the previous night.

He was the dazzling Irish poet and supreme apostle of Aestheticism, a man who argued that life itself should be lived as a piece of art. Yet, the celebrity of this tour masked a tragedy waiting in the wings. In England, his passionate, volatile relationship with Lord Alfred Douglas would ultimately lead to his downfall. In 1895, the defiance that once delighted audiences became evidence against him, resulting in a conviction for "gross indecency" and two years of hard labor in prison. In Lynn, however, before the cage claimed him, he was simply the velvet-clad star, briefly illuminating the gray manufacturing town with the blinding light of his own artistry.

http://www.elisarolle.com/queerplaces/klmno/Oscar%20Wilde.html

Oscar Wilde with Lord Alfred Douglas in 1893.

# THREE

## The Lavender Aristocracy

1900 - 1950

As the 20th century dawned, the North Shore transformed into a playground and haven for the "Lavender Aristocracy." This was the era of the "Glass Closet," a time when immense wealth provided a glittering shield for those who lived outside the norm. In the exclusive enclaves of Gloucester and Manchester-by-the-Sea, a vibrant, semi-underground colony flourished. Here, the "confirmed bachelor" and the "eccentric maiden aunt" were not figures of pity,

but the architects of a brave, new way of living. The bond between these neighbors was so strong that, eventually, Joanna Davidge, A. Piatt Andrew, Cecilia Beaux and Henry Davis Sleeper called their collection of summer houses on Eastern Point "Dabsville," with "DABS" standing for the initials of their surnames.

Figures such as A. Piatt Andrew, Henry Davis Sleeper, and John Hays Hammond Jr. used their fortunes to build literal fortresses of solitude and celebration. In castles perched on the granite rocks, they created interiors that mirrored their complex inner lives—rooms filled with collected beauty, secret passageways and the laughter of like-minded friends. They lived in plain sight, protected by the armor of their class, hosting parties where the gender norms of the outside world were left at the door.

Yet, this freedom was a paradox. It was a liberty purchased with privilege, a world where one could be "eccentric" but never explicitly "out." Despite these constraints, these trailblazers refused to be invisible. They defined American style, influenced national politics and created art that challenged the status quo. This section explores the lives of those who turned their private exile into a public masterpiece, proving that even within a gilded cage, the spirit can soar.

# Congressman

A. PIATT ANDREW

If one were to conjure the image of an early twentieth-century Harvard economics professor, the picture would likely be staid, buttoned-up and predictable. A. Piatt Andrew (1873–1936) was the spectacular antithesis of this stereotype, a man described by contemporaries as a fusion of the Whitmanic and the Wildean. Blessed with matinee-idol looks, boundless charisma and a narcissism that led him to hang a full-length portrait of himself in a secret, mirrored bedchamber. Andrew was the gravitational center of a rich, strange world he built on the rocky shores of Gloucester, Massachusetts.

Andrew's presence on Eastern Point transformed the landscape into a stage for a home game of closeted but intense bohemianism. In 1902, he built Red Roof, a house that was far more than a bachelor's retreat; it was a strangely dark, Gothic cottage honeycombed with secret rooms, hidden passages, and bedchamber peepholes. Red Roof was a

A. Piatt Andrew in 1911. Isabella Stewart Gardner Museum, Boston.

place of liberation, a "lavender" stronghold where the rigid morals of the mainland didn't seem to apply. Gossip whispered of peculiar pastimes within its walls, fueled by architectural features like a hidden alcove above the library books—too low to stand in but equipped with a mattress and covers—where guests could look down through a hole into the room below.

Here, he hosted legendary stag parties and cultivated a circle that included his devoted neighbor, Henry Davis Sleeper, and two men 15 years younger: the inventor John Hays Hammond Jr. and the actor Leslie Buswell. His letters and diaries document a world of "boyology"—his term for the camaraderie and affection of his male circle—filled with "frightful roughhousing" and intimate encounters. He recorded mornings of nude sunbathing with recent Harvard graduates like Ray Atherton and Jack Mabbett, sometimes noting in his diary when a young man "slept with me" or "spent the day in my bed."

A. Piatt Andrew campaign poster.

The dynamic between these men was electric and complex. Andrew was the undisputed "kingpin," and his neighbors orbited him with a mix of devotion and jealousy. Across the harbor, Hammond erected a medieval-style castle. Local legend has it that on calm evenings, the two men engaged in "acoustic battles," blasting their phonographs at one another across the water in a curious duel of musical sophistication.

Yet it was Henry Sleeper who loved him most enduringly. Sleeper served as his anchor, managing Red Roof during Andrew's long absences. Sleeper's letters to Andrew vibrate with a physical longing that transcends mere friendship. After receiving a medal from Andrew, Sleeper confessed to a ritual that brought the object into his most private sphere: "I haven't had it off for an hour since I put it on... every night it goes into the pocket of my pajamas!" On another occasion, aching for Andrew's presence, he wrote of visiting Andrew's empty shore to inhabit his space physically: "I went down to your beach & lay, for an hour, breathing the sea. You always seem so near when it is still there." Perhaps most telling was Sleeper's frank acknowledgement of Andrew's potent sexual charisma, describing how another male rival was "conscious & jealous of yr. lure—and fears it."

Andrew was also a close friend of Isabella Stewart Gardner (1840–1924), whom he called "Y" or "Ysabella." She was more than a famous art collector; she was the fierce patron saint of the North Shore's "lavender" gentlemen. At her Prides Crossing estate, she cultivated a devoted court of "bachelors," including Andrew. Finding conventional society stifling, she celebrated the eccentricities of men like Andrew, Sleeper and John Singer Sargent. Her flamboyant life—walking lions and wearing diamonds to breakfast—was a rejection of Edwardian norms, making her a natural ally. She used her immense social capital to

Isabella Stewart Gardner in 1894

shield these men, creating a safe harbor where their queer genius could authentically thrive.

Andrew inherited his wealth and supplemented it by his career as a Harvard economics professor, Director of the U.S. Mint, Assistant Secretary of the Treasury and later a U.S. Congressman.

Andrew's impact extended far beyond the social intrigue of Eastern Point. A brilliant economist who laid the foundations for the Federal Reserve System, he pivoted to martial glory when World War I broke out. He founded the American Field Service (AFS), organizing a volunteer ambulance corps composed of the "flower of American youth" from Ivy League colleges. In Andrew's conception, this all-male force echoed the ancient Theban Sacred Band—an army of lovers and friends united in a heroic cause. He filled Red Roof with Roman war relics, underscoring a classical,

A. Piatt Andrew with Isabella Stewart Gardner at Red Roof. Isabella Stewart Gardner Museum, Boston.

martial aesthetic that merged his public service with his private ideals. Later serving as a Republican U.S. Congressman and Secretary of the Treasury, Andrew navigated the halls of power in Washington, D.C. as a respected politician while maintaining a private life that was fundamentally queer, protected by his status and the loyalty of his friends. He remained a deepening riddle to the public: mysterious, magnetic and restlessly unfulfilled, living boldly at the center of a world he created to safeguard his own complex desires.

Evans, R. Tripp. The Importance of Being Furnished: Four Bachelors at Home.

http://www.elisarolle.com/queerplaces/a-b-ce/A. %20Piatt%20Andrew.html

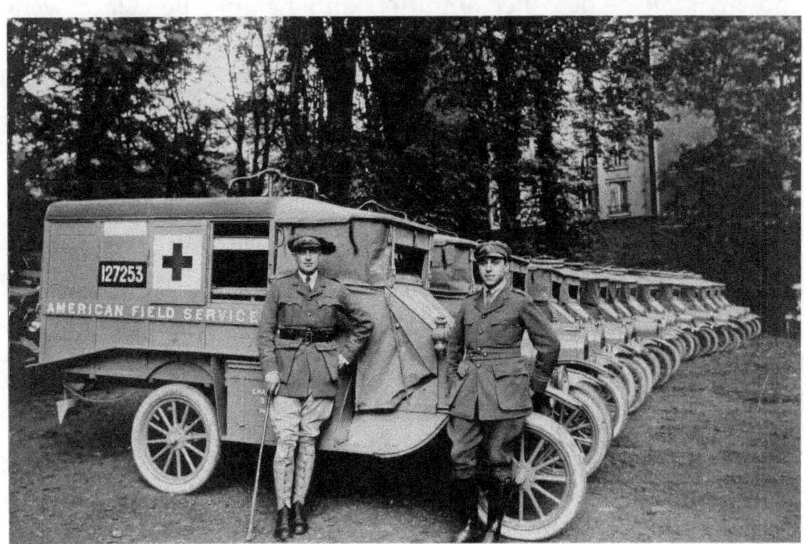

Inspector General A. Piatt Andrew and Assistant Inspector General Stephen Galatti at the AFS headquarters in Paris, France. 1917. Photograph by H.C. Ellis. Courtesy of the Archives of the American Field Service and AFS Intercultural Programs (AFS Archives.)

# Sacred Calling

The drinks were poured, the laughter was loud, and the company was exclusively "lavender." At Green Alley, her estate on the Gloucester coast, Cecilia Beaux (1855 - 1942) presided over a salon that defied the gender rules of the early 20th century. Surrounded by her queer neighbors from Eastern Point—Henry Davis Sleeper and A. Piatt Andrew—Beaux felt a freedom she couldn't find in the stifling drawing rooms of Philadelphia. She had rejected marriage as an impediment to her "sacred calling" of art, choosing instead this chosen family where her ambition and her independence were celebrated, not suppressed.

Cecilia Beaux in 1894.

Cecilia Beaux stands as one of the premier American portraitists of the late nineteenth and early twentieth centuries, achieving a level of acclaim comparable to her contemporary, John Singer Sargent. She viewed the domestic obligations of a wife as incompatible with the demands of high art and instead cultivated deep, sustaining relationships with women, such as during her time living with Agnes Irwin, the dean of Radcliffe College. Her work was often critiqued in gendered terms, praised for possessing both masculine strength and feminine sentiment; it reflects a life that quietly defied heteronormative expectations.

Beaux's professional contributions were monumental. She was the first woman hired as a full-time faculty member at the Pennsylvania Academy of the Fine Arts and became a National Academician. She commanded high fees for portraits of the elite. Her subjects ranged from intimate portraits of her family to high-profile commissions, including First Lady Eleanor Roosevelt. Her ability to capture the American ruling class with psychological insight and technical brilliance earned her gold medals at international expositions. In 1933, Eleanor Roosevelt honored her as "the American woman who had made the greatest contribution to the culture of the world." By embracing the cult of "single blessedness" and forging her own community in places like Dabsville, Beaux secured a legacy not only as a master painter but as an independent woman who lived on her own terms.

Green Alley.

A Little Girl by Cecilia Beaux.

The Velie Boys by Cecilia Beaux.

# Most Famous Brush

In the grand studios of London and Paris, John Singer Sargent (1856–1925) painted the velvet and pearls of the aristocracy with a cool, detached brilliance. But in the privacy of his sketchbook, the velvet vanished. There, with charcoal in hand, he obsessively traced the contours of the male form—specifically the body of Thomas McKeller, a Black elevator operator and model. These sensual, intimate drawings, hidden away from his society patrons, reveal the

John Singer Sargent in his studio with *Portrait of Madame X*, circa 1885.

"glass closet" of a man who lived in plain sight, channeling his forbidden desires into the quiet stroke of a pencil.

Sargent was the most famous brush in the world, the man who defined the look of the Edwardian aristocracy. He earned a massive fortune through commissions from the wealthiest figures in Europe and America. He created masterpieces like *Madame X* (1884), whose scandalous strap caused a sensation in Paris, and *The Daughters of Edward Darley Boit* (1882), a moody, psychological portrait of four sisters.



Sargent's North Shore connection was woven through his friendship with Isabella Stewart Gardner. He was a frequent guest at her properties and later at her Museum in Boston. He also visited the queer enclave in Gloucester, specifically visiting A. Piatt Andrew at Red Roof. Though he found Red Roof's master, A. Piatt Andrew, "unaesthetic," Sargent's presence in this queer-friendly space highlights his integration into New England's artistic and bohemian circles. The North Shore offered him respite from the demands of London; here, he could paint for pleasure, capturing the rocky coastlines and the relaxed intimacy of his friends. It was in these unguarded moments that the "real" Sargent emerged—not

John Singer Sargent - Study for Sorrowful Mysteries.

the society painter, but the sensitive observer of beauty who found solace in the company of other artistic men.

He lived authentically by sublimating his desires into his art, creating a body of work that is both publicly celebrated and privately coded. His refusal to marry, in an era that viewed bachelorhood with suspicion, was a quiet but firm stance. His contribution to culture is immeasurable, but for the queer history of New England, Sargent represents the "glass closet"—a man who lived in plain sight, loved by all, yet whose deepest passions were reserved for the canvas. He dared to capture the world's sensuality, leaving behind a legacy that whispers of the love he could not speak.

http://www.elisarolle.com/queerplaces/fghij/
John%20Singer%20Sargent.html.

Portrait of Nicola D'Inverno (1892), by John Singer Sargent.

# Beauport

Henry Davis Sleeper (1878–1934) stood in the "South Gallery" of his architectural masterpiece, Beauport, but he wasn't looking at the art. He was staring through a window he had specially designed to frame exactly one view: the roof of the house next door. Inside that house lived A. Piatt Andrew, the man Sleeper loved with a quiet, devastating intensity. Every room in Sleeper's labyrinthine castle was a stage set for a life he couldn't fully claim, and this window was his private observatory, a permanent monument to a love that lived just across the garden wall. To the outside world, Henry Davis Sleeper was a figure of gentle paradox: a shy, constitutionally frail bachelor who lived with his widowed mother, yet who somehow conjured into existence one of the most theatrical, rule-breaking, and socially vibrant homes in America. He was a man with no formal education who listed his occupation as "none" until his forties, yet whose aesthetic legacy would eventually influence museums like Winterthur and the Metropolitan Museum of

Henry Davis Sleeper.

Art. But beneath the surface of this quiet connoisseur beat a heart of intense romantic passion, a passion he sublimated entirely into the creation of Beauport, his masterpiece on the rocky shores of Gloucester, Massachusetts.

*Sleeper deliberately designed his own bedroom suite, the South Gallery, to face Andrew's property.*

Sleeper's time on the North Shore began in childhood with summers at Marblehead Neck, but his destiny was sealed in 1906 when he met A. Piatt Andrew, a charismatic Harvard economics professor. Andrew's magnetic personality and his "bachelor's castle," Red Roof, on Eastern Point, Gloucester, captivated Sleeper. Despite Andrew's reputation for having a "roving eye" and a preference for athletic young men, Sleeper fell deeply in love. In a move that fused architectural ambition with romantic devotion, he used his substantial inherited wealth to buy the lot next door to Red Roof. He began constructing a home that was ostensibly a summer

Beauport, Gloucester, MA, in 2016.

cottage but in reality a lifelong love letter to his neighbor. He named it Little Beauport, a nod to Samuel de Champlain's name for Gloucester Harbor, but also possibly a sly reference to the "beau" he hoped to secure.

Sleeper's life at Beauport was defined by the queer "Dabsville" community he was the last to join and helped anchor—an enclave of artists and intellectuals, including Joanna Davidge, A. Piatt Andrew, and Cecilia Beaux. Within this safe harbor, Sleeper's sexuality was an open secret, accepted and integrated into the social fabric.

Sleeper had enjoyed a previous romantic relationship with the writer Guy Wetmore Carryl (1873–1904), a brilliant American humorist and poet known for clever works like *Grimm Tales Made Gay*. He lived in a Swampscott cottage, which he wittily named "Shingle Blessedness," a retreat where he cultivated artistic camaraderie. His life was tragically cut short at thirty-one by injuries sustained while fighting a fire that destroyed his home.

Carryl shared a deep romantic bond with Sleeper and publicly immortalized their connection by dedicating his novel to him. *Far From the Maddening Girls*, to Sleeper as his "dear friend and comrade." Sleeper enshrined this lost love, keeping Carryl's photograph in his bedroom for decades and noting he never expected to find such a companion again.

Guy Wetmore Carryl.

Sleeper's connection to Andrew, though, was the

defining emotional axis of his life. Though Andrew likely did not return Sleeper's romantic love—Andrew was known for his "boyology" circle of younger men—Sleeper made himself indispensable. He became the caretaker of Red Roof during Andrew's long absences in World War I, polishing his shoes, tending his garden, and even sleeping in his house to be closer to his spirit.

Professionally, Sleeper blossomed late but brilliantly. Beauport became his laboratory, a place where he defied the rigid rules of Gilded Age design. He mixed high and low art, combining priceless antiques with flea-market finds, and used color and light to create "moods" rather than historical recreations. His genius lay in his "mannerist" approach—installing a window with 138 panes to frame a specific view, or painting a dining room solely to match a set

The library at Beauport.

of red toleware. This unique aesthetic eventually attracted wealthy clients such as Henry Francis du Pont and Hollywood stars such as Joan Crawford, launching Sleeper's career as one of the first professional interior designers in the modern sense. He was celebrated for his "witchery" with light and space, transforming the staid world of interior decoration into an expressive art form.

Sleeper's legacy is preserved in the labyrinthine halls of Beauport, now renamed The Sleeper-McCann House, a National Historic Landmark. The house remains a physical manifestation of his complex identity: a "queer gothic" fantasy in which secret staircases, hidden rooms, and carefully coded tributes to male beauty stand as silent witnesses to a life lived largely in the "glass closet." His "Golden Step Room," with its view of the harbor and his "Souvenir de France" room, a tribute to his time with Andrew in Paris, are not just design triumphs but chapters in an autobiography written in wood, glass and color. In the end, Sleeper proved that a home could be more than a shelter; it could be a stage for a self-invented life, a sanctuary for forbidden love and a lasting monument to the power of beauty.

Evans, R. Tripp. The Importance of Being Furnished: Four Bachelors at Home. Rowman & Littlefield, 2024.

https://www.historicnewengland.org/property/beauport-sleeper-mccann-house/

Beauport window.

# The Inventor

To the terrified fishermen of Gloucester Harbor, it looked like witchcraft. A forty-foot boat, the Natalia, was tearing through the Atlantic at thirty knots with absolutely no one at the wheel. High above on the cliffs, watching through a telescope, stood John Hays Hammond Jr. (1888-1965), tapping a telegraph key that steered the "ghost ship" using invisible radio waves. This stunt in 1914, which nearly caused a riot on  docks, proved the viability of the remote-controlled torpedo. Still, it was merely the public face of a man whose private life was far more complex than his military contracts suggested. John Hays Hammond Jr. was a living contradiction: a futurist who built a medieval fortress as his home but soon opened it to the public as a museum; a scientist who developed radio control yet spent his evenings trying to contact the dead; and arguably America's most prolific queer scientist, a bisexual man who found his true family not in his famous lineage, but in a bohemian brotherhood.

Long before the stone towers of "Abbadia Mare" rose to dominate the coastline, Hammond found his sanctuary in his circle of friends, Leslie Buswell, A.

John Hays Hammond Jr. in 1915.

Piatt Andrew and Henry Davis Sleeper. Together, they forged a queer utopia on the shores of Gloucester Harbor during the dying light of the Gilded Age. In an era that demanded rigid moral conformity, they created a world where their fluidity was not a secret to be choked down, but the very bond that held them together.

That bond was tempered in the fire of the Great War. Hammond shows his love in this letter to Buswell, who was in France, "...But let this sadness be a passing shadow, for we shall win each other by the very strength of the thing that makes us suffer. We shall take this sacred friendship and we shall always treat it with wonder and reverence thus it will never die. Remember, that where you are, my heart is; you who have become the pivot of my existence and the goal to which all my efforts lead. I love you."

Hammond's journey to this rocky promontory began with a childhood steeped in genius. At the age of twelve, his father took him to West Orange, New Jersey, to visit Thomas Edison's laboratory. The young Hammond was so inquisitive that the "Wizard of Menlo Park" gave him a personal tour, igniting a lifelong passion for scientific invention. Edison gave him the philosophy, "inventing must be a money-making proposition." But it was Alexander Graham Bell who truly molded his professional

The radio-controlled Natalia in 1914.

discipline. On Bell's specific advice, Hammond, by then a Yale graduate, took a humble job as a clerk in the U.S. Patent Office. It was a strategic masterstroke; by studying the legal architecture of invention, Hammond learned how to protect his ideas with ironclad precision. This legal savvy and his brilliant inventive mind would eventually help him secure over 430 patents. In the castle's laboratory, shielded by lead-lined walls, he developed the "variable pitch propeller," a crucial innovation that helped Allied fighter planes maneuver in World War II. He also created a "telescope for the ears" that could detect enemy aircraft through fog. His radio control technology is still widely used today. Although Hammond inherited a fortune, he earned his own millions by selling patents to the U.S. military and corporations like RCA.

The Hammond Castle Museum, Gloucester, MA.

Yet, Hammond was not merely a scientist of the past; he remained a patron of the avant-garde until his final days. While the Gilded Age faded, Hammond's engagement with the queer artistic community did not. In the early 1960s, as a new counter-culture began to swell in Gloucester, the elderly inventor quietly bridged the gap between the Edwardian aesthetes and the Beat Generation. He invited poet Gerrit Lansing and artist Harry Martin, who became his lover, to Gloucester. He became a financial supporter of *Set*, a radical literary

The cover of *Set* magazine, #2, 1963, drawn by Harry Martin.

magazine edited by Lansing. In its pages, alongside works by Charles Olson and Robert Duncan, Hammond's name appeared as a patron, linking the "lavender" aristocracy of his youth with the gritty, mystical post-modernism of the Gloucester poets. It was a testament to a mind that refused to stagnate, recognizing a kinship with the rebels and visionaries of a new era.

> *Remember, that where you are, my heart is; you*
> *who have become the pivot of my existence and*
> *the goal to which all my efforts lead. I love you.*

Inside those lead-lined walls, the drama of his life played out. Even after Hammond married spiritualist Irene Fenton, his connection to Leslie Buswell remained the emotional anchor of his existence. In a gesture that defied explanation to outsiders but made perfect sense to Hammond, Buswell built his own massive estate, Stillington Hall, a mile away from Hammond's drawbridge. For decades, they lived as neighbors—two kings in adjacent fortresses, their lives intertwined in an architectural embrace. Sadly, they had a falling out around 1930 and stopped speaking. They died within months of each other in the mid-1960s, the silence between their castles marking the end of an era where they had dared to live, invent and love on their own terms.

Shand-Tucci, Douglass. The Crimson Letter: Harvard, Homosexuality, and the Shaping of American Culture.

Lopez, Russ. The Hub of the Gay Universe: An LGBTQ History of Boston, Provincetown, and Beyond. Shawmut Peninsula Press, 2019.

https://hammondcastle.org/

# Dashing Young Actor

LESLIE BUSWELL

He came to America to play a part on a stage, but Leslie Buswell (1890–1964) found his true role in a chance encounter that felt like gravity. In 1913, the dashing young British actor crossed paths with the "Dabsville" trio—A. Piatt Andrew, Henry Davis Sleeper and John Hays Hammond Jr.—and was instantly pulled into their

Leslie Buswell, left, with John Hays Hammond, Jr., Stokowski and Donahue.

"scintillating" orbit. He abandoned the touring life for the granite cliffs of Gloucester, joining a queer bachelor brotherhood so tight-knit that he eventually used his inherited wealth to build his own castle, Stillington Hall, just a mile from Hammond's, cementing his place in a landscape defined by male affection. Born in Richmond, England, and educated at Cambridge, he possessed a charisma that was both immediate and disarming.

He became a central pillar of New England's most exclusive bohemian queer enclave on Eastern Point. While the group was outwardly defined by artistic patronage and intellect, its inner life was fueled by a complex and often painful geometry of desire. Buswell found himself at the heart of a jagged love triangle that tested the bonds of their brotherhood. The inventor John Hays Hammond Jr. was "spellbound" by the handsome Briton, entranced by his beauty and spirit. Buswell, however, was caught in a difficult emotional riptide. While he was fond of Hammond and deeply respected his genius, he struggled to conceal a potent attraction to

Leslie Buswell, left, with A. Piatt Andrew in Paris. Isabella Stewart Gardner Museum, Boston.

the older, magnetic A. Piatt Andrew, the group's undisputed leader. This dynamic did not go unnoticed; Henry Davis Sleeper, whose own devotion belonged entirely to Andrew, observed that Buswell's feelings were an open secret. Hammond, acutely aware of the threat, was reportedly jealous of Andrew's lure, fearing the power his friend held over the man he loved.

*He left the stage for the cliffs of Gloucester, finding his role in a brotherhood of bachelors.*

Despite these romantic tensions, the group proved to be men of action when the world demanded it. With the outbreak of World War I, Buswell was among the first to volunteer for the American Field Service (AFS) ambulance corps, which Andrew organized. He traded the drawing rooms of Gloucester for the mud of the Western Front, serving as an ambulance driver with conspicuous gallantry.

Stillington Hall, Gloucester, MA. Courtesy of Cape Ann Museum Library and Archives.

His letters home, visceral and haunting, were collected and published as *Ambulance No. 10*. The book became a sensation, providing a gripping, firsthand account of the war's devastation and helping to sway American public opinion toward intervention.

After the war, the romantic rivalries settled into a lifelong, productive proximity. Buswell returned to Gloucester, not to the stage, but to the laboratory, assisting Hammond with his pioneering electronics research.

Though he later married and served as an Air Force colonel in World War II, Buswell's legacy remains rooted in that rocky promontory, where he lived, loved and created within a circle that dared to defy the conventions of their time.

http://www.elisarolle.com/queerplaces/klmno/Leslie%20Buswell.html

*Ambulance No. 10* by Leslie Buswell.

# Forty Steps

To the mid-century public, Charles Hammond Gibson, Jr. (1874–1954) was a living relic. This "Proper Bostonian" caricature wandered the Back Bay of Boston in a raccoon coat and stiff collar, seemingly oblivious to the modern world. Yet, behind this carefully cultivated façade of eccentric gentility lay a life defined by intense romantic passion, artistic rebellion and a tireless effort to enshrine a queer identity that society refused to acknowledge. Gibson was not merely a guardian of the past; he was the architect of his own immortality, transforming his family home into a museum that served as a temple to his own vanished youth and desires.

Born into the heart of Brahmin privilege, Gibson spent his life oscillating between the rigid social grid of Boston's 137 Beacon Street and the rugged, romantic coast of the North Shore. It

Charles Hammond Gibson, Jr. in 1900.

was at "Forty Steps," the family's summer estate in Nahant, that Gibson found his true fairyland. While he eventually turned the Beacon Street townhouse into a monument to Victorian domesticity, Forty Steps was the canvas for his horticultural genius. There, he created elaborate Italianate rose gardens that became a celebrated showplace of the North Shore. For Gibson, these gardens were more than a hobby; they were a sanctuary where he could indulge his aesthetic passions freely, creating a "festival of roses" that drew thousands of visitors and allowed him to reign as a sort of horticultural prince, far removed from his austere father's disapproval.

A scandalous and transformative love affair with Maurice de Mauny, a self-styled French count, defined Gibson's emotional life. They met in 1891. Their relationship blossomed during an idyllic tour of Europe, where they lived as "kindred souls joined together in immaterial marriage." When they returned to Boston in 1894, their intimacy shocked the conservative social set. De Mauny's presence in the bedroom adjoining Gibson's at the family home sparked gossip that labeled the Frenchman an "imposter" and Gibson a deviant. The family eventually forced de Mauny out, but the heartbreak fueled Gibson's literary output for decades. He sublimated this loss into his novel *Two Gentlemen in Touraine*, a thinly veiled, coded romance that celebrated their time together, and volumes of poetry such as *The Wounded Eros*, which chronicled the pain of unrequited and forbidden love.

Gibson inherited his wealth from his wealthy Boston Brahmin family. His father was a successful cotton broker. Professionally, Gibson dabbled in real estate and served a colorful, controversial term as Boston's Parks Commissioner. He famously wore a fur coat to his office, demanded a touring car and fought a public battle to build a replica of the *Petit Trianon* on Boston Common to serve as a public lavatory. This proposal baffled the city but perfectly aligned with his Francophile aesthetic.

In his final years, Gibson cemented his legacy by creating the Gibson House Museum. While he pitched it as preserving a Victorian interior, it was, in reality, a shrine to himself. He meticulously labeled his own manuscripts, preserved his clothing and curated the space to reflect the golden era of his youth—the era before his heart was broken and his beauty faded. Today, the Gibson House stands not just as a time capsule of Boston society but as a pioneering site of queer history, preserving the world of a man who refused to be erased by the passage of time or the strictures of convention.

https://www.thegibsonhouse.org/our-lgbtq-history

The Gibson House, aka Rose Cottage, right front, in the early 1900s. Forty Steps Beach, Nahant, is in the foreground. All four houses in this image were designed by Cornelius Coolidge in the early 1800s.

# American Modernist

Exhausted and spiritually adrift, the modernist painter Marsden Hartley (1877–1943) wandered into Dogtown and felt the earth shift beneath his feet. The massive, erratic boulders of the abandoned settlement looked to him like "a cross between Easter Island and Stonehenge." Here, among the rocks and cellar holes of the past, Hartley found a desolate, "druidic" landscape that matched his own jagged loneliness. He set up his easel in this wasteland, painting the *Rock Doxology* that would become a rugged, silent prayer for a life lived on the margins. Born Edmund Hartley in Maine, he spent his life seeking both artistic truth and a place to belong, a search complicated by the isolation of being a gay man in an era of silence.

He poured his desolation into a celebrated series of paintings, such as *Rock Doxology*, *Blueberry Highway*, and *Dogtown*, which used bold, expressionist forms to capture the primal energy of the land. These works are now considered pivotal, marking his return to New England themes and

Marsden Hartley in 1916

cementing his legacy as one of the greatest Early American Modernists.

Hartley's accomplishments extended far beyond Gloucester. He was a key figure in the Alfred Stieglitz circle in New York and the first American to fully embrace European avant-garde styles, such as Cubism and German Expressionism. His earlier *Berlin series*, painted while he was in love with a German officer named Karl von Freyburg, is a coded, vibrant memorial to his fallen partner—a fearless assertion of queer love amidst the devastation of World War I. From the tragic romance of Berlin to the granite solitude of Dogtown, Hartley ultimately transformed his exclusion into a visionary language, proving that the margins of society could birth the very center of American modernism.

http://www.elisarolle.com/queerplaces/klmno/Marsden%20Hartley.html

Weinberg, Jonathan. Speaking for Vice: Homosexuality in the Art of Charles Demuth, Marsden Hartley, and the First American Avant-Garde. Yale University Press, 1995.

*The Old Bars, Dogtown* by Marsden Hartley, 1936.

# Radical Pacifist

HARRY DANA

Harry was crying, running down the hallway of his grandfather's mansion, chasing the young author John Cheever. "How can you be so cruel?" he shouted, a moment of raw, desperate longing shattering the decorum of the Longfellow House. Whether being arrested for "morals charges" in 1935 or turning his family estate into a sanctuary for Harvard first-year students discovering their sexuality, Dana lived with a reckless, open-hearted courage that constantly threatened to topple his Brahmin pedigree.

Henry Wadsworth Longfellow ("Harry") Dana (1881–1950) walked the halls of history in slippers, often with a drink in hand and a roguish glint in his eye. To the outside world, he was the dutiful

The Longfellow House, Cambridge, MA.

grandson of America's most beloved poet, a distinguished scholar of Russian drama and the keeper of the flame at the Craigie (Longfellow) House in Cambridge. But behind the heavy drapes of 105 Brattle Street and along the rocky, salt-sprayed coast of the North Shore, Harry lived a life that vividly defied the stiff collar of his Brahmin heritage.

*How can you be so cruel?*

Stark, often dangerous contrasts defined his world. In academia, he was the radical pacifist dismissed from Columbia University for his anti-war activism during World War I, a man who pivoted from the classroom to become the "live-in curator" of his grandfather's mansion. Yet, his life was not confined to the dusty archives of Cambridge. On the family's sweeping estate at Dana Beach in Manchester-by-the-Sea, Harry found a respite from the political friction stirred up by his progressive views. The North Shore was his ancestral summer playground, a place of amateur theatricals and ocean air, geographically and socially proximate to the queer enclaves of Gloucester's "Gold Coast." It was here, between the city and the sea, that the rigid expectations of his lineage seemed to soften. He inherited significant family wealth and the Longfellow House in Cambridge.

In the end, Harry Dana did more than just survive the scrutiny of his era; he preserved the past while boldly inhabiting his own truth. He transformed the Longfellow House into a national treasure, meticulously cataloging a history that tried to erase men like him. He died in the home he saved, honoring his famous ancestors not by imitating their lives, but by possessing the courage to live entirely scandalously, as himself.

Shand-Tucci, Douglass. The Crimson Letter: Harvard, Homosexuality, and the Shaping of American Culture.

# Secret Court

KEITH SMERAGE

The sentence was handed down in the summer of 1920, but it took ten years for the execution to be carried out. Keith Smerage (1898 –1930), a promising student in the Class of 1921, was a casualty of Harvard's infamous "Secret Court," a clandestine tribunal convened to purge the campus of "homosexualism."

Smerage's nightmare began with the suicide of his friend, Cyril Wilcox. When private letters revealed a social circle of gay men, President Abbott Lawrence Lowell unleashed a witch hunt. Smerage was dragged before the tribunal, interrogated without representation and forced to confess. The verdict was absolute erasure: expulsion, immediate exile from Cambridge, and a vindictive order to inform his parents and block him from other universities. The irony was suffocating. While President Lowell ruthlessly dismantled Smerage's life for loving men, his own sister,

Keith Smerage as a young boy.

the cigar-smoking, renowned poet Amy Lowell, lived openly in a "Boston marriage" with actress Ada Dwyer Russell just across the river.

Denied his degree, Smerage attempted to reinvent himself. He soon left the "ivory tower" for the world of the performing arts. Adopting the stage name "Richard Keith," he found a new voice as a gifted pianist and baritone. He secured a singing role in the traveling operetta *Blossom Time* and appeared in numerous companies throughout the Boston area. Back home in Topsfield, he became a soloist in the Congregational Church Choir, trying to build a life of beauty from the ashes of his reputation.

*I am one of at least ten times that number.*

But Smerage could not outrun the shadow of the court. In a vicious, heartbroken letter to the administration, he laid bare the institution's hypocrisy. He insisted that Harvard's "reputation for this sort of thing... is nationwide" and admitted he was "sore at being one of eight expelled" when he knew he was just one of "at least ten times that number." He even dared to point the finger back at the ivory tower itself, noting that locals aware of the scandal had a sharp retort for the administration: "Tell them to look to their faculty."

Yet, it was guilt that haunted him most. He confessed his deep regret for naming friends under pressure: "To tell would expel them, while a word of warning, a helping hand, without the 'jolt' of ruining their life careers, could help them out." That jolt had ruined his own career. On September 8, 1930—a decade after his expulsion—Keith Smerage became the third member of the circle to die by suicide, the final tragic victim of a secret war.

Paley, Amit R. "The Secret Court of 1920." The Crimson, Harvard University, 21 Nov. 2002, https://www.thecrimson.com/article/2002/11/21/the-secret-court-of-1920-at/.

Wright, William. Harvard's Secret Court: The Savage 1920 Purge of Campus Homosexuals.

Keith Smerage with violin.

# White Blackbird

Margarett Sargent (1892–1978) lived two lives. To the artistic underground, she was "The White Blackbird"—a rare, rebellious talent. To the polite society of Boston's North Shore, she played the role of Mrs. Quincy Adams Shaw McKean, the perfect mistress of a 54-acre estate in Beverly. But beneath the garden parties and polo matches, Sargent was a radical trapped in a gilded cage.

Born into the stiff "Brahmin" elite as a cousin of the famous painter John Singer Sargent, she rejected the rules of her ancestors. She painted bold, psychological portraits that exposed the unease behind wealthy faces. While her husband lived a traditional life, Margarett smuggled the bohemian world into conservative Beverly, turning her "Prides" mansion into a secret salon for avant-garde artists.

Her deepest rebellion happened behind closed doors. Trapped in an unhappy marriage, Margarett loved women. She had passionate affairs that defied

Portrait of Margarett Sargent, 1919.

the script of her class. Her lovers included the writer Jane Bowles and Isabel Pell, a dashing future French resistance fighter whom Sargent found "wonderfully handsome." Pell visited the estate often and was known to the children simply as "Cousin Pell." This code allowed Margarett to hide her true self in plain sight.

*It just got too intense.*


The pressure of this double life eventually broke her. In 1936, she abandoned her art forever, telling her granddaughter, "It just got too intense." She retreated into silence and alcoholism. Her story almost vanished, but the 1996 biography, *The White Blackbird*, written by her granddaughter, Honor Moore, finally revealed the truth. Margarett Sargent was not a failed socialite; she was a brilliant, tragic pioneer who fought to breathe inside a velvet box.

Moore, Honor. The White Blackbird a Life of the Painter Margarett Sargent by Her Granddaughter.

# FOUR

## The Creative Underground

1950 - 1990

By the mid-20th century, the doors of the "Glass Closet" had blown wide open. The North Shore was no longer just a retreat for wealthy men hiding behind velvet curtains; it became a crucible for a gritty, vibrant and unapologetically public creative underground. In this era, the "queer" spirit moved from the parlor to the street, finding its voice in the ink of Beat poets, the lens of daring photographers and the roar of motorcycles on the coastal roads.

This was the age of the bohemian rebel. In Gloucester, the "Warlock Poet" Gerrit Lansing transformed a dusty room above a bar into a portal for the occult and the avant-garde, drawing icons like Allen Ginsberg to the fishing docks. It was a time when artists did not just create beauty; they documented survival. From the "whimsical figurines" that hid profound truths to the street-wise poets who turned their pain into verses, these heroes used their creativity as a weapon against a conformist world.

But this freedom was not without cost. This section explores the internal battles of those who fought to find peace in a society that often called them "sick." It honors the "painful witnesses" who navigated mental health struggles and addiction to find the other side of sobriety. These were the trailblazers who proved that living authentically wasn't just a stylistic choice—it was a radical, necessary part of staying alive.

# Warlock Poet

Gerrit Lansing

To find the magic in Gloucester, you had to climb past the smell of stale beer. Above the Rigger bar on Main Street, up a narrow staircase, lay the sanctuary of the Abraxas bookstore. Here, amidst piles of occult books and poetry, Gerrit Lansing (1928–2018) held court like a wizard in a fishing village. He transformed a dusty room into a portal where local teenagers and famous authors like Allen Ginsberg could escape the blue-collar grit. Lansing was not merely a poet; he was a mystical anchor who turned a seaside town into a haven for the avant-garde.

Lansing arrived on the North Shore through his friendship with multi-talented and multi-media artist Harry Martin. He moved into Abbadia Mare, a medieval-style fortress perched on the cliffs, where Jack Hammond lived above the Hammond Castle Museum. There, he became a central figure in a legendary mid-century "gay haven." Shielded from a conservative era by stone walls, Lansing and his circle indulged in a life of "exuberant and restless disorder." They hosted nude

Harry Martin, left, with Gerrit Lansing.

swimming parties and literary games, blurring the lines between art and sexuality. A rediscovered sketch by the artist Ellsworth Kelly shows Lansing swimming in the castle pool—a snapshot of a hidden, vibrant world.

While he lived for art, Lansing found his anchor in Deryk Burton, a sailor. Together for thirty-five years, they navigated the Atlantic on private yachts as well as the cultural currents of the North Shore. This stability allowed Lansing to create his complex, magical poetry, collected in *The Heavenly Tree Grows Downward*.

*Above the smell of stale beer, he built a sanctuary of magic.*

But his greatest gift to the town was Abraxas. It was more than a bookstore; it was a clubhouse for the outcast. Lansing treated local teenagers with the same seriousness he gave to visiting scholars. He offered them books by Jean Cocteau for a dollar and told casual stories about dining with famous writers, making the world feel vast and accessible. When he died in 2018, the community gathered in the Great Hall of the Hammond Castle Museum to honor him, proving that magic was not found in ancient texts, but lived daily on the edge of the sea.

Cook, Greg. "Midcentury Gay Haven In Gloucester Revealed In Long Lost Ellsworth Kelly Drawing." Wonderland, 8 June 2024, https://gregcookland.com/wonderland/2024/06/08/hammond-castle/

Grundy, David. Never by Itself Alone: Queer Poetry, Queer Communities in Boston and the Bay Area, 1944-Present. Oxford University Press, 2024. .

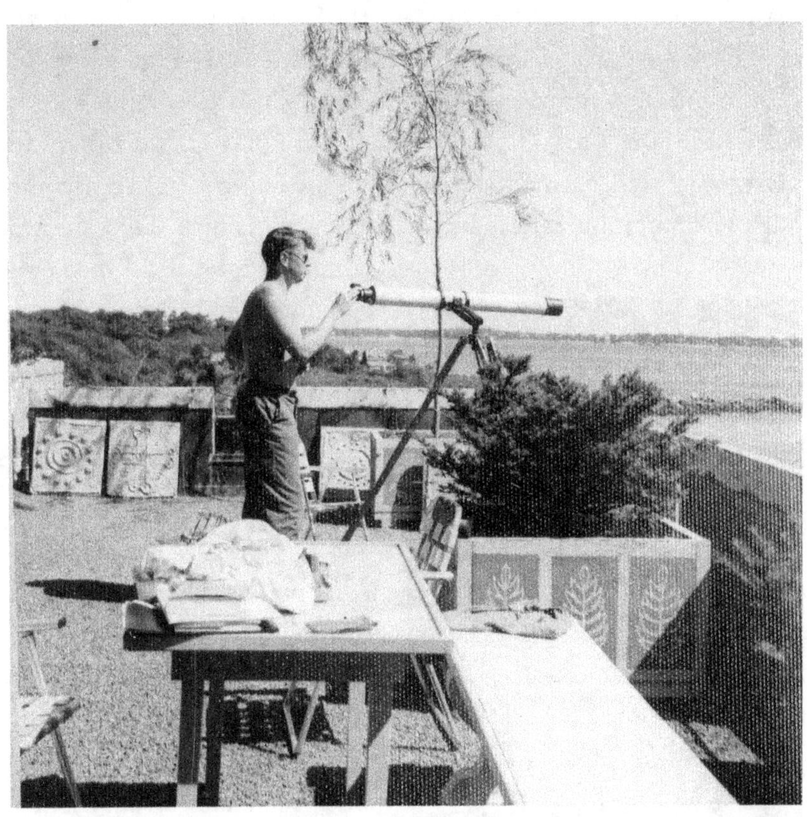

Gerrit Lansing atop the Hammond Castle Museum.

# Whimsical Figurines

HARRY MARTIN

One moment, Harry Martin (1927–1984) stood at the center of the universe, sipping drinks with Tennessee Williams on Broadway; the next, he stood in the salt-spray silence of a Gloucester castle. The sudden death of his partner, the lyricist John Latouche, had shattered his world, leaving him adrift. But a lifeline came from an unlikely source: the eccentric inventor John Hays Hammond Jr. Hammond invited Martin to come to Gloucester and live at Abbadia Mare, now known as the Hammond Castle Museum. Martin accepted, fleeing the ruins of his life in New York to become not just Hammond's guest, but his lover, trading high-stakes theater drama for the medieval grandeur of the North Shore.

In Gloucester, Martin found his voice within a unique intellectual brotherhood. He became a founding member of "Les Cinq," a literary circle that met weekly in the castle's museum. Composed of Martin, Hammond, the poet Gerrit Lansing and his partner Deryk Burton and a local man named Paul Oakley, the group would spend hours

Harry Martin.

playing elaborate literary games and setting creative prompts for one another. It was a salon hidden in stone, where the "Lavender Aristocracy" of the past mingled with the new bohemian energy of the future.

No longer just a supporting character, Martin created art that celebrated his neighbors. He crafted whimsical papier-mâché figurines—vibrant, loving caricatures of Gloucester's ordinary citizens. These weren't just dolls; they were joyful snapshots of a town he learned to love. He was also a skilled and respected photographer, graphic designer, sculptor and filmmaker.

Martin served as the living link between the wealthy, hidden queer elite of the 1920s and the radical counterculture of the 1960s. Though he often stood in the shadow of dazzling personalities, his steady presence held these eras together. He proved that while fame is fleeting, the art of witnessing a community is a masterpiece that endures.

https://www.capeannmuseum.org/news/2025/12/05/cape-ann-cosmos-harry-martins-people/

Papier mâché figurines by Harry Martin: James Joyce; Fisherman; Charlie Chaplin.

# Street-wise Poet

In a cramped apartment on the backside of Beacon Hill, Boston, the lights flickered on, powered by electricity stolen from the landlord. Under this illicit glow, Stephen Jonas (1921–1970)—street hustler, poet genius—held court. He was a phantom living in the service entrance of American culture, scavenging food from dumpsters to feed his friends while crafting poetry that would influence a generation. A queer, African American artist, Jonas rejected the grand experiment of traditional success for a life among thieves and junkies.

He served as a vital link between the gritty Boston streets and the artistic coast of Gloucester. He frequently traveled north to visit his champion, Gerrit Lansing, bringing his Boston lingo—a fusion of jazz slang and occult knowledge—to the salt air of Pigeon Cove. In works like *Exercises for Ear* and *Orgasms,* he treated the page like a musical score. His lines

Stephen Jonas book cover.

evaporate into silence like a jazz trumpet fading in a smoke-filled room.

*A phantom in the service entrance of American culture.*

Jonas acted as a fountain of books for fellow gay poets like John Wieners, even though Jonas struggled with mental health and served prison time for stealing those very books. He lived on the razor's edge of poverty. The emotional reality of his life lives on in a surviving audio recording. In the middle of reading a poem, Jonas simply stops and breaks down weeping. It is a moment of raw, piercing vulnerability. He died young, leaving behind a legacy of unflinching music that proves the most vital history often unfolds in the shadows.

**Jonas, Stephen, et al. Arcana: A Stephen Jonas Reader.**

# Painful Witness

JOHN WIENERS

Outside Beacon Hill, Boston's Charles Street Meeting House in September 1954, Hurricane Edna battered the city. Winds howled, and rain lashed the windows. Inside, a young John Wieners (1934–2002) sat transfixed, watching the poet Charles Olson read as if he were commanding the storm itself. In that moment of violence and beauty, Wieners decided to give his life to poetry.

He became the glamorous tragedy of the North Shore, a man who turned the wreckage of drug addiction and psychiatric wards into lyrics of heartbreaking purity. To polite society, he was a problem to be solved—a junkie, a hustler, a mental patient. But to the region's underground history, he is a saint of the impossible.

> *He turned the wreckage of his life into lyrics of heartbreaking purity.*

His spiritual compass frequently pointed north to Gloucester. There, he found sanctuary among the "Occult School" of poets visiting the mystic Gerrit Lansing to discuss magic. Unlike the rugged masculinity projected by his mentor Olson, Wieners lived an unapologetically queer existence. He navigated a "nightworld" of anonymous encounters and unrequited longing that the Puritan soil of Massachusetts tried to bury. He became the "poet laureate of gay liberation" long before the movement had a name.

Wieners, through the "Good Gay Poets" collective (an offshoot of the *Fag Rag* journal), published the pamphlet *Playboy* (later titled *We Were There! A Gay Presence at the Democratic Convention*), which documented the group's radical presence at the 1972 Democratic National Convention. During the convention, members of the collective—including Charley Shively—drove to Miami to present a list of demands that included the abolition of the nuclear family, the military and prisons, while Wieners' poetry from this period articulated a politics of queer survival and resistance against state oppression.

He found a champion in Allen Ginsberg, who revered him as a "pure poet." While Ginsberg shouted his defiance to the world, Wieners whispered his heartbroken confessions. In his masterpiece,

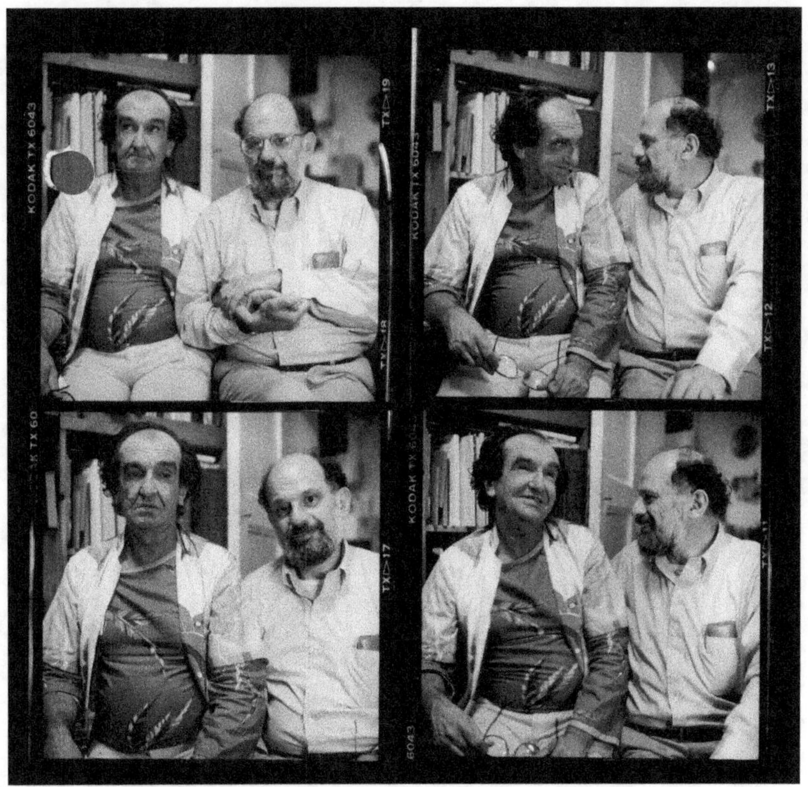

John Wieners, left, with Allen Ginsberg.

*The Hotel Wentley Poems*, and the later *Asylum Poems*, he chronicled the "hurts of wanting the impossible." He wrote of addiction and asylums not as a sociologist, but as a survivor. His legacy is a beautiful, painful witness—a reminder that history includes those who burned out trying to live authentically in a world that had no place for them.

Wieners, John, and Michael Seth Stewart. Stars Seen in Person: Selected Journals of John Wieners.

. Grundy, David. Never by Itself Alone: Queer Poetry, Queer Communities in Boston and the Bay Area, 1944-Present

# A Great Swim

The sketch lay hidden in an archive for decades. It was a simple line drawing labeled, *"It was a great swim, Jack."* But this doodle reveals a secret history. The artist was Ellsworth Kelly (1923–2015), a master of modern art known for cold, silent shapes. The subject was the poet Gerrit Lansing, swimming naked in the pool of a medieval castle in Gloucester. This fleeting moment captures the "double life" of a painter who balanced his rigid art with the warm, chaotic heart of the North Shore's queer underground.

To the world, Kelly's work looks like a monument to silence—massive, vibrating blocks of color detached from human emotion. But for those tracing queer history, his sharp lines are not a refusal of feeling; they are a container for it. He forged his vision in the heat of a life that stretched from Manhattan lofts to the gothic eccentricities of New England.

Archivists found the proof of his secret world in a guest book at the Hammond Castle

Ellsworth Kelly in 2008.

Museum from March 1960. We don't know how often he visited, but that sketch proves he was deep inside the castle's "queer haven." He wasn't just an observer; he was swimming and sketching alongside Lansing and John Hays Hammond Jr., shielded by the stone walls during a time when being queer could ruin a career.

Kelly lived through the "Lavender Scare," a time of government crackdowns from the late 1940s into the 1960s on queer people. He learned to express his queerness through tension, not confession. His breakup with artist Robert Indiana was so volatile that it reportedly inspired Indiana's famous *LOVE* image. Kelly, conversely, poured that passion into paintings where colors kiss but never bleed—vibrating with strictly controlled desire.

His legacy is one of ecstatic silence. Unlike poets who shouted their pain, Kelly distilled his into perfect forms. But that sketch in Gloucester—a friend in the water—reminds us that behind the hard edges of the canvas lived a man deeply embedded in the affections of his time.

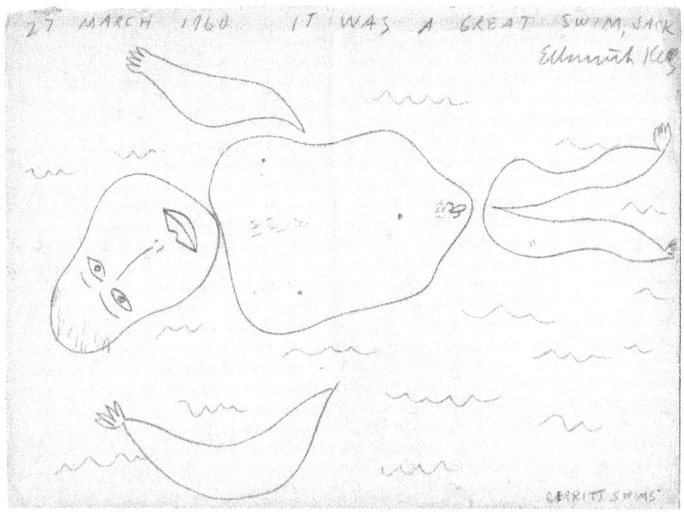


Ellsworth Kelly sketch of Gerrit Lansing.

Robert Indiana, LOVE, 1967.

Ellsworth Kelly, Red Blue Green, 1963. Courtesy of Museum of Contemporary Art, San Diego.

# Maestro

Leonard Bernstein (1918 – 1990) did not just conduct music; he became it. On the podium, he was a vessel of kinetic energy, leaping and sweating, channeling a passion that was too vast to be contained by a single genre—or a single identity. Born in Lawrence, Massachusetts, to Jewish immigrant parents, Bernstein became the first American-born conductor to achieve worldwide fame. But behind the tuxedo and the baton lived a truth that fueled his artistry as much as it complicated his life.

Leonard Bernstein conducting at The Albert Hall in 1973.

While the world saw a devoted husband and father, Bernstein navigated a "double life" that was an open secret among his inner circle. He was, as his collaborator Arthur Laurents bluntly stated, "a gay man who got married." He was a member of the extraordinary quartet of gay Jewish geniuses—alongside Laurents, Jerome Robbins and Stephen Sondheim—who created West Side Story, infusing the American musical with a depth of longing and outsider status that mirrored their own experiences.

Bernstein's life was a symphony of contradictions. He loved his wife, Felicia Montealegre, deeply, and they were married for 25 years. Yet, his sexual and romantic connections with men were constant and vital. From his early infatuation with conductor Dimitri Mitropoulos to his later relationship with Tom Cothran, for whom he briefly left his marriage in 1976, Bernstein refused to stifle his capacity for love.

He was a man who brought the forbidden into the mainstream, whether by blending jazz with symphonies or by advocating for civil rights and nuclear disarmament, even when it was dangerous to do so. To classify Bernstein merely as "bisexual" or "gay" is almost too

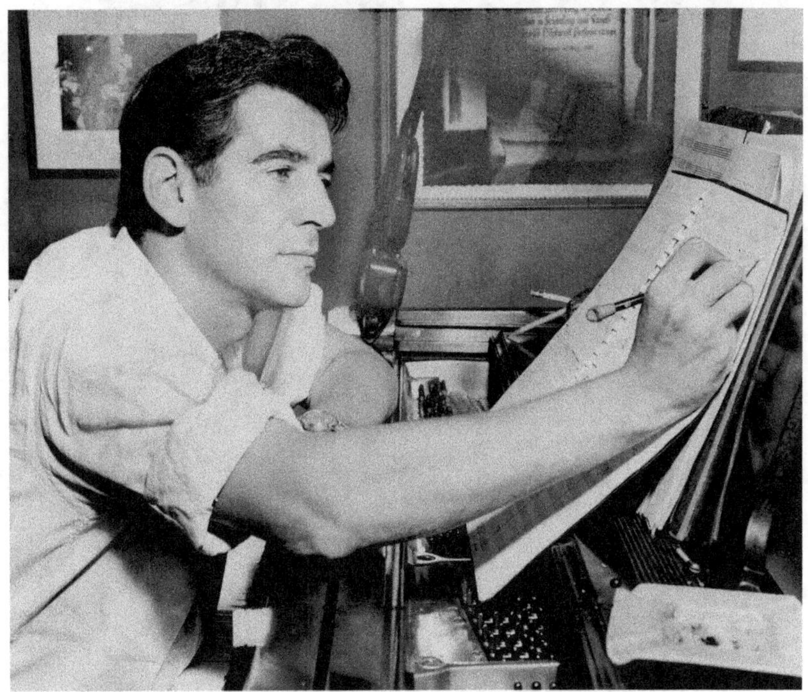

Bernstein at the piano, annotating a musical score, 1955.

small for a man of his appetite; he was a pan-everything enthusiast who loved people passionately.

Today, we reclaim Leonard Bernstein not just as a musical titan but as a queer hero who navigated a homophobic century with flair. He proved that one could be the most celebrated figure in American culture while holding a private world that defied its conventions. In the end, the "Maestro" didn't just teach America how to listen; he taught us that a life lived without passion—in all its forms—is a life not worth living.

Bernstein, Leonard, and Nigel Simeone. The Leonard Bernstein Letters.

Bernstein conducting the New York City Symphony in 1945.

# Danny and Andy

DANNY WILLIAMS & ANDY WARHOL

"You won't have to worry about me being gay anymore."

Danny Williams said it quietly, almost conversationally, to his brother David as they sat outside the family's old Rockport house on a muggy July evening. Locals called it "The Witch House"—legend had it Elizabeth Proctor was sent there when her pregnancy spared her from the noose during the Salem trials. To Danny, just back from New York, the place seemed to sag under the weight of history and rumor. He looked thin. Haunted. As though whatever he'd fled had carved something out of him.

Danny Williams.

After dinner, he told his mother, gently, that he needed a change. Could he borrow her car? She handed him her car keys without a word. He drove toward Pigeon Cove, the sun sinking behind him in molten streaks, lighting the road in a strange, burning glow. At the breakwater, he undressed, alone except for the harbor seals resting on the rocks, their dark eyes following him. What did they see? No one ever saw or heard from Danny again.

Danny had once seemed destined for brilliance. After graduating from Harvard in 1961, he sharpened his film editing on Al Maysles' *Showman,* which helped land Maysles the job of documenting the Beatles. Danny moved to New York and fell into the gravitational field of Andy Warhol's Factory—its whir of creativity, danger and amphetamine-driven possibility. Warhol and Danny became lovers, and Warhol treated him with a rare tenderness. He handed Danny his prized Bolex, a Swiss-made camera of exquisite precision. With it, Danny made more than twenty short films, forgotten for decades until the Andy Warhol Film Project rediscovered them in an archive. Clips now appear in his niece Esther B. Robinson's 2007 documentary, *A Walk Into the Sea*. Scenes flash in and out in a strobe effect he achieved by turning the camera on and off.

Danny was gifted not only with film but with light itself. A circuitry wizard, he pioneered the stroboscopic techniques that electrified Warhol and the Velvet Underground's *Exploding Plastic Inevitable* tour—gyrating bodies flickering in violent bursts of shadow, sadomasochistic pantomimes slicing across screens while the band roared and improvised. His experiments—lighting in rapid pulses— became a foundation of psychedelic light shows.

But the Factory, fueled by methamphetamine and shifting alliances, was merciless. Warhol eventually moved Danny out of his townhouse and into the cold, impersonal studio. Danny showered once a week at the YMCA across the street. Then, little by little, he was pushed out altogether. Disheveled, unwashed, glasses broken, he returned to Rockport with nowhere else to go.

What happened that night at Pigeon Cove remains unknowable. A body was never found. Did he rendezvous with someone and vanish into a new life? Slip from a slick rock? Swim too far into the dark? Or did he walk deliberately into the sea—exhausted, rejected, carrying more sorrow than he could bear?

No one can say. Only the tide remembers.

Robinson, Esther B., director. A Walk Into the Sea: Danny Williams and the Warhol Factory. Arthouse Films, 2007.

Pigeon Cove, by Emma Fordyce Macrae, c. 1930

# Riding for Liberation

ROBERT DOW

On warm nights, the sound of Bob Dow's Harley echoed off the narrow streets of Lynn, Massachusetts — the deep, steady growl of a man determined to be seen. You can imagine the bike gleaming with chrome, a bold white lambda painted on the windshield — the ancient Greek symbol newly reborn as the banner of queer liberation. In 1973, that alone was a declaration of war.

"If you're going to ask people to come out of the closet," Bob liked to say, "then you'd better show an example."

Robert Dow circa 1970.

He had learned that the hard way. When WNAC-TV in Boston asked him to speak about gay rights, Bob — then president of the Homophile Union of Boston (HUB) — spoke with his back to the camera. The words were his, but the shame was visible. He drove home that night, furious at himself. "Never again," he vowed. And he meant it.

From that moment forward, Robert Dow — a working-class man from Lynn, the oldest of five brothers — was all in. When he became HUB's president in 1971, his face and name became inseparable from the movement. He rode across New England — from Boston to Providence, up the coast to Portland, through the Berkshires — talking, arguing and recruiting. "Visibility," he said, "is our weapon."

At the time, visibility came with a cost. Bob knew it well. After the TV appearance, he was fired from his job at Lynn's J.J. Nissen Baking Corporation because his bosses thought his visibility reflected badly on them. Years earlier, he had been dismissed from the Essex County School of Agriculture after someone "turned him in" for a homosexual encounter. Later, in the Navy, he'd been dragged from his ship and locked in the brig after being outed by fellow sailors. When his discharge papers came through, rumors ran wild—drugs, theft, insubordination. Bob climbed onto a table in the crowded barracks and shouted, "It's because I'm queer! Didn't you ever see a faggot before?" The silence that followed was deafening, but he felt free for the first time.

The discharge haunted him long after he came home. Because of it, the Massachusetts Registry of Motor Vehicles refused to renew his driver's license. For seven years, he fought the denial through every legal channel. Finally, one day, he slammed his fist on a clerk's desk and demanded his rights as an American citizen. He walked out with a license—and a story he would tell for the rest of his life. "I'm known to be violent," he said, "but I'm more enraged that I should be driven to violence."



Advertisement for Robert Dow's 1973 appearance on WNAC-TV.

That anger, honed into purpose, became his political engine. By the early 1970s, Boston was becoming one of the few cities where queer people could organize openly — but even then, the work was dangerous. Bob fought for unity among fragmented queer groups, trying to keep the movement from splintering. "In Boston," he said, "if there's trouble with one organization, there's trouble with them all." He believed in solidarity — the belief that survival meant sticking together.

Barney Frank and Elaine Noble — both rising political figures — often sent young activists to learn from him. They found a man who was fiery, restless, impatient with hypocrisy, but generous to anyone willing to stand up and fight.

He and his partner, Don Meuse, lived together in Lynn, though the movement rarely left Bob enough time for home. Don called him "hyperactive," a man who thrived on too little rest. Weekends were spent on the road — HUB meetings in Boston, strategy sessions in Cambridge, and a rally in Providence.

By 1974, HUB was thriving in ways few had imagined when it was started just a few years earlier by members of the Mattachine Society. That summer, the group held a picnic on Lynn Beach, not far from where Bob had grown up. One can imagine the sun was high, the waves gentle. Families, friends and lovers gathered on blankets, laughing in the open air. A small crowd sang "We Shall Overcome" as the tide rolled in. To passersby, it might have looked like any seaside gathering. But for those who had spent years hiding, it was a quiet revolution: the first time many of them had held hands, kissed, or simply *been* in public without fear.

HUB will hold a picnic today on Lynn Beach. Person can gather at the beach at 1 pm, or call HUB at 536-6197 for more information before 9 pm, on Friday, May 31. Bring your own hamburgers and hot-dogs. Chips and rolls will be provided.

Advertisement for 1974 picnic.

Bob arrived on his Harley, the lambda bright against the

blue sky. He kicked down the stand, nodded to friends and looked out over the beach. "This," he said quietly, "is what pride looks like." That picnic wasn't a parade or a protest. It was the movement made ordinary—and visible.

For Bob, liberation was not abstract. It was about living in daylight. He knew anger. He knew loss. But what made him remarkable was what came next — the transformation of fury into leadership. He didn't see himself as a hero, just a man who refused to turn away again. And so he rode through the winding roads of New Hampshire, the fog along the Maine coast, the brick neighborhoods of Boston — a man with a lambda and a purpose.

Each time his Harley roared to life, it was a declaration: that he was here, that he was out, and that he would never again turn his back to the camera.

"Focus On Robert Dow." Gay Community News, 17 Nov. 1973, p. 3.

Postcard of Lynn Beach.

# The Love Part of This

Long before Grace Schrafft forged a path of radical authenticity, she was a wild child on Eastern Point who stole her mother's new car and totaled it, earning a prompt exile to Catholic boarding school. She had grown up in the eccentric orbit of Gloucester's elite, giving summer tours of Henry Davis Sleeper's Beauport mansion and reading in the *Gloucester Daily Times* of John Hays Hammond Jr.'s funeral, where his friend Cardinal Cushing humorously described the inventor as a "queer fellow." But the queer love that would define her own life arrived later, in the form of Grace Moceri (1945–2010).

In the early 1970s, both women were living traditional lives as wives and mothers. Then, lightning struck, and the best friends fell in love. Compelled by a bond they couldn't ignore, they dismantled their conventional worlds, leaving their husbands and packing

Grace Schrafft, left, with Grace Moceri.

up their two infant children—including Moceri's son Jesse, who later grew up to claim his own gay identity—to start a new life in the West. Their path was guided by intuition and psychedelics; Schrafft decided to move the family to Mariposa after woodland sprites told her to do so while she was tripping. There, in the shadow of Yosemite National Park, they built a rustic life where Schrafft's fondest memory was the simple, grounding act of milking the goats.

*Compelled by a bond they couldn't ignore, they dismantled their conventional worlds.*

Their commitment to justice was as deep as their roots. Before leaving the North Shore, Moceri, the daughter of a fishing captain, had already made history by co-founding the Gloucester Fishermen's Wives Association in 1969. Together, they co-founded the Judith Sargent Murray chapter of the Cape Ann Feminists,

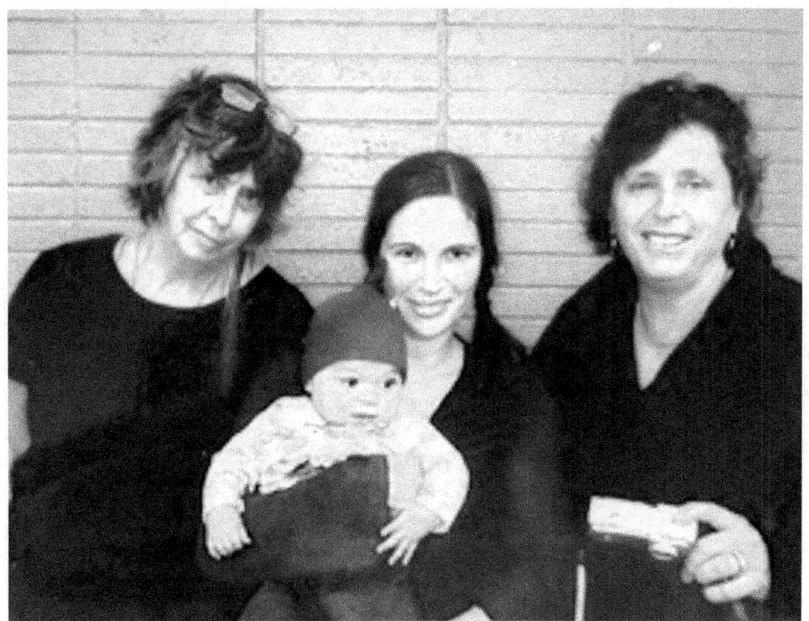

Grace Schrafft, left, Lena holding Hazel and Grace Moceri, whose son, Jess, was the sperm donor for Lena. Lena is Hazel's mother.

establishing a crucial child care and nursery cooperative, consciousness-raising groups, and safe houses for victims of domestic violence.

Their conscience knew no borders. Enraged by the 1997 Acteal massacre—the slaughter of 45 Indigenous pacifists at a prayer meeting in Chiapas—they traveled to Mexico to stand witness, and later to Nicaragua to celebrate the anniversary of the 1979 Sandinista revolution. Schrafft even spent four months in jail for selling pot, a testament to her lifelong refusal to bow to arbitrary authority. Their nearly 40-year partnership, captured in the 2013 documentary *The Love Part of This*, culminated in their 2004 marriage, proving that, for the two Graces, living authentically was the ultimate revolutionary act.

Guerra, Lya, director. *The Love Part of This*.

# Photographer



For decades, Fran Dalton was Newburyport's eyes. Known to most as Frank, she rode through town on an old English bicycle, a camera hanging from the handlebars, capturing a city in the midst of a profound transformation. From the urban decay of the 1960s to the revitalization of the 1980s, her lens documented it all: the crumbling architecture, the riverfront's industrial grit, and the faces of neighbors who called this shifting landscape home.

Frances Martina Dalton.          Frank Dalton.

But while Fran was documenting the city's transition, she was also navigating her own. Born and raised as male, she lived much of her life with a secret that she only fully revealed in her later years. In the mid-1980s, at the age of fifty-eight, Fran transitioned, finally stepping into the world as the woman she had always known herself to be. It was a brave act of authenticity in a time and place where such journeys were rarely visible.

Her legacy was preserved by friends Frank and Colleen Stiriti, who compiled her thousands of slides into a book, ensuring her dual journey—of a city reborn and a woman self-realized—would not be lost. Today, Fran Dalton is remembered not just as a chronicler of Newburyport's history, but as a quiet pioneer who proved that it is never too late to become who you really are.

Stiriti, Frank and Stiriti, Colleen. Images of Life, Change & Beauty: Photographs, Poetry & Art - Selections from the Works of Fran Dalton,

Frank Dalton behind a mannequin.

The Ghost of Inn Street by Fran Dalton.

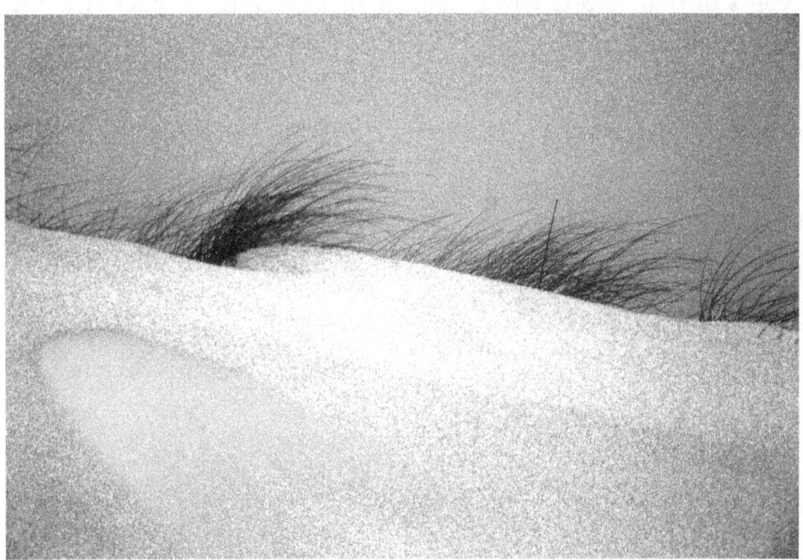

Photograph by Fran Dalton.

# My Search for Peace

JIM ZIPPER

Jim Zipper was a brilliant engineer who was tormented by self-loathing. Working with a priest, Jim started Homosexuals Anonymous in 1961 as a support group. The priest betrayed him and used the group to shame homosexuals. This led Jim to attempt suicide on the tracks of the MTA and was the first of many hospitalizations.

Once Jim got sober, he started going to Alcoholics Anonymous. Yet even in AA, he recognized that queer people needed something more: a place where they could share their stories without code words or shame. So he founded the first gay AA meeting in Lynn, held at the Lynn Hospital. That act was revolutionary—not only because it offered support to others, but because it signaled Jim's own healing. He was no longer hiding. He was creating a community.

The following is from "A Gay Man's Search for Peace," *North Shore Sunday*, December 18, 1983:

"I am a gay man and have lived in Lynn all my life. I like

Jim Zipper in 1980.

Lynn and plan to spend the rest of my life here. However, I find some of the people here have little or no use for me or people like me. They apparently believe we're out to seduce their men and boys. I don't believe this to be true at all. My experience tells me most of us gays just want to be accepted and treated as equals.

"The following is my story. Looking back over my life, I knew as a child of seven or eight that I was gay. Gay wasn't the word used in those days, however. I'm 45 now.

"Man, was it scary being gay. There was no one to talk to. I couldn't talk to my family or friends, I knew how they felt. I couldn't talk to my church, God, school or teachers, I knew how they felt. To say the least, this left me alone and isolated. In my younger years this wasn't so bad. But in my high school years the isolation hurt a lot. I was alone, an outcast.

"Just to be able to live, I learned to please other people. I never let my feelings, thoughts or desires be known. Outwardly. I did, acted and said what others expected. Inwardly, I was scared, rejected and hurt. I kept busy during those years going to school and working. I was a good student, a good employee and a good son.

"From high school I went into the Air Force. If I thought high school was painful, man was I in for a sorrowful awakening. All hell broke loose there. We had open barracks and common showers. Most of the time I was scared stiff. I was fearful someone would notice my glance or sense my desire to be close. They talked openly about their hatred for queers and faggots. They led me to believe that my feelings and affections weren't okay. That I was truly no good. That I had no right to exist.

"I drank anything and everything I could whenever I could. Escape from this hell was all I cared about. After four years of that torture I was a broken human being. Sometime in the next couple of years I sought help from my church. What a disaster that was. It ended when they firmly convinced me I was no good and I attempted suicide.

"This was the prelude to my next 20 years of living hell. This brought craziness, mental wards and tranquilizers. When I wasn't crazy or drunk, I was drugged. Horror, stark terror, insane fear, total hate and despair ran me. I had no control over myself and whatever happened, happened.

"Today, I'm in my fifth year of sobriety. Some of this time I've spent in therapy. All of the time has been spent trying to rebuild my life.

"Today, I like myself. That's the most beautiful feeling. I wake up and am thankful to be alive. I walk along the beach and am thankful for its restful sounds and comforting sights.

"Today, after much hell, I realize that it's okay to be me. That it's okay to have and express my feelings and affections. That it's okay to love those of my choice. Today, I do my best not to get angry at people who call me names and laugh at me. I do my best to realize that they have problems and hope that they also will find peace.

"I look forward to the day when insight and awareness will allow us all to walk hand in hand, to be open and honest about our feelings and affections. Maybe not in my lifetime, but someday.

"Unreal? I hope not. I plan to spend the rest of my life working toward that goal. I'm sure others are doing the same. Till then, peace."

"A Gay Man's Search for Peace." North Shore Sunday, 18 Dec. 1983.

*Lynn, MA* — North Shore Gay AA weekly meeting. Lynn Community Health Center, 86 Lafayette Park. 7pm. Info: 599-5928.

Advertisement for 1981 Gay AA meeting.

# FIVE

## Claiming Space

For the queer community of the North Shore, survival required more than just courage; it required territory. In a society that demanded their invisibility, claiming physical space was a radical act of defiance. This section explores the "sacred geography" of the region—the gritty bars, the vibrant dance floors and the quiet living rooms where the isolated finally found their tribe and built their chosen families.

Interview.

It began in the shadows, often on the rough edges of industrial towns. At places like the Light House Café in Lynn—later reopened as Fran's Place, the oldest queer bar in Massachusetts—lesbians and straight male sailors forged an unlikely alliance, creating a "safe harbor." These venues were not just businesses; they were life rafts. Inside the doors of queer bars a generation found a spiritual home on the sticky dance floor, discovering more compassion in the nightlife than in the pews of the churches that rejected them.

But visibility came with a price. To claim space was to invite the gaze of the police and the fists of those who hated difference. This history honors the resilience of those who faced the raids, the "bashings," and the systemic harassment, yet refused to abandon their sanctuaries. From the underground house parties to the public pride of the Salem Rainbow Stroll, these heroes proved that a community is not just a group of people—it is a place where you can finally walk through the door, exhale and be entirely, unapologetically yourself.

# Safe Harbor

KATHY CLAY

"Sure, I've been to the Light House — and I've got the scar to prove it," says bar patron Pat Ferguson with a half-smile, running her finger from her eyebrow down to her chin. "I heard a knock at the back door, opened it and whoosh! She was waiting there with a broken bottle, trying to get somebody else."

The Light House Café in Lynn was that kind of place — dangerous, unpredictable, but somehow still a refuge. For many women, it was more than a bar. It was a haven, a hidden harbor for lesbians long before there was anywhere else to go.

Kathy Clay, right, at Fran's Place in 1983.

The story begins back in 1937. Hugh and Mary Collins had wanted to open a restaurant on Union Street that March, but City Hall stood in their way. So they set their sights elsewhere and, that December, opened the Light House Café on Washington Street, right across from Lynn Harbor.

From the beginning, lesbians were part of the story. At first, it was a sailors' bar — loud, boisterous and filled with men who'd just come back from the sea with pockets full of money and a hunger for life on land. "It started out as a seamen's bar," remembered longtime patron Jim Zipper. "Actually, the lesbians started going there first for prostitution — getting the sailors' money. It was the attraction of those people to the big money of the seamen that brought the gay and lesbian crew there."

Jay Collins, whose grandfather founded the place, remembered the mix of worlds colliding inside those walls. "We used to get a lot of Navy people," he said. "But then when it became gay, it was technically supposed to be off-limits to servicemen — though they still came."

The Light House Café, Lynn, MA, in 1974.

When the harbor was filled in during the 1950s, and the shipping business died down, the sailors stopped coming. The bar changed with the times — and by then, the Light House had become a place that truly belonged to the lesbians who had always found their way there.

Interview.

It was still rough, though. No one walked through those doors without knowing there was a chance things could turn ugly. "When you walked in there, it was totally crazy," said Kathy Clay. "You didn't know if you were going to make it home alive. You'd just be sitting at the bar and shotguns, and .22 bullets galore would come flying through the door."

Once, a biker gang stormed in and took everyone hostage. "They started drinking down the bar and smashing bottles in the corner." Clay pleaded. "The only thing we asked was, if you're going to kill us, can we get drunk, too? So they let us drink too."

For women like Kathy, the Light House was more than a wild bar — it was salvation. As a teenager, Kathy refused to wear dresses. Her family didn't understand her, branded her as "rebellious," and they had her committed to Danvers State Mental Institution. Just before her release, a nurse slipped her a note. "When you get out of here," the nurse whispered, "I want you to go to this place." It was the address of the Light House.

"When I finally walked in," Kathy remembered, "one of the first people I saw was that nurse. And I thought, Oh God, it's not me. I'm not crazy. Finally — jeez — it's not me. Look at them all."

The Light House may have been rough and rowdy, but for countless women, it was the first place where they could breathe.

https://www.unitedlynnpride.com/topics/fran%E2%80%99s-place-and-the-light-house

# A Palace

JOANNE PATRIZZI MACDONALD

"It was a palace; they had gays and lesbians from all over. It was wild." These are the words of the late activist Jim Zipper, remembering a brief, shimmering moment on the Lynnway when the Aquarius Lounge defied the gritty norms of 1960s queer nightlife. Rising from the waterfront like a neon mirage in 1969, the Aquarius was not a hidden dive but a declaration of luxury. It was Lynn's first new queer bar in thirty-two years, a beautiful, big venue that rivaled the flashy establishments of Route 1. But like many bright flames of that era, it burned hot and fast, meeting a

Joanne Patrizzi, left, in 1983.

suspicious, fiery end in the ocean just two years later.

Interview.

At the center of this opulent experiment was Joanne Patrizzi MacDonald (1940–2015), a woman whose life was as dramatic and textured as the club she helped build. Born into a world of sharp edges and high stakes, Joanne was a lesbian navigating a treacherous landscape of family expectations and underworld whispers. Rumors persisted that mob money fueled the Aquarius's plush carpeting and ornate French mirrors, a suspicion deepened by Joanne's own colorful history. She was a hustler in the most resourceful sense, admitting to "wheeling and dealing and selling hot stuff" just for the thrill of it. She once worked as an escort in Florida to escape the drudgery of Lynn shoe factories, always chasing the next connection, the next deal, because she "didn't care about money" as much as the action itself.

Her personal life was equally constrained by the heavy hand of tradition. Despite her identity, she was forced into a marriage with a man, a desperate ultimatum delivered by her family: marry or lose her inheritance. She complied, securing her financial future but never compromising her spirit. She poured her ambition into the Aquarius, envisioning a "perfect place" with nice rooms and elegant decor, a sanctuary that demanded respect. "I even put in French mirrors," she recalled with a touch of bitterness regarding the club's violent end. "I tell you, they destroyed them."

The Aquarius Lounge operated only from 1969 to 1971; it was destroyed by a fire of suspicious origin that many believed was no accident. Today, it exists only in the memories of patrons, who recall a fleeting "palace" on the water where the carpet was plush, the crowd was wild, and the queer community of the North Shore partied in style.

# Welcoming to All

TISHA STERLING

The first time Robert Muise looked in the mirror and saw Tisha Sterling staring back, the fear vanished. The lashes were heavy, the sequins caught the dim light of Fran's Place and the shy boy from Gloucester was gone. In his place stood a queen who could command a room with a lip-sync and an arched brow. Tisha wasn't just a character; she was armor. For the next forty years, she would stand at the door of that bar, a glittering guardian for every other lost soul who needed to know that they, too, could be royalty.

Robert Muise grew up in Gloucester feeling half-visible, as if he were watching life through a window no one else could see through. He knew he was different long before he had a name for it. Gloucester in the 60s and 70s wasn't a place where a boy could say he wanted to wear women's clothes, or that he felt more alive when he imagined himself on a stage, sequins catching the light. He kept all that hidden and moved quietly through the world, waiting for somewhere—anywhere—to open its arms to him.

He found it on a cold night in Lynn.

He had heard whispers about a bar on Washington Street—Fran's Place—one of only two queer bars on the North Shore. A place where men danced together, where women who'd been pushed to the margins found each other in the glow of colored lights. "I've gone into bars," one patron once said in a newspaper story about

Fran's, "and when I went into the bar, there were all those people just like me. Wow."

Robert pushed open the door for the first time sometime in the late 1970s and felt exactly that—Wow. The mirror ball turned lazily overhead, catching little stars of light on every wall. Music poured from the speakers. People were laughing, drinking, and dancing. No judgment, no fear. He later said that he knew, almost instantly, "Fran's was home."

It wasn't long before he tried something he had only dreamed of: he experimented with makeup, wigs, and dresses. Tentative at first— lashes that trembled, lipstick uneven—but then braver, bolder,

Tisha Sterling performing.

freer. The staff encouraged him. Patrons cheered him on. Someone said, "Honey, you belong on that stage." And they were right.

He created his drag persona: Tisha Sterling.

And Tisha, unlike Robert, was incandescent.

She emerged under the lights in a cascade of sequins and attitude, lip-syncing Cher so perfectly that crowds swore they were seeing the real thing. Her timing was exquisite, her expressions fearless, her energy magnetic. Before long, she wasn't just performing—she was organizing full drag revues, theme nights and eventually a drag competition that became a staple of Fran's nightlife. Sunday nights, Tuesday karaoke, Wednesday oldies—Tisha kept it all humming, turning the bar into a glittering circus of joy and rebellious authenticity.

"She could have dressed like a chicken, and it wouldn't matter," a longtime patron joked years later. "We're about having a good time,

Outside Fran's Place in 1983.

not judging anybody." That spirit—open, defiant, welcoming—was what made Fran's Place thrive.

Interview.

Tisha rose from performer to bartender to manager. By the 1980s, at the height of the AIDS crisis, she was leading Night of 100 Stars, a drag fundraiser that brought performers from all over to raise money for people living with HIV. At a time when stigma ran rampant and funerals were constant, the bar was a lifeline. "Fran's Place has been like home," Tisha would later say. "Before gay marriage and equal rights came about, holidays were like you would typically go home to your birth family. Many people were not accepted by their families and would come to Fran's."

During the worst years—when hateful messages and even vandalism hit the building—the community stood by the bar. They always had. Fran's was welcoming to everyone: gay, straight, bisexual, transgender, drag queens, seniors, curious newcomers, the lonely, the lost, the joyful. It didn't matter. As one manager said to the press, "It's just a place for everyone to come in and have a good time."

> *Leave your problems at the door. This is about
> having a good time, about music and dancing.*

By 2016, when Fran's finally closed its doors, Tisha Sterling was the longest-serving employee, having worked there for decades. The closing was more than a business decision—it was the end of an era. The building at 776 Washington Street had housed a queer bar in the Collins family for nearly 79 years, dating back to The Light House Café in 1937—the oldest queer bar in Massachusetts. Drag shows, strippers, comedy nights, karaoke, Latin nights, disco, pinball—it had all lived within those walls, shaping generations.

When the owner announced the property's sale, Tisha stood in the nearly empty sports bar. Reporters wrote that the hardest part for her wasn't losing the job—it was losing the people, the community, the constancy of showing up for everyone who needed her.

But Lynn did not forget.

In 2022, Tisha Sterling received an official citation from the Mayor and City Council in recognition of her decades of service to the queer community. The kid from Gloucester who once felt invisible was celebrated as an icon—a queen who brought light, laughter and a safe family to thousands.

At Fran's Place, she had once said, "Leave your problems at the door. This is about having a good time, about music and dancing."

And for forty years, she made that true. Tisha turned a bar into a home, a stage into a sanctuary, and a life once lived in shadows into a legacy that will outshine the mirror ball forever.

https://www.unitedlynnpride.com/topics/fran%E2%80%99s-place-and-the-light-house

Tisha at the *Through a Rainbow Lens* exhibit opening in 2024.

# Working Class

PAT GOZEMBA

On a Halloween night in the early 1980s, the patrons of Fran's Place in Lynn, Massachusetts, witnessed a scene that perfectly encapsulated the irreverent, fearless spirit of Pat Gozemba. Dressed in full habits—surplus costumes from a production of *The Sound of Music*—Gozemba and her girlfriend, Judith Holmes, swept into the working-class bar. "The bar goes into an uproar," Gozemba recalled, describing the moment the crowd realized two "nuns" were

Wendy Robinson, left, with some founding members of The History Project, Pat Gozemba, Janet Kahn, Chris Czernik and Libby Bouvier at Fran's Place circa 1984.

hitting the dance floor. As the music swelled, Judith began stripping off the wimple and veil, sending the room into a frenzy of laughter and applause. It was a moment of pure, subversive joy, but beneath the antics lay a profound and serious purpose. Gozemba was there not just to dance, but to bear witness. She was there to ensure that the women of the North Shore—the factory workers, the "butches" and "femmes," the survivors of a harder era—were not erased from history.

*Rather than retreat, Gozemba wrote a letter to the student newspaper, outing herself and effectively becoming the first openly lesbian faculty member on campus.*

Gozemba is a North Shore queer icon, a title earned through decades of refusing to be silent in a world that preferred secrets. Born in 1940 into an Irish working-class family in Somerville that

Patrons at Fran's Place in 1984.

later moved to Waltham, Gozemba grew up in the shadow of hypocrisy. She watched her mother maintain a decades-long affair with a priest—a man who would eventually stand at the altar at Gozemba's own wedding to a man in 1967. That marriage, and the silence required to sustain the family's image, forged a steely resolve

Paper.

in Gozemba to live authentically. She later noted that she was someone "very disturbed by family secrets," realizing that the only antidote to shame was visibility. By 1969, she had fallen in love with a woman and began claiming her own identity, eventually divorcing her husband amicably.

This commitment to visibility defined her tenure at Salem State College where she taught English and Women's Studies. In 1975, amidst a fight for salary equity for women, a university vice president dismissed the activists as "man-hating dykes." Rather than retreat, Gozemba wrote a letter to the student newspaper, outing herself and effectively becoming the first openly lesbian faculty member on campus. She did it for the students, knowing they needed to see that a queer person could hold a job, buy a house and live a full life. She became a force for labor rights, serving as the faculty union president and fighting tirelessly for equal pay.

Her activism naturally bled into her scholarship. As a founding member of The History Project in Boston, Gozemba was critical of how queer history often focused on the wealthy or the male. She wanted to find the "working-class women," the ones who toiled in Lynn's shoe factories and found sanctuary in bars like The Light House. Armed with a camera and her gregarious charm, she attended reunions at Fran's Place, convincing wary patrons to share their stories. The resulting work, *In and Around the Light House*, co-authored with Janet Kahn, remains a seminal text on working-class lesbian bar culture, documenting a world of violence, poverty

Interview

and fierce, life-saving friendship. She honored these women not as victims, but as survivors who navigated a hostile world with grit.

Gozemba's drive to correct the record continued well into the new millennium. She pushed the North Shore Gay Alliance to become the North Shore Gay and Lesbian Alliance (NSGLA), refusing to let lesbians be subsumed under a generic label. When the fight for marriage equality reached its fever pitch in Massachusetts, she was there on the front lines. With her wife, Karen Kahn, and photographer Marilyn Humphries she co-authored *Courting Equality: A Documentary History of America's First Legal Same-Sex Marriages*, ensuring that the grassroots struggle for civil rights was preserved for posterity.

Today, living in Salem Willows with Karen and their cat, Sparky, Gozemba remains a formidable guardian of her community. Her activism has evolved to encompass the planet itself; as a leader of the Salem Alliance for the Environment (SAFE), she has fought against polluting gas leaks and advocated for environmental justice communities. State Senator Joan Lovely perhaps summarized Gozemba's impact best: "There is no one fiercer than Pat Gozemba, fighting for marginalized populations to bring justice, fairness and equity to all." From the dance floor of Fran's Place to the picket lines of Salem State and beyond, Gozemba has spent a lifetime proving that history belongs to those brave enough to write it.

Kahn, Karen, and Patricia A. Gozemba with photographs by Marilyn Humphries, Courting Equality: A Documentary History of America's First Legal Same-Sex Marriages.

Kahn, Janet, and Patricia A. Gozemba. "In and around the Lighthouse: Working-Class Lesbian Bar Culture in the 1950s and 1960s." Gendered Domains: Rethinking Public and Private in Women's History.

# Saving Fran's Place

TONY LECONDINO & DOMINIC SERINO

On the bitterly cold November night in 1981, Lynn felt half-asleep under a crust of frost. At Fran's Place on Washington Street, one of the only queer refuges on the entire North Shore, the mirror ball had finally stopped its lazy spinning. The disco beat had died out. The dance floor—hours earlier alive with a Saturday night crew of drag performers, queer couples and friends who had nowhere else to feel at home—was now a sticky patchwork of spilled beer.

Tony Lecondino, known throughout the bar scene as Tony the Tiger, was the last person inside. He wasn't just the manager—he was the builder, the fixer, the DJ, the protector. He had already lived a life before Fran's: a Catholic kid from Revere, a misfit who loved music, a teen who snuck into Boston's queer clubs for the first time and a U.S. Navy veteran who had served on the U.S.S. *Farragut* off the coasts of Spain and Cambodia. He had learned patience there, discipline, grit. He had learned how to hold his ground when everything around him felt uncertain.



The Great Fire of Lynn, 1981.

That would matter more than he could imagine.

Tony was cashing out the drawer, snapping rubber bands around neat stacks of bills, wiping down the counter. It was past 2:30 a.m.; all he wanted was to go home. But something felt wrong—an unnatural heat pressing against the windows. He stepped to the door, cracked it open, and the smell hit instantly: thick, acrid smoke rolling down Washington Street like a living thing.

Five blocks away, flames had erupted inside one of the old Oxford Shoe buildings—abandoned, dry, explosive as tinder. Within minutes, the structure blew open, sending columns of fire into the sky. The wind caught them and dragged them east and south, igniting factory after factory, building after building. The fire swallowed everything: Dyer Leather, Marshall's Wharf, entire rows of shoe factories that firefighters had called "a disaster waiting to happen." The blaze spread so violently that crews from more than 30 cities—Boston, Cambridge, Salem, even Salem, New Hampshire—responded. Five hundred firefighters were eventually on the ground, many saying afterward that they had "never seen anything like it."

Tony watched the orange glow swell higher, closer, hotter. The temperature inside Fran's climbed. He shut the door. Locked it. And he made the decision that defined the night.

He wasn't leaving.

The pounding on the door came fast. "You have to evacuate the building!" the firefighters shouted. But Tony looked around the bar, he had transformed from a dark, dingy, unfriendly place into a dance club and sanctuary—one of the only places on the North Shore where lesbians, gays, bisexuals, drag queens, trans people and anyone who'd been rejected elsewhere could dance side by side. Fran's Place had become a nightly miracle, a home when home wasn't safe.

He told the fire department, "I'm not going to leave the building."

Then he locked the door again.

While flames clawed up and down Washington Street, Lynn Ladder #1, parked across from the bar, grew so hot that the truck itself caught fire and collapsed. The air was filled with sparks blown sideways by the wind. The temperature in the bar climbed toward ninety degrees despite the air conditioners blasting. Tony could hear the roar of the fire—an animal sound, deep and furious.

Then, through the chaos, he heard it: "Hello? Hello? Hello?"

Outside stood a cluster of seniors from a nearby building, evacuated into the freezing night, some without coats, some in slippers, some terrified and half-frozen. Tony opened the bar doors wide and ushered them in. Over the next several hours, they huddled in the overheated, smoky nightclub as Tony moved through the room

Tony, The Tiger, Lecondino tending bar.

checking on them, calming them, offering water to both them and the firefighters who slipped inside for brief, gasping breaks.

He stayed on the phone with the fire chief, repeating the same words: "I'm not leaving." Those words changed everything. The department realized that if they pulled back, Tony—and therefore Fran's—would be lost. So they boxed the bar in with protection. One hose truck on Sagamore Street. Another directly in front of Fran's. Both aimed nonstop streams of water at the roof. The bowling alley next door was saved. The block was saved. And Fran's Place—the queer heart of the North Shore—survived because one man refused to walk out the door.



The seniors stayed with him for nearly three hours until the Red Cross arrived. The heat inside remained brutal, the air thick with smoke, but the building held. Tony watched through the windows as walls of nearby buildings collapsed, fountains of sparks shooting into the air. Firefighters staggered past, exhausted, some injured. The Blue Note Tavern went up in flames. The Hotel Edison was evacuated. Hundreds were displaced. Veteran firefighters stood on the street at dawn, shaking their heads, saying they had never experienced anything so intense.

But Fran's Place still stood—scorched, soaked, steaming, but standing.

Tony didn't brag about it later. He just said, "If it wasn't for me refusing to leave the building, the building would be gone." The firefighters agreed.

He had held the line with nothing but nerve and stubborn resolve, a Navy man's steadiness and the fierce loyalty of someone who understood what Fran's meant to the people who needed it.

If Tony the Tiger had stepped outside that night—if he had listened, or panicked, or surrendered to fear—Fran's Place would have burned like everything around it.

Instead, one man stayed inside

while a city burned around him,

and saved a home that had saved so many others.

Lynn suffered another catastrophic fire earlier the same year. In February 1981, a fire that began at the gritty queer bar Tamany Hall consumed much of Central Square. A dozen businesses burned. The Poultry Center, Sherman Jewelry and the Coral Room ignited one by one as 500 firefighters fought the inferno.

Owner Dominic Serino was not convicted of arson, but of mail fraud. He had mailed "puffed" invoices to boost his insurance claim—half of Central Square burned for a $56,000 scam.

Fran's Place—Tamany Hall's rival—had its own share of mysterious fires. "Through that time, it was extremely tough... and I was getting the word... it was the guy up the street," recalls Jay Collins, owner of Fran's. After Serino's conviction, Collins told the fire inspector. "I can guarantee you you will never see another fire in Fran's," he told him. "And we never did have one."

https://www.unitedlynnpride.com/interviews/tony-lecondino

# The Guide

GARY DOTTERMAN

Gary Dotterman (1944–2023) learned the cost of justice when he was just a teenager in Oklahoma, feeling the baton of a police officer crack against his ribs for helping Black citizens register to vote. He didn't stop. He carried that fire from the Jim Crow South to the jungles of Vietnam and finally to the printing presses of Lynn. When he launched *The Guide to Gay New England* in 1980, it wasn't a business decision; it was a continuation of the same fight— a roadmap for survival handed to a community that was being hunted in the streets.

The Guide to Gay New England.

Gary Dotterman lived a life that defied simple categorization, evolving from an anti-racist organizer in Jim Crow Oklahoma to a Vietnam veteran who turned against the war and finally emerging as an "irrepressible and fearless" pioneer for queer rights. Born into poverty in Tulsa, Dotterman's political awakening began early; by age 12, he was volunteering on campaigns and helping Black citizens register to vote. His time in Vietnam, where he witnessed the brutality of imperialism firsthand, radicalized him further, transforming him into a lifelong peace activist who later sought personal reconciliation with the people of Vietnam.

> *If we don't write our own guide to survival, no one else will.*

Although his activism took him from Washington, D.C. to Brazil, Dotterman left an indelible mark on the North Shore of Massachusetts and Boston. After moving to the area, he became a fixture in the local political scene, serving as a staffer for gay Boston City Councilor David Scondras. However, his advocacy came at a personal cost; he was fired under pressure from right-wing opponents for his queer rights work, a battle he fought in court and won. Beyond politics, he was also an entrepreneur and community builder, opening queer bars in Boston that provided vital social spaces for the community.

Gary Dotterman, left, with Tony Lecondino.

Dotterman's influence reached even further through the printed word. While living in Lynn for a time, he produced the seminal publication *The Guide to Gay New England*. Printed at various locations around Massachusetts and known simply as "The Guide," this magazine became a lifeline for queer people across the region. Tony Lecondino, the manager at Fran's Place in Lynn, remembered his close friend's publication as essential reading: "It became very popular and became national.....It told you where you could go. Gay bars in different countries and even different states. It was very informative."

A committed socialist, Dotterman eventually joined the Communist Party USA, where he became a driving force in pushing the organization to renounce its past homophobia and fully embrace the queer movement. His life was a testament to the idea that the fight for justice is universal, spanning from the shop floors of Tulsa to the political offices of Boston and the queer bars of Lynn, leaving behind a legacy of solidarity that refused to be silenced.

Atkins, C.J. "Remembering Gary Dotterman: Anti-Racist Oklahoman, Vietnam Vet for Peace, and Irrepressible Gay Communist."

# North Shore Bars

"It was the best church I'd ever been to."

That confession by Rev. Donna, a regular of 47 Central who had been told all her life that queer people were "the scum of the earth," reveals the true nature of the North Shore's nightlife. In a history book filled with human courage, we must also honor the brick-and-mortar heroes: the bars themselves. These venues were not merely businesses; they were our silent partners in survival, the only places

Mr. Dominic's at 212 Broad Street, Lynn, MA in 1984. This address was the site of six queer bars in the 1980s.

where we could "strip off" the armor required to navigate the daylight world and finally be at home.

Step inside, and the gray industrial streets of Lynn vanished, replaced by a sensory overload that signaled safety. The air was a thick, heady mix of stale beer, expensive perfume and the sharp chemical tang of hairspray and adrenaline. Under the spinning glitter of the mirror ball, the tacky floor became holy ground. Here, the bartenders were more than drink-slingers; they were the best friends who guarded your secrets and the therapists who listened when the world turned its back. The DJs were the high priests, spinning the anthems that kept the party going until the 1 a.m. lights came up.

It was a world of dizzying possibilities. On any given night, you might find yourself cheering at the "Dating Gayme," marveling at the glamour of "Miss Gay North Shore," or throwing dollars at the stage during the legendary "Night of 100 Stars" charity drag revue. You squeezed into private booths for stolen moments, navigated the

Hat from Joseph's Restaurant, Lynn, MA.

haze for a hookup, or locked eyes with a future spouse across the room—or perhaps the one that got away.

But this sanctuary had an edge. It was a place of exotic dancers and hushed drug deals, where the joy was often spiked with danger. Fights broke out, and the threat of the police was real. At Fran's Place, a button at the door would flash the lights to warn of a raid, prompting men to grab women and pretend to be "straight" couples on the dance floor. Yet, despite the raids and the risks, we kept coming back. In a city that demanded invisibility, these bars were the miracle where we could finally be ourselves in the open—glittering, loud and unafraid.

https://www.unitedlynnpride.com/trl-map

https://www.unitedlynnpride.com/trl-timeline

https://www.unitedlynnpride.com/trl-photos

Joseph's Restaurant owner, Joe Grover, at the bar.

## North Shore Queer Bars

Byfield: HyWay Inn; 1960s

Gloucester: Hotel Delphine; 1950s

Haverhill: Friend's Landing

Ipswich: Fantasy's

Lynn: The Light House Café; 1937-1975, Aquarius Lounge; 1969-1971, Mr. Dominic's; 1975-1980, Fran's Place; 1976-2016, Mr. Dominic's II; 1977-?, Tamany Hall Lounge; 1978-1981, Dom's Lounge and Barbeque; 1980, Billy Gee's; 1981, JR's Ranch; 1981-1982, The Gay Blade; 1982, Marco-Marco; 1983, Mr Dominic's; 1983-1988, Joseph's Restaurant; 1988-2004, The Pub at 47 Central; 1999-2009, Club Central; 2004-2004, Max's Pub; 2009-2012, Northern Nights; 2011-2014, Cirque @ 47 Central; 2012-2013, Pub 47 Central; 2013-2015

Peabody: Stars

Rockport: The Spirit

# The Best Bar

GEORGE CHAKOUTIS

"Sit against the wall. Face the door. Know your exit."

This wasn't advice for a soldier; it was George Chakoutis teaching his friends how to have a drink in a queer bar in 1980s Lynn. In a city where smoke bombs and fists were common hazards of a Friday night, George turned 47 Central into a fortress of joy. He didn't just pour drinks; he held the line, creating a sanctuary where, for a few hours, the strategy of survival could be replaced by the simple freedom of a dance.

Nelio Dossantos, George Chakoutis, Amanda Stevens in 2007.

From a landscape of caution and shadow, Chakoutis built something luminous. When he took the helm of 47 Central, he didn't just open a business; he cultivated a community. Under his stewardship, the venue transformed from a mere watering hole into the beating heart of the

Interview.

North Shore's queer life. It was a place where the fear of the outside world dissolved into music, laughter and solidarity. His efforts were undeniable; in 2007, WBZ-TV named 47 Central the "number one gay and lesbian bar on the North Shore," a testament to the vibrant, inclusive atmosphere he had fostered.

*Know your exit. But while you're here, dance.*

But George's legacy extended far beyond the accolades or the nightly receipts. He was a force of nature when it came to giving back, earning a reputation in the *Daily Item* as a "phenomenon of fundraising." Whether it was rallying support for addressing the AIDS crisis or hosting benefits for local organizations, he turned 47 Central into an engine of charity, proving that the community was not just looking out for itself but for the city as a whole.

47 Central Avenue, Lynn, MA in 2004, now Eclipse.

Though 47 Central closed its doors in 2015, the light of community George Chakoutis ignited never truly faded. He created more than a bar; he created a memory of safety and joy in a city that had once offered neither. Today, the reunions he organizes are filled not just with nostalgia, but with the enduring gratitude of a generation that found a home and a family under his roof.

https://www.unitedlynnpride.com/topics/47-central

Lunch menu from 47 Central, Lynn.

# Female Impersonator

SHAWNA DIXON

"Dolly Parton" sashayed onto the stage, her bosom straining against a red sequin dress. The illusion was flawless, but the hunger was real. She dragged a child's red wagon piled high with 14 first runner-up trophies. "What's a girl gotta do to get a f##king tiara around here?" she quipped, dripping with attitude.

This was the electric presence of Shaun Watson—better known as

Shauna Dixon—who headlined shows across Ipswich, Boston, Lynn, Peabody, Methuen and Haverhill throughout the 1990s and early 2000s. With perfect female impersonations, Shauna didn't just imitate people like Dolly Parton, Stevie Nicks, Olivia Newton-John and Annie Lennox; she embodied them. She wowed audiences, captured the heart of a community, and yes, she

Shauna Dixon.

finally got her tiara, winning the title of "Miss Gay North Shore" in 1994 at Fran's Place.

But the sequins often hid a darker reality. In 1994, Shauna became the center of a controversy in Salem when the licensing board threatened legal action to stop her scheduled show at Carmelina's. Officials claimed the restaurant's entertainment license, which permitted karaoke, did not cover a drag show. A media firestorm ensued, fueled by headlines like "Padlock on the make-up case" and "Both sides in guys as girls dispute dig in their heels." While Carmelina's owner pursued an appeal that ultimately failed, the fallout was personal: Shaun lost his day job at a salon.

It was a jagged era when applause barely drowned out the fear of men following her home with baseball bats, and the AIDS crisis claimed friends faster than the music could play. Yet, Shauna never faltered. Whether raising thousands of dollars for a fire victim or lap dancing for a room full of men she did not know were priests, Shauna Dixon proved that while a tiara is nice, true royalty is earned through survival.

Shauna Dixon.

# Bashed

LINDA NICHOLS, JAY GILBERT & DAVID MCLANE

**Linda Nichols** On a grim November afternoon in 1985, the pavement of Lynn became a witness to a brutality that defined an era of terror. Lee Cunningham didn't just assault Linda Nichols; he pummeled her until she lost consciousness, fueled by a hatred so casual it chilled the blood of the few who dared to watch. The violence was public, visceral and terrifyingly prolonged. When spectators, paralyzed by a mix of fear and shock, finally urged him to stop, Cunningham didn't flee or offer an excuse. He simply retorted, "She's queer." In his mind, those two words were not just an explanation, but a complete moral justification for nearly killing a woman in the street.

Jay Gilbert's reward offer in 1980.

But this assault was not an isolated explosion of rage; it was the crescendo of a violent epidemic that had systematically targeted the North Shore's queer community for years. By the time Linda Nichols fell to the ground, the streets of Lynn had long been unsafe for anyone who dared to live openly. The atmosphere was thick with a specific, suffocating dread, where a casual outing could turn into a fight for survival in an instant.

*He simply retorted, "She's queer."*

The roots of this terror reached back to October 1979, outside the sanctuary of Fran's Place on Washington Street. The bar was supposed to be a refuge, but the darkness outside hid a gang of young men lying in wait, hunting for sport. They arrived armed for a massacre, wielding knives and a leather-covered pipe designed to inflict maximum damage without leaving fingerprints. When two men exited the bar, the trap snapped shut. The assault was bloody

Protest supporting Linda Nichols outside Lynn District Court in 1985.

and calculated, a message delivered with cold steel and blunt force: *you are not welcome here.*

The terror soon escalated, claiming ownership of public spaces one by one. In June 1980, the sanctity of Red Rock Park was shattered when two men were viciously attacked at Lynn Beach. This was no scuffle; they were beaten by a man who lashed out with a chain, screaming, "Faggots, get off my beach!" The message was clear: the parks, the streets and the beaches belonged to the violent, and existence itself was a provocation.

It took immense courage to break the silence surrounding these crimes, a courage embodied by Jay Gilbert. A fixture of the political scene who had run for City Council and state representative in the early 1970s, Gilbert had spent a decade shaking hands and asking for votes while carrying a secret that could destroy his career. But when the violence against the local queer community exploded in 1979, Gilbert decided the price of hiding was too high.

Refusing to let the violence outside Fran's Place go unanswered, the local businessman—known to many as the friendly florist from Lafayette Park—stepped out of the closet. He publicly condemned the attacks and put his own money on the line, offering a $200 reward for information

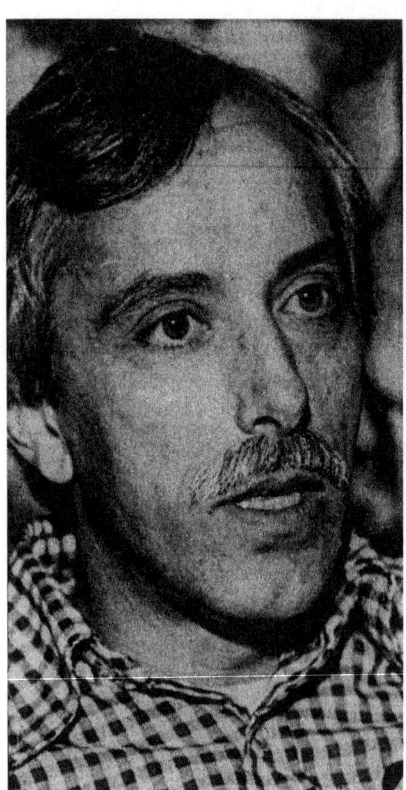

Jay Gilbert in 1979.

leading to the arrest of the attackers. Days later, he sat down for a bombshell interview with *The Daily Item*. Under the headline "Growing Up Gay," Gilbert shattered his carefully built facade. He forced his neighbors to see him not just as a politician, but as a gay man who refused to be terrorized. "People are always afraid of something they don't know," he declared. He didn't ask for tolerance; he demanded dignity.

Violence.

*People are always afraid of something they don't know.*

The loud protest outside Cunningham's hearing in 1985—where a dozen women finally stood as a wall against the apathy—was a watershed moment. However, it would be a mistake to view these scars only as history. While the specific era of terror in Lynn began to fade with fewer assaults, the geography of hate simply shifted, moving from the exposed pavement of downtown Lynn to the shadowed trails of the neighboring coast.

**David McLane** In September 1988, the true face of homophobia revealed itself in Gloucester. Three teenagers set out with a brutal goal: to "roll a fag." They lured David McLane to his apartment, where a night of drinking devolved into a nightmare. The attackers beat and stabbed him to death, shouting anti-gay slurs. The savagery of the attack—leaving knives protruding from the victim's head— marked it as one of the state's most notorious hate crimes, a terrifying reminder that for some neighbors, the mere existence of a gay man was considered a capital offense. Three men were eventually convicted for the murder of David McLane.

Cunningham's retort—"She's queer"—was never just about one woman. It was the creed of a decade that has stretched into a generation. Whether it is a chain on a beach in 1980, a knife in an apartment in 1988, or a boot in the woods in 2024, the creed remains chillingly the same: the price of being yourself on the North Shore is still, too often, paid in blood. Yet the legal system has rarely delivered full justice for that cost. Cunningham was not locked up.

*He opened a conversation that the North Shore had tried to suppress for generations, ensuring that the victims of violence were no longer invisible.*

Yet, against this backdrop of recurring darkness, Jay Gilbert's legacy stands as a necessary light. At a time when solidarity could cost a person their livelihood, Gilbert risked everything to tell the truth. By turning his personal secret into a political weapon, he challenged the bigotry fueling the bloodshed on Washington Street. He proved that true leadership is about standing up when it matters most. He opened a conversation that the North Shore had tried to suppress for generations, ensuring that the victims of violence were no longer invisible. Gilbert planted the seeds of a movement that would eventually outgrow the fear he fought so hard to uproot, reminding us that while hate may persist, it can no longer thrive in the silence he so bravely broke.

https://www.unitedlynnpride.com/topics/discrimination-and-violence

# Police Abuse

BLUISTON DEYOUNG

"Hey, you can't do that. You can't just do that!"

That was all Bluiston DeYoung meant to say—just a human objection, a hand raised against injustice happening in real time. Moments earlier, the cruiser had drifted past, then circled back. "The cops come by," DeYoung remembered, "and at one point, one of them yells out the window and calls us 'Dykes.' He says, 'F#cking dykes, go inside and have your fight,' or something." One of the women snapped back. "My friend said something to them—I don't know what she said, but she mouthed off—and that was all it took. They backed up really quickly, got out of the car, grabbed her, slammed her violently on the hood of the car and were going to proceed to cuff her."

"I walk up. So, I go over to the police officer, and I'm like, 'Hey, you, you can't do that. You can't just do that.' And he hauls off and hits me. So, I

**Women Charge Police Abuse**

By David Morris

LYNN, MA—Three women claim that Lynn police abused them physically and verbally and deprived them of their constitutional rights during recent incidents outside a bar and later at the local police station.

DeYoung and Arista Navickas of Boston and Ramona Maliawco of Lynn told *GCN* that eight police officers beat them with clubs, maced them and shouted obscenities at them beginning about 8:00 pm on Sunday, March 22, while arresting them on charges of disorderly conduct and other offenses and later at the police station, where they refused to let the women make telephone calls once they had been jailed.

The three women said that after spending about an hour at Fran's Place, they were having a heated discussion on the street outside when police officers drove up and told them to go back into the bar. The women said they refused because their argument might create a disturbance inside. They claim the police grabbed them, handcuffed them, maced them and hit them with billy clubs, then summoned more police. Three more cruisers and a paddy wagon soon appeared, they said.

The women said that after handcuffing them, police officers threw them into the paddy wagon and sprayed mace at them before closing the doors.

The women quote officers at the station as saying laughingly, "There's three fucking lesbians here." One officer is alleged to have told them, "If you want to be men, we'll treat you like men."

DeYoung, Navickas and Maliawco told *GCN* that they were not informed of the charges against them until some time after they had been jailed. They said they were told telephone calls would be made on their behalf by police officers.

Maliawco was released on bail at about 1:30 am but DeYoung and Navickas were held until about 8:30 am on Monday, March 23.

When contacted by *GCN*, Lynn police refused comment on the case.

Boston attorney John Ward, who will represent at least one of the women, told *GCN* their trial has been set for April 14.

Article about police abuse outside Fran's Place in 1981.

hit him back. They all came at me at that point," DeYoung said. "So it was me and probably six police officers, I would guess. I got my ass kicked. And when he hit me, I reacted. The reason why is because when I was twelve, I got beat up by a cop in my hometown for nothing, and he, too, thought I was a boy. So my first reaction, at that point, was reflex, and that's why I hit him."

*If you want to be men, we'll treat you like men.*

The attack that night—March 22, 1981—was not the first burst of violence outside Fran's Place, though it became one of the most infamous. For years, the sidewalk between the bar and the bowling alley had been a zone of danger. Cars full of young men slowed to shout slurs or throw bottles. People walking to their cars were followed, cornered, or shoved. "Oh yeah, God, there was lots of harassment," DeYoung said. "When you were in Fran's, we weren't going to take any shit from anyone." But strangers were one thing. Police were something else entirely.

Bluiston DeYoung today.

According to *Gay Community News*, officers ordered them back inside, then grabbed them, handcuffed them, maced them, beat them with billy clubs and threw them into a paddy wagon, spraying them with mace again once the doors were closed. At the station, officers mocked them—"three f#cking lesbians"—and one warned, "If you want to be men, we'll treat you like men."

Interview.

But the paper could not convey the chaos as DeYoung lived it: the cruiser jolting backward, the friend slammed onto the hood, the fist to DeYoung's face, the instinctive swing back, then the sudden avalanche of bodies. "It was an army of cops," DeYoung said. "They weren't arresting her anymore. They all came at me."

The charge was assault and battery on a police officer, a terrifying accusation for a queer person in 1981. But the queer community of Fran's—people who risked being outed, people who were afraid but came anyway—showed up at the arraignment to testify. Many had never spoken publicly about their sexuality. Many feared retaliation. But they came.

"They were witnesses to it," DeYoung said. "My friends came with me." Their presence shifted the ground in the courtroom. A queer legal team stepped in. In the end, the case ended without a finding. The officers faced scrutiny. Their violence attracted press attention beyond Lynn.

Afterward, DeYoung noticed the difference. "I don't think we got harassed after that so much... they got into a lot of hot water."

It didn't undo the years of fear or the bruises from that night. But it marked a turning point—earned not through mercy, but through solidarity and courage.

Decades later, when the Pulse nightclub was attacked in Orlando, grief rippled through Fran's Place. Old memories surfaced—blue lights, threats, beatings. But Lynn was different now. Manager Tisha Sterling recalled the moment vividly: "When the incident at Pulse happened, the police chief assigned two cruisers to sit outside of

Fran's. That, to me, was above and beyond... And I was like, 'Thank you, thank you, thank you.'"

The same sidewalk where queer people once feared cruisers now saw them as protection.

It took decades of resistance, bruises, courtroom battles, and queer witnesses who dared to stand up. But in the end, Lynn listened.

https://www.unitedlynnpride.com/topics/police-relations

# House Parties

Pat Gozemba & Peter Abate

While the neon flicker of the bars offered a necessary escape, for many in the North Shore's queer community, the most vibrant nights didn't happen on a public dance floor, but in a living room. In an era where being out in public could still invite harassment or violence, the house party became a critical institution—a sanctuary within the city where the community could be fully, unapologetically themselves.

Pat Gozemba, center, at her house party in the late 1970s.

In the late 1970s, 17 Ocean Terrace became one such refuge. The home of Pat Gozemba and Marilyn Humphries was the site of legendary gatherings that functioned as both parties and performances. Here, away from the prying eyes of neighbors or the potential brutality of the police, friends staged elaborate drag lip-sync pageants. As preserved in photographs by Marilyn Humphries, these nights were explosions of camp and creativity. The safety of the private home allowed for a level of vulnerability and expression that even the bars, with their dark corners and bouncers, couldn't always guarantee. These photos capture a joy that is defiant in its privacy, showing a community building its own culture from the ground up.

As the decades passed, this tradition of domestic gatherings evolved from a necessity for safety into a sophisticated social network. By the 1990s, Lynn's Diamond District had transformed into a quiet mecca for gay and lesbian homeowners. At the center of this shift was Peter Abate, a Lynn English graduate and co-founder of the social group "Lynn Side Out." Abate, who had met his husband

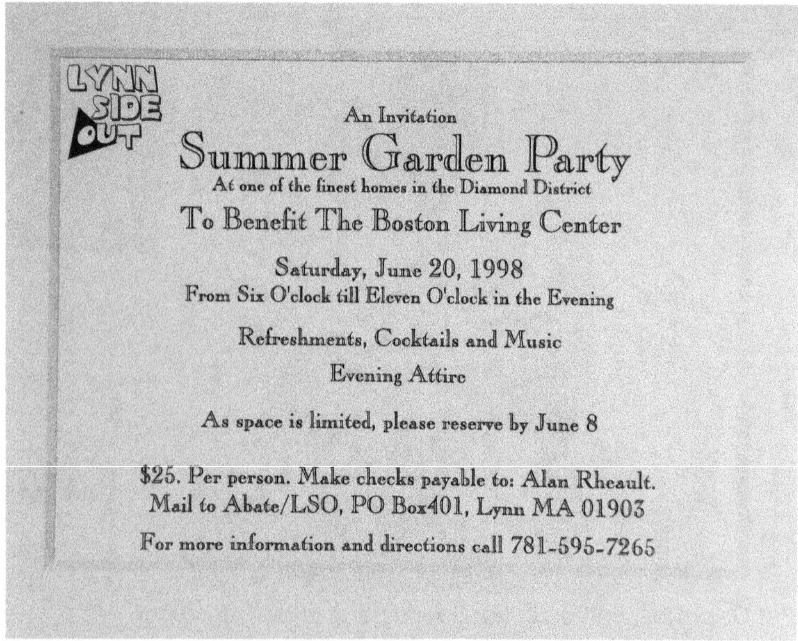


An invitation to a garden party held by Lynn Side Out in 1998.

David in 1983, understood that the community needed connection beyond the barstool.

Interview.

Lynn Side Out grew to over 120 members, publishing newsletters and organizing a social calendar that rivaled any nightclub. Instead of smoke-filled rooms, they hosted progressive dinners where guests would wander from one Victorian home to another for cocktails and courses, hiking trips and garden parties. For Abate and his peers, these events were about weaving a tighter social fabric, turning a neighborhood into a chosen family. While the bars provided the spark for Lynn's queer revolution, it was the house parties—from the drag pageants on Ocean Terrace to the dinner parties in the Diamond District—that kept the fire burning, proving that the strongest community is often the one you build at home.

https://www.unitedlynnpride.com/images/house-parties

https://www.unitedlynnpride.com/images/lynn-side-out

Pat Gozemba, center, at her house party in the late 1970s.

# Staying Home

STEPHEN GALANTE & BILL PLUCKHAHN

The bountiful bouquet filled the office with sweet perfume as Stephen Galante opened the note, his heart pounding in his chest. He had been dating his boyfriend, Bill Pluckhahn, for several months when the call came that Stephen had been approved to adopt—a decision so momentous that Bill had needed to take time to think about it. Stephen feared he had asked too much, but the card nestled in the flowers did the simple math of their future: "1+1+1+ love equals a family."

That note in 1993 launched a courageous journey of fatherhood that defied every convention of the time. As the first openly gay client at his adoption agency, Stephen, alongside Bill, built a family of five children, intentionally welcoming mixed-race children and those with special needs born of trauma. It wasn't just society that doubted them; even queer friends whispered that a child "needs a mother and a father." But Stephen and Bill silenced the critics by simply living their truth in Beverly. Through countless soccer games, YMCA trips and Stephen's devoted 20-year tenure as PTO president, they showed the world that a family with two dads was beautifully, perfectly normal.

This unshakeable confidence was a hard-won victory for a man who had been teased relentlessly in high school, clueless as to why until he read a health textbook chapter on homosexuals and realized, with a jolt, "Oh my god, that's me." It was his first Boston Pride in 1980 that whispered the possibility that being queer wasn't a bad thing, and leaders like Joe Antonelli at the North Shore Gay and Lesbian Alliance (NSGLA) who taught him he could just be himself. Stephen eventually served as president of the NSGLA, bringing his signature "100 percent" commitment to the cause.

Today, with their oldest child now 38, Stephen and Bill's love has been consecrated three times over: a holy union, a Vermont civil union and a big Italian wedding in Massachusetts. Looking back, the life they built stands as a testament to the fact that the strongest families are those forged not by expectation, but by an abundance of love.

Kahn, Karen, and Patricia A. Gozemba with photographs by Marilyn Humphries, Courting Equality: A Documentary History of America's First Legal Same-Sex Marriages.

Bill Pluckhahn, center left, and Steve Galante with their children, Ben, Zach, Amanda, Mary, Grace and Deon.

# Go Out Loud

THOMAS MACDONALD

When the city of Salem held its inaugural Pride flag raising over a decade ago, officials realized they didn't actually own a rainbow flag. They had to borrow one from Thomas MacDonald. That moment perfectly encapsulates Thomas: a man who hasn't just shown up for his community, but has literally provided the fabric for its visibility.

Born in 1953 in Bermuda, Thomas found his truth after moving to the United States. In New York City, meeting his first boyfriend sparked his coming out, a journey supported by his parents and marked by self-discovery. He later chronicled this path in his autobiography, *Here Is What Happened: A Black Man's Discoveries and Decisions*.

Upon settling in Salem, Thomas found a quiet queer scene and decided to turn up the volume. Alongside Chris Sicuranza, he launched "Go Out Loud," an organization dedicated to the radical act of queer joy. What began as intimate socials, game nights, and boat rides exploded into legendary events, including a "Halloween Scream" at the Hawthorne Hotel that drew 1,000 revelers. He was a founding member of North Shore Pride.

Thomas's impact is intersectional and profound. As a Black gay man, he brought a vital perspective to Mayor Kim Driscoll's Race Equity Taskforce, driving necessary conversations about diversity training and visibility within the Salem Police Department. His leadership extends across the region, from the welcoming committee of his church to the boards of the Salem Theatre, HAWC (Healing Abuse Working for Change) and the Essex National Heritage Commission.

Now, whether traveling the world with his husband, Bill Henning, or advocating for local equity, Thomas continues to lead by example. He didn't just come out; he went out loud, and Salem is infinitely brighter for it.

MacDonald, Thomas, Here Is What Happened: A Black Man's Discoveries and Decisions.

Thomas MacDonald, left, and Bill Henning at Machu Picchu.

# Music Theatre

BILL HANNEY

Bill Hanney is the impresario who saved the North Shore Music Theatre (NSMT) from silence. In 2010, he purchased the shuttered venue, adding it to a portfolio that includes Rhode Island's Theatre By The Sea and a chain of cinemas. His mission is simple: provide great entertainment where everyone belongs.

This inclusivity shines in his support for the queer community through "OUT AT THE NORTH SHORE." Sponsored by North Shore Pride, this series transforms select performance nights into dedicated celebrations. The premise is inviting: "When the show's over, the party's just getting started!" Audiences gather for a free post-show reception in the Broadway Club featuring live music, open mics and cast appearances. Through these evenings, Hanney ensures the theater remains a sanctuary where all share the spotlight.

https://www.nsmt.org/outnight.html

# Rainbow Stroll

LEMARIS BELL

"It wasn't a bummer." When a sightseer offered this feedback at the end of a tour, Lemaris Bell took it as the highest praise. Too often, queer history is reduced to a somber march from oppression to AIDS. Bell founded the Salem Rainbow Stroll in 2022 to shatter that narrative, proving that queer history in the Witch City is vibrant, resilient and occasionally magical.

A favorite stop on the tour is the bronze statue of Samantha from *Bewitched*. Bell delights in revealing that the beloved television show was written as an allegory for homosexuality, featuring a cast that had more than one queer actor (most notably Paul Lynde and Dick Sargent)—a pop-culture beacon hiding in plain sight. But the tour digs deeper than TV magic, offering the inside story on notable residents like the diarist Reverend William Bentley, the brooding author Nathaniel Hawthorne and the scandalous sculptor Louisa Lander. By weaving these lives together, Bell transforms Salem from a site of historic hysteria into a landscape of belonging. For Bell, the Rainbow Stroll is about reclaiming space, ensuring that visitors leave knowing that queer joy has always walked these cobblestones.

https://www.salemghosttours.com/Pride.html

Lemaris Bell stands next to the *Bewitched* statue in Salem, MA.

# SIX

## Mobilizing Mercy

When the shadow of the Acquired Immunodeficiency Syndrome (AIDS) epidemic fell across the North Shore, it did not distinguish between the quiet farm roads of Topsfield and the gritty, thumping dance floors of Lynn. It arrived as a "sudden, brutal silence," a crisis that demanded a response when the world turned its back. This section chronicles the extraordinary mobilization of a community that refused to die in the dark.

Interviews.

The response was as varied as the landscape itself. In the rural suburbs, Jack Armitage and Peter Konrad founded "Strongest Link," the country's first rural Human Immunodeficiency Virus (HIV) organization, serving a terrified county where anonymity was both a shield and a cage. Across the North Shore, activists like 3rian King, Kirsten Freni and the group Prism replaced fear with radical compassion, parking medical vans outside nightclubs to meet people exactly where they were.

We also hear the roar of the individual voice. Paul Monette transformed his "borrowed time" into a weapon of truth, writing from the trenches to dismantle the silence. And we follow Jack Noseworthy, who carried the union values of his Lynn upbringing to Broadway, helping to weave a safety net for a generation of artists under siege. Together, these stories form a map of survival—proof that when institutions failed, neighbors became saviors and love became the most powerful medicine of all.

# Strongest Link

JACK ARMITAGE & PETER KONRAD

It was a Friday night in 1984, and the crew was all dressed up, ready to hit the discos in Boston. Jack Armitage turned to his tight-knit group of friends and asked the question that would change the trajectory of his life: "Where's Jim?" The reply came back ominous and brief: "He's in the hospital with pneumonia." Jim died on Sunday. That sudden, brutal silence where laughter should have been was the catalyst. Grieving but determined, Jack pulled together with Peter Konrad and other friends to do something impossible. Jack moved to Palm Springs to work with dying patients. When he returned two years later, they founded Strongest Link AIDS Services.

What they created in Topsfield was the first rural HIV organization in the country. The need was instant and overwhelming; the phone started ringing as soon as they opened the doors. Strongest Link became the "only game in town" for Essex County, tasked with the massive challenge of reaching a terrified population spread across suburbs and rural towns. Their efforts were soon joined by North Shore AIDS Health Project (NSAHP) and Sam Berman in Gloucester, and by the wonderful holistic team he cultivated.

Jack Armitage became the hands and feet of the operation. Living on a farm in Topsfield, Jack was not a social worker by training, but he was one by nature—driven by an innate desire to help. He became the organization's first Executive Director, driving a green

VW bus to shuttle people to hospitals and bridging the gap between isolation and care.

If Jack was the heart, Peter Konrad was the spine. Born in Holyoke in 1954 and armed with an MBA from Dartmouth, Peter was building a corporate career at companies like General Electric and NYNEX. Serving as the founding board president of Strongest Link, Peter handled the unglamorous but vital work that kept the organization from collapsing—managing budgets, filing for non-profit status and setting agendas with help from the board's CPA and attorney. If the account were short one month, Peter would

Peter Konrad and Jack Armitage.

quietly cover the difference with a personal check, ensuring the doors stayed open.

The board of directors was a carefully chosen group of people who dove in and got things done. It is difficult to describe the energy and vigor that spontaneously shepherded this grassroots effort. Together, they built a comprehensive safety net. Strongest Link provided far more than just emotional support; it built an infrastructure for survival. They offered case management and referrals to a brave network of practitioners—infectious disease specialists, acupuncturists and spiritual comforters willing to treat the stigmatized. They established support groups that met for 104 consecutive weeks, offering a lifeline of consistency. To combat ignorance, they launched speakers bureaus in schools and businesses. They utilized the arts, specifically the "Memories of Eddie" photography exhibit by Forest Foundation's Loel Poor, to foster empathy through education. They fiercely advocated for

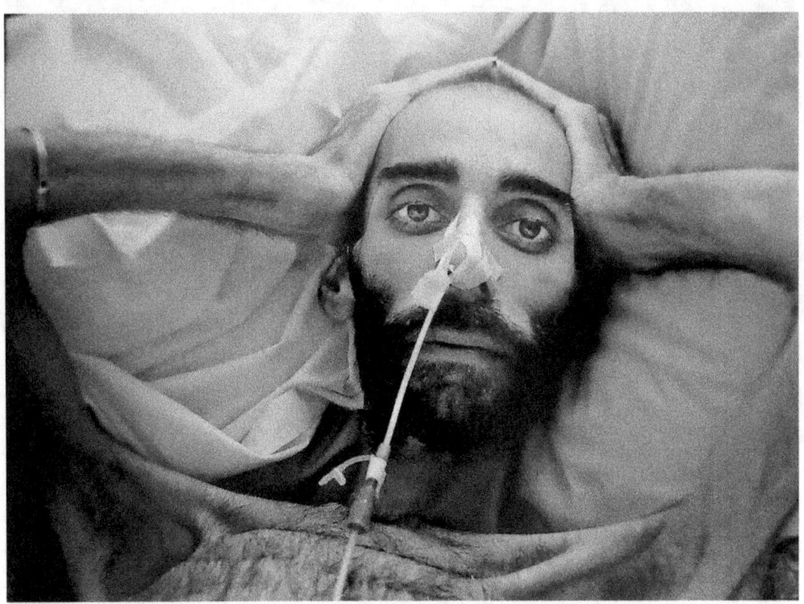

Photo of Eddie Garabedian from the exhibit, Memories of Eddie, by Forest Foundation's Loel Poor.

access to emerging medications, often having to soften the defenses of local pharmacies wary of engaging with their clients.

As they worked, a shocking reality emerged. They were surprised to calculate that 70 percent of their client base was not comprised of gay men, but of women and their children. This demographic shift, emerging from Lynn, Salem and Gloucester, was traced back to needle users who transmitted the infection to their families. Jack and Peter found themselves battling not just a virus, but the stigma of addiction. Inside the support groups, however, social barriers dissolved. A hemophiliac boy from Hamilton, Scott, became a symbol of this unity. He was tough, sitting in groups alongside

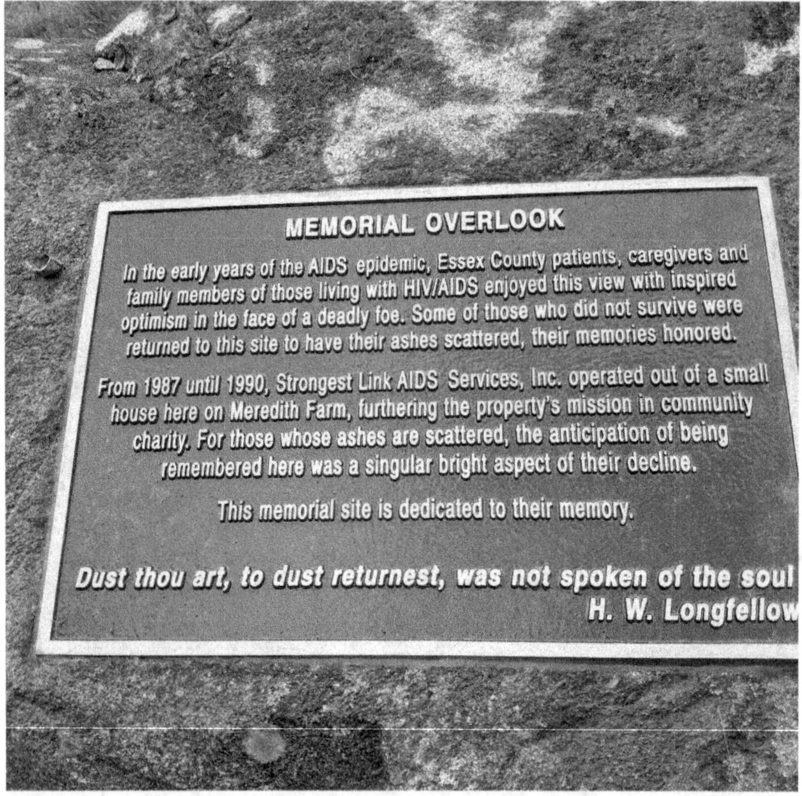


When burial services were unavailable, clients arranged to have their ashes scattered on a Topsfield hilltop near where Strongest Link began.

recovering intravenous drug users and gay men, standing up to the disease with incredible courage.

The work was grueling, often involving battles with a reluctant medical establishment and the heartbreaking logistics of death. In 1989, Neil Harrington, the mayor-elect of Salem, proclaimed there was no point directing funds to HIV prevention because "they are all going to die anyway." That statement didn't defeat Strongest Link's angels; it radicalized them. When burial services were unavailable, clients arranged to have their ashes scattered on a Topsfield hilltop near where Strongest Link began.

The organization evolved to outlast the crisis of those early years. Jack stepped down as Executive Director in 1991, handing the reins to Maddy St. Amand, who professionalized the agency's services. In 2005, Strongest Link acquired the Cornerstone Wellness Center in Lynn to provide direct food and wellness services. Finally, in 2011, recognizing the changing landscape of healthcare, Peter and Jack returned to the board of directors and worked with ten-year Board President Janet Santa Anna to steer the organization into a merger with the AIDS Action Committee, Boston, ensuring the mission would continue. Larry Kessler, Executive Director at AIDS Action, Committee described Strongest Link as "Unique in that it serves rural, suburban and urban communities."

Looking back on those impossible years, Jack Armitage reflected, "It was satisfying to know that I had led with my gut to do the right thing. As it turned out, it was not only the right thing; it was the ONLY thing." Today, a faded grey sign that reads "Strongest Link AIDS Services" still hangs near the Liberty Tree Mall, a quiet ghost of a time when a VW bus, a personal checkbook and a group of friends were the only things standing between a community and the dark.

https://fenwayhealth.org/aac/

# Borrowed Time

PAUL MONETTE

The war didn't start with a gunshot; it started with a doctor's voice in a sterile room. In March of 1985, when Paul Monette (1945-1995) heard the diagnosis for his partner, Roger Horwitz, the comfortable, literary life he had built evaporated instantly. He picked up his pen like a weapon. No longer content to be a poet of the abstract, Monette began to write from the trenches of the AIDS epidemic, chronicling the IV drips and the night sweats, determined to scream the truth of their love into the face of a government that was letting them die.

Monette was not supposed to be a warrior. Born in Lawrence, Massachusetts, into a working-class French-Canadian family, he was educated at Phillips Academy and Yale. He began his career as a poet and novelist, writing witty, sophisticated works that seemed destined for a comfortable literary niche. But history had other plans. When the AIDS epidemic

Paul Monette.

crashed into his life, it transformed him from a quiet observer into one of the most ferocious and eloquent voices of a generation under siege.



Monette's memoir, *Borrowed Time: An AIDS Memoir*, is a searing chronicle of their battle against the disease—a love story written in the shadow of death. It stripped away the clinical detachment often associated with the epidemic, revealing the raw, agonizing humanity of loss. When Roger died in 1986, Monette didn't retreat into silence; he roared. His subsequent work, including the National Book Award-winning *Becoming a Man: Half a Life Story*, dissected the closet he had lived in for so long, linking the internal shame of growing up gay in a homophobic society to the external negligence of a government that let thousands die.

Monette's memoirs are testimonies from a man who decided that if he were going to die, he would die speaking the truth. In the end, Paul Monette didn't just leave behind books; he left behind a map of how to survive despair with your voice intact.

AIDS Memorial Quilt in Washington, DC.

# Funeral Mass

The welcoming congregation of St. Pius V Catholic Church in Lynn contributed a panel to the AIDS Memorial Quilt, saying: "Our local funeral director and our parish community are welcoming to all people, and as a result, the AIDS Action Committee often referred people to us. We have not placed any names on our panel so as not to leave someone off and out of respect for those who desire privacy. Our prayers, love and concern travel with this panel."

https://www.aidsmemorial.org/quilt

https://www.hostcatholic.org/

The St. Pius V communitiy's panel for the AIDS Memorial Quilt.

# Prism

3RIAN KING, DAVID GOUDREAU, CATHERINE O'CONNOR, KEN GLOVER, COCO ALINSUG & KIRSTEN FRENI

The bass thumped inside the nightclub, a pulse of escape and sweat. Outside, a mobile medical van was parked right on the curb, its doors thrown open to the cool night air. It was a radical, jarring sight in the early 2000s—bringing HIV testing directly to the party. The team didn't wait for the community to come to a sterile clinic; they brought the clinic to the dance floor, understanding that to save lives in the midst of an epidemic, you had to meet people exactly where they were, shame-free and face-to-face.

When the shadow of the AIDS crisis first fell across the North Shore in the early 1980s, it didn't arrive as a medical statistic, but as a phantom that began quietly emptying bar stools and silencing dance floors. In Lynn, a city known for its grit and tight-knit neighborhoods, the devastation was intimate and relentless. Between 1987 and 2022, the virus claimed one hundred and fifty lives in the

3rian King.

city alone, a grim accounting that left no corner of the queer community untouched.

For those living through it, the fear was atmospheric—a constant, low-level hum of dread. George Chakoutis, the owner of the beloved bar 47 Central, recalled the visceral reality of that era: "People we knew were dying every day." It wasn't just the loss of friends; it was the terrifying lottery of survival. As Peter Abate, a Lynn native and community leader, remembered, "You never knew whether it would be you next."

In this climate of fear, the queer bars of Lynn—Fran's Place and 47 Central—transformed from mere watering holes into sanctuaries

The GBMHP mobile medical van.

and command centers. They became the places where information was whispered, grief was shared, and resistance was funded. At Fran's Place, the legendary "Night of 100 Stars" wasn't just a drag show; it was a lifeline, raising critical funds for AIDS support. Similarly, 47 Central became a fundraising engine for Strongest Link, an organization dedicated to helping those stricken by the disease.

But the community needed more than money; they needed a strategy. This work began in the late 1990s under the leadership of David Goudreau, the first director of the Gay & Bi Men's Health Program (GBMHP) in Beverly. Under David, the program became the first in the country to conduct internet outreach, meeting men where they were virtually—on sites like Gay.com and Manhunt. net—to connect them with healthcare. David also built community offline, founding "CAMEN" (Cape Ann Gay & Bi Men), a weekly discussion group, and co-founding the Cape Ann Pride Committee, which hosted coffeehouse concerts and a Pride Dance at Gloucester City Hall.

It was at a CAMEN meeting that David met a young man named 3rian King. Raised in Gloucester, 3rian had grown up feeling the

The GBMHP team and friends at 47 Central, Lynn, MA. Right side, front to back, Coco Alinsug, Kirsten Freni and 3rian King.

sting of being different. Bullied in school and stripped of his Stevie Nicks records by a mother who feared his queerness, he found his salvation not in a clinic, but in a bookstore called Abraxas. There, the poet Gerrit Lansing mentored him, showing him that a queer life could be lived with intellect, magic and unapologetic pride. David hired 3rian as an outreach worker, and when David left for Provincetown, 3rian stepped up as director, ready to expand the mission.

Rebranding the program as Prism LGBT Health, 3rian knew that to save the next generation, he had to physically go to the party. He approached the Massachusetts Department of Public Health with a pilot idea: parking a testing unit right outside the nightclubs. This wasn't a solo mission, but a powerful collaboration. 3rian partnered with Catherine O'Connor, a nursing instructor at Northeastern University, who shared his passion for going the extra mile. Catherine secured the university's "Health Innovations" van and staffed it with nursing students, turning the curb into a classroom of compassion.

The success of the van hinged on trust. "One of the reasons we were so successful," 3rian recalls, "was the strong relationships we had built with the bar owners." George Chakoutis at 47 Central and Tisha Sterling at Fran's Place didn't just allow the van; they championed it. Often, bartenders and bar staff were the first to step onto the van to get tested, setting a powerful example that stripped away their patrons' fear. The "Health Innovations" program continues to this day under Catherine O'Connor, recently proving its worth again by providing hundreds of vaccines during the Mpox outbreak.

To support this mobile mission, 3rian assembled a team that became local legends. There was Coco Alinsug, who would later become a city councilor, using his charisma to bridge the gap between public health and the public. Then there was Kirsten Freni, whose journey into this work began when she first met 3rian in 2003 at Club Central. By 2006, following Coco's departure, Freni broke barriers by joining the program as its first female employee. To step into this world, she had to navigate a unique bureaucratic hurdle: completing training to become a "Certified Male," a designation required for her to officially conduct outreach in spaces strictly designated for men who have sex with men.

Embracing the role with characteristic boldness, Freni became the "Condom Queen of the North Shore." She traveled everywhere with her "booty box," a kit stocked with lube, condoms and gifts designed to break the ice. She didn't wait for clients to find her; she met them where they were, whether at queer bars or in public sex environments like parks and truck stops. Her presence was often strategic, helping to legitimize health outreach in stigmatized spaces where police often targeted queer men; the presence of a woman changed the dynamic, allowing her to remain and provide counseling and resources without the same fear of intervention.

Ken Glover as Miss Syphillis with Coco Alinsug.

And then there was Ken Glover. Ken understood that in a dark bar, a pamphlet was easy to ignore, but a six-foot drag queen was not. Developing the persona "Miss Syphilis," and later "Blanche Debris," Ken turned outreach into performance art, wading through crowds with a giant martini glass filled with condoms.

While the bars and outreach teams fought for the living, the dignity of the dead was often threatened by stigma. In the early years, many religious institutions turned their backs on people living with AIDS. In this spiritual desert, St. Pius V Catholic Church in Lynn emerged as an oasis of mercy. When other doors were locked, St. Pius threw its doors open, performing funeral services for those the world wanted to forget.

Today, the landscape has shifted. The terrifying acute crisis has evolved into a chronic condition for many. 3rian King continues his work, now as a case manager at the North Shore Health Project in Gloucester. His focus has turned to a new chapter: helping long-term survivors age with HIV. The story of Prism and its partners is a testament to a community that refused to let its members die in the dark—a history written by those who stepped up, from the internet chat rooms to the curb outside the club, when the rest of the world stepped back.

https://healthproject.org/index.html

https://healthq.org/

# From the Heart

KIRSTEN FRENI

"It was never work because it was about people." This simple truth is the heartbeat of Kirsten Freni's decades-long legacy on the North Shore. Her activism wasn't born in a boardroom but in the trenches of the AIDS crisis. Losing her close friend, John, to the epidemic in 1985 ignited a fire in her that has never dimmed. In an era defined by fear and stigma, Freni moved toward the vulnerable, becoming the North Shore's "Condom Queen." Famous for her "booty box"— a treasure chest of safe sex supplies—she went into bars and onto street corners, providing HIV testing, education and compassion where it was needed most. She organized solemn vigils and AIDS walks, ensuring that those lost, like John, were never forgotten.

Freni is a weaver of community, stitching together disparate threads like a master quilter. Her influence has "tentacles" that reach into every corner of queer life north of Boston. She was on the board of North Shore Pride along with Hope Watt-Bucci, 3rian King and Thomas MacDonald. She served as the architect of its spectacular entertainment. With a flair for the dramatic and a rolodex to match, she brought powerhouse acts and celebrity Emcees Randy Price and Fast Freddy to the Salem Common, turning a local gathering into a world-class celebration. For the first two years, Prism offered HIV counseling and testing at North Shore Pride. As the event grew, Prism brought in the Northeast Health Van, which has been a staple every year, providing testing and other health services.

Her dedication to youth is her most profound legacy. As the longest-serving board member and a long-term president of the North Shore Alliance of LGBTQ+ Youth (NAGLY), Freni was a lifeline. She didn't just govern; she drove the van, shuttling teenagers to the State House to fight for their rights. She drove the van for NAGLY's

Kirsten Freni, the "Condom Queen."

annual educational outings to Provincetown and Ogunquit. She launched the organization's first "Gaysgiving," ensuring that no young person would have to spend the holiday alone or hungry.

Crucially, Freni understood that passion alone couldn't sustain a movement; it needed resources. Realizing that growing NAGLY into a permanent safe haven required money, she worked with lawyer Bob Goldman, who worked pro bono,  to formally incorporate the organization. This vital step allowed NAGLY to receive donations and grants, transforming it from a grassroots effort into a sustainable institution. With the foundation laid, she launched a series of fundraisers to keep the lights on and the doors open, including the amazing Red Party, which became a legendary event for fueling the organization's mission. The Red Party, with performances over the years by The Platters, Suede, James Mazzone and JuJube from RuPaul Drag Race, became one of the hottest tickets in Salem.

In Lynn, her impact is etched into the city's history. Alongside Tisha Sterling, she organized the city's first Pride flag-raising in 2010, and, with Coco Alinsug, spearheaded the inaugural Pride event at the Lynn Museum in 2016. It was her vision that sparked the Lynn

NAGLY at Goldfish Pond, Lynn, MA.

Lynn's first Pride Flag raising in 2010. Center left to right, Tisha Sterling, Mayor Judy Flanagan and Kirsten Freni.

LGBTQ+ history project, an initiative that later won a national award for preserving stories that might otherwise have been lost.

Whether leading a lesbian spirituality group to nurture the soul or organizing community health outreach, Freni has always worked from her heart. Her relentless advocacy was formally recognized in 2022 with citations from Lynn Mayor Jared Nicholson and Senator Brendan Crighton. Still, her true accolade is the vibrant, interconnected community she helped build—one act of kindness at a time.

https://www.nagly.org/

Peter Konrad with Kirsten Freni at NAGLY's Red Party.

# Broadway Cares

JACK NOSEWORTHY

"That experience that happens between the actors on stage and the audience, something that can only happen once with that group of people, was like a drug. It was something, oh God, I just want to feel that again!" For Jack Noseworthy, this insatiable hunger for connection defined his early life, propelling him from the blue-collar streets of Lynn, Massachusetts, to the bright lights of Broadway and Hollywood. Growing up near Flax Pond in a two-family home he shared with his uncle's family, Noseworthy was raised in a strongly union household. His father and uncles were all ironworkers in

Broadway and Hollywood actor, Jack Noseworthy.

Interview.

Local Seven. While Jack spent one summer as an ironworker, his father never wanted Jack to follow in his footsteps. Still, the union values of solidarity and providing a safety net for the community stayed with him and later became the bedrock of Noseworthy's second act as a humanitarian.

In his youth, however, Noseworthy was singularly focused on his own ascent. He describes himself as a "diamond in the rough" who viewed high school and college not as a time for romance or self-discovery, but as a training ground for his inevitable stardom. This intense drive paid off. He graduated from the Boston Conservatory and launched a successful career that spanned three decades. He made his mark on Broadway in *A Chorus Line* and *Jerome Robbins' Broadway*, where he holds the distinction of being the only male actor to perform the role of Peter Pan. His talent soon took him to Hollywood, where he landed memorable roles in films such as *The Brady Bunch Movie*, the sci-fi horror cult classic *Event Horizon* and the submarine thriller *U-571*. Later, he would garner critical acclaim for his portrayal of Robert F. Kennedy in the National Geographic film *Killing Kennedy*, acting opposite Rob Lowe.

Yet, his journey was shaped by the silence and privilege of the era. As a handsome, white, cisgender male, Noseworthy fit the mold of the leading man, a "privilege" he acknowledges allowed him to ascend professionally while keeping his identity as a gay man largely unspoken in an industry that was not yet ready for positive queer representation. But the real world devastatingly intruded on his theatrical dreams. Noseworthy landed his first professional job in 1987, just as the HIV/AIDS epidemic was ravaging the theatre community. What began as a distant crisis became tragically personal when, within eighteen months, five of his friends and colleagues died—all men under the age of thirty-five.

The emotional weight of that era was profound and left a heavy footprint on his life. Among the losses was Dan McCoy, a talented actor from the *Cats* company whom Noseworthy now recognizes as his first same-sex crush, though he lacked the vocabulary to acknowledge it at the time.

Amidst the grief, Noseworthy found a way to fight back, leaning into the collective strength he learned from his union upbringing. He began participating in benefit concerts for Broadway Cares and Equity Fights AIDS, organizations that were circling the wagons to protect a community ignored by the government. Today, Noseworthy serves as a professional development officer for Broadway Cares/Equity Fights AIDS, a role he views as a way to honor the friends he lost. He stands on their shoulders, ensuring that the safety net his father prized is available for people facing illness and crisis today. Life eventually offered Noseworthy the personal happiness he had deferred for so long; he now lives in New York City with his husband, Sergio, and their son, teaching the next generation that giving back is the most rewarding role of all.

https://broadwaycares.org/

## Lynn's Noseworthy to star on CBS-TV sitcom, 'Teech'

**By BILL BROTHERTON**
**Item Staff**

Jack Noseworthy, English High class of '82, the only male to ever play Peter Pan on Broadway, is going to give television a try.

The son of Thelma and John Noseworthy, 13 Atkins Ave., Lynn, is a cast member of "Teech," a new situation comedy that will air on CBS this fall. The show is about a black teacher working in an all-white boys school, and Noseworthy will portray the "class brain."

Noseworthy has enjoyed incredible success in the entertainment industry since he graduated from the Boston Conservatory with a degree in dance in 1987. He has performed on Broadway, toured Europe with a theater troupe and been interviewed by Ted Koppel on ABC's "Nightline."

Now he's about to undertake the rigors of a weekly prime-time network show.

"I was hired as a guest star on the pilot episode," said Noseworthy, speaking via telephone from the Los Angeles home he's renting. "They liked me and asked me back the next week and then the next week ... and before I knew it I was in all six episodes."

At first, Noseworthy had one or two lines. By the fifth show, his character was central to the plot. But he was still not a regular cast member. When word came that the network was pleased with the show and wanted another seven episodes, he was certain the contract would be in the mail.

It wasn't.

**NOSEWORTHY, Page 11**

**JACK NOSEWORTHY**
**Lynner wins TV role**

Jack Noseworthy starred in the TV sitcom, *Teech,* in

# SEVEN

## Protest & Power

Politics is power, and for centuries, queer people on the North Shore were denied both. We were the subjects of the law, never its authors. But in the late 1970s, the tide began to turn. This section charts the revolutionary journey from the margins to the mayor's office, a shift that transformed us from a "problem" to be managed into a constituency to be courted.

It started not with a roar, but with a flyer slipped through a mailslot.

In 1978, David Newton and the North Shore Gay Alliance began the quiet, terrifying work of door-to-door education in Beverly, proving that the most radical political act is often just introducing yourself to your neighbor. That spark ignited a movement. We moved from asking candidates for support to becoming the candidates ourselves, claiming seats on School Committees and City Councils where our "out" voices had never been heard.

But this history is not just a victory lap; it is a battle map.

As recent conflicts over Drag Queen Story Hours and the rise of Christian Nationalism demonstrate, the public square remains a contested space. This section honors the trailblazers who endured the glare of the spotlight to secure our rights, and the modern defenders who stand firm against the rollback of progress. It is the story of how we stopped asking for permission to exist and started demanding the right to lead.

# The Alliance

DAVID NEWTON, JOE ANTONELLI, STEPHEN GALANTE & PAT GOZEMBA

In the autumn of 1978, the North Shore of Massachusetts was not a place where most queer people announced themselves. It was a region of quiet streets and closed doors, where safety lay in silence. But for David Newton, a professor of chemistry and physics at Salem State College, the silence had become untenable. His journey into activism began on his neighbors' doorsteps. Motivated by the gubernatorial election, Newton and his partner, Jim Greenhaw, drafted a questionnaire for the candidates, asking them to go on

NSGLA members at Boston Pride.

record regarding the rights of queer teachers and citizens. When they received a response, they didn't file it away. They printed flyers and walked from house to house, slipping the truth through mail slots—a quiet, subversive act of political education in a time when such visibility could cost a person their livelihood.

> *They didn't know if there were other queer people around, or who they were.*

It was this initial foray into political action that crystallized a larger idea. Newton, the first out gay professor at Salem State College, realized that a temporary campaign was not enough; the North Shore queer community needed a permanent political arm. He sent out a notice, a simple call to action for those who might be willing to gather. He opened the door to his own home on Ober Street in Beverly.

NSGLA hat.

The response to that first invitation in October 1978 was modest but profound. About a half-dozen people arrived. They stepped over the threshold of a private home and into something entirely new. They were almost entirely closeted, people for whom a public meeting would have been unthinkable. Newton had envisioned a political machine, a group that would fight for legislation and rights. But as he looked around his living room, he realized that the people sitting there had a more primal need. They weren't just there to march; they were there to breathe. As Newton later recalled, it became obvious right away that the attendees had no interest whatsoever in any political activity. They were interested in social events because they were people who, without exception, were closeted. They didn't know if there were other queer people around, or who they were.

> *Standing there, ready to answer questions, they forced their colleagues and students to reconcile the monsters of their imagination with the human beings standing before them.*

Thus, the North Shore Gay Alliance (later the North Shore Gay and Lesbian Alliance, or NSGLA) was born. It became a lifeline where the political and the social intertwined, often with the social taking precedence as a form of survival. The group's calendar exploded with activities designed to knit a fragmented population into a community. They didn't just meet in secret; they claimed space. They organized roller-skating nights, beach parties, and boat cruises, turning the North Shore's recreational landscape into a backdrop for queer joy. They fielded softball and volleyball teams and hosted brunches and potlucks.

While the membership sought connection, Newton and the steering committee ensured the group remained a potent force for education and advocacy. They didn't retreat from the public eye;

they engaged with it. They hosted "Gay History Week," connecting their local struggle to a broader legacy. They sat for interviews with the *Boston Globe*, *North Shore Sunday* and the *Salem Evening News*, refusing to let their stories be told just by others. They polled candidates, testified before State House committees and appeared on radio and TV programs, challenging the narrative that queer people were deviants or criminals.

Visibility was their most potent weapon. At Salem State College, the group staked a claim to public space during a theater department production, setting up a table in the lobby with a sign that read, "Some of your best friends are gay." Standing there, ready to answer questions, they forced their colleagues and students to reconcile the monsters of their imagination with the human beings standing before them.

It was at one of the group's film nights—another cultural lifeline they established—that a young student named David Rowand, fresh from a breakup and looking for connection, found the group. He approached Newton and his colleague Pat Gozemba after the film, a meeting that led to his immediate integration into the local fold. He became the group's treasurer.

Pat Gozemba's NSGLA membership card.

When David Newton, the founder of the North Shore Gay Alliance, moved to San Francisco in 1983, the baton of leadership passed to Joe Antonelli. A distinct energy shift accompanied the transition. While, Newton had planted the seeds of political action, Antonelli, who ran a shop called "Town Hall Antiques and Collectibles" in Salem's marketplace, was ready to take the group even more public. Under his tenure, the organization explicitly broadened its mandate to become the North Shore Gay and Lesbian Alliance (NSGLA), a decision Antonelli championed to reflect the reality of the women who were integral to the movement. His most audacious move was organizing the group's fifth anniversary celebration at the historic Old Town Hall in Salem. Leveraging his connections with the Chamber of Commerce, Antonelli secured a permit for a queer dance with a full liquor license—a first for the Witch City—turning a quiet support network into a visible cultural force that drew over 250 attendees to the heart of civic power.

Antonelli's leadership was defined by a refusal to remain hidden. He transformed the Alliance into a political entity, hosting "candidates' nights" where local politicians were invited to seek the queer vote, and organizing contingents to march in Boston Pride and the National March on Washington. He used his shop's community bulletin board to post queer news alongside general community events, subtly weaving queer existence into the daily fabric of Salem.

By the time Antonelli prepared to move to Florida in 1990, the NSGLA had evolved from a small social cluster into a recognized political constituency. He passed the leadership to Stephen Galante, leaving behind a legacy of "loud and proud" visibility that had permanently altered the North Shore's social landscape.

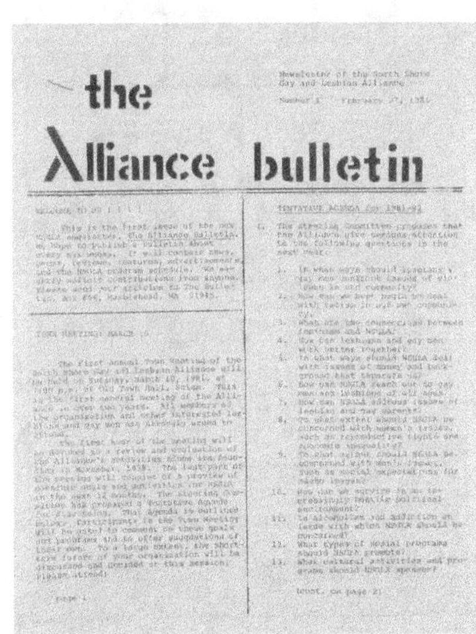

The NSGLA newsletter.

The work was not without its costs. Newton faced intense harassment at his home in Beverly, a reminder that the safety of his living room did not extend to the street. He endured a constant barrage of obscene phone calls and individuals driving past his house shouting slurs. On one terrifying occasion, a gang of post-adolescent youths physically prevented guests from leaving a party. The threats eventually escalated to a chilling peak in August 1979, when a group called his home over twenty times in a single day, warning him that he had "one hour" to get out of Beverly or they would come to his door and blow his head off with a shotgun.

Gozemba was also the target of threats. One evening in the early 1980s, a young man called her house 10 times, saying he knew where she lived, could see the lights on in her house, had a gun and was coming to get rid of her and save innocent students from her.

NSGLA T-shirt.

Yet, looking back, Newton sees the era not just as a time of fear, but of momentum. He admitted he was "kind of swept away" by what was happening in the world, spending as much time on queer events as on his faculty duties. By the time the AIDS crisis began to cast its long shadow in the 1980s, forcing a shift from liberation to survival, the NSGLA had already achieved something monumental. They had proven that the North Shore was not a wasteland for queer people. They had built a foundation of potlucks and protests, of film reels and flyers slipped through mail slots. David Newton and the founding members of the NSGLA didn't just organize a group; they terraformed the social landscape of Essex County. They carved out a space in Salem and Beverly, cities famous for their history, and wrote a new chapter of resistance and community, ensuring that those who came after would never again have to wonder if they were alone.

https://througharainbowlens.vrticalmedia.digital/

https://www.bostonprideforthepeople.org/

NSGLA members build a Lavender Lobster float for Boston Pride in Sue Sherry's Wolcott St. garage in Lynn.

# Sex Education

MARGOT ABELS

Margot Abels lives in a purple house on a busy intersection in Lynn, where the ocean air mixes with the grit of the city. To the neighbors who stop to chat while she gardens, she is the professor, the mother, the widow who has weathered the storms of life with a quiet, fierce dignity. But to understand the steel in her spine, you must look beyond the domestic tranquility of her garden to a life defined by a refusal to flinch in the face of danger. Long before she became a reluctant figure in the national media, Abels was already walking through fire, forging a legacy of authentic, unapologetic survival.

Margot Abels.

Her courage was not learned in a classroom, but on the pavement. Born in 1964 and raised by Jewish socialist parents who viewed political action as a moral imperative, Abels spent her young adulthood on the front lines of the culture wars in New York City. Working at an abortion clinic during the violent peak of

Interview.

Operation Rescue, she escorted terrified women through gauntlets of screaming protesters. She endured bomb threats and the constant, grinding stress of a job that made her feel "dirty and broke," yet she never abandoned her post. This was the crucible that formed her—a belief that protecting the vulnerable was worth any personal cost.

> *They were unaware that they were being illegally recorded.*

That belief would be tested to its breaking point in March 2000. While working as an HIV/AIDS prevention educator for the Massachusetts Department of Education, Abels co-led a workshop for queer youth where students could submit anonymous questions. One index card, written by a teenager seeking clarity in a world of silence, asked simply: "What is fisting?" Abels read the card aloud, and her co-presenter, Michael Gaucher, answered clinically. He clarified that the partner's hand is not formed into a fist, but cupped to be smaller; he stressed the absolute necessity of safety, lubrication and communication.

They were unaware that they were being illegally recorded. A conservative operative hidden in the room captured the audio, which was later manipulated—spliced with a homophobic voiceover to strip away the educational context and paint the educators as predators. The resulting firestorm turned Abels' life upside down.

The backlash was immediate and terrifying. The narrative spun by the Right—that state employees were "recruiting" children into "prurient" acts—brought news vans to her street in Lynn, waiting for a glimpse of the "monster" they had manufactured. Her phone rang with vitriol and threats, the safety of her home shattered by the rage of strangers. She was fired, publicly humiliated and isolated. Perhaps most painful was the abandonment by parts of the queer community, who were then focused on respectability politics. "Those people who really felt like you needed to separate 'gayness' from sex... thought that what we were doing put the work in jeopardy," Abels recalled. Though she eventually sued the state with the support of her union and won her job back, proving her methods were sound, the "chilling effect" of this incident effectively ended direct sex education by DOE employees for decades.

But to let this incident define Margot Abels is to let her enemies win. Her true victory lies in the rich, defiant life she built away from the cameras. In 1999, she and her partner, Bridget McGuiness, chose Lynn not for its quiet, but for its noise and diversity, deliberately avoiding the polished, Whiter suburbs. She threw herself into the community, serving on the original board of directors for NAGLY

Bridget, left, and Margot at their wedding on Lynn Beach, the first same-sex marriage in Lynn.

(North Shore Alliance of LGBTQ+ Youth), ensuring the next generation had the support she fought for.

When marriage equality finally arrived in Massachusetts, Abels and Bridget didn't just get married; they made history. Alongside a male couple, they stood on the beach at the end of their block and became the first same-sex couples to marry in Lynn. It was a ceremony that was both a political act and a declaration of profound love, celebrated with the sand beneath their feet and their community around them.

It was in Lynn that the abstractions of politics became the concrete reality of community. Abels transformed from a target of national hate into a pillar of local love. She became a fierce advocate for her daughter within the special education system and a familiar face in the youth hockey world. When Bridget fell terminally ill, the true heart of their life was revealed. Night after night, as Bridget lay dying, neighbors—some who knew their politics, some who just knew their hearts—came to their home. They didn't intrude; they simply lit candles on the stairs and stood outside in a silent, glowing vigil. It was a testament to a life lived so openly and generously that it commanded reverence.

Today, Abels teaches at Northeastern University, warning a new generation that the rights they enjoy are fragile. She sees the tactics used against her in 2000—surveillance, distortion and moral panic—reflected in the modern assaults on trans rights and bodily autonomy. "It was us twenty years ago, it's somebody else now," she warns. "It could be us again." But her warning comes with a blueprint for survival. Margot Abels is proof that you can walk through the fire of public hatred and come out the other side not just whole, but triumphant—standing in the sun, in front of a purple house, living a life that is entirely, beautifully your own.

Kiristy, Laura. "A Bittersweet Victory At Last." Bay Windows, 30 Aug. 2001, pp. 1–5.

# Gender Talk

NANCY NANGERONI & GORDENE MACKENZIE

"The best way to win people over is to make friends."

For Nancy Nangeroni and Gordene MacKenzie, this isn't just a slogan; it is a battle-tested strategy. Laws can change, they argue, and when you enforce change solely by law, you often drive the opposition underground where it festers. But when you make friends, you dissipate the opposition entirely. Friendship endures where legislation might be reversed.

This philosophy of connection began with a simple question in a crowded room at the Texas "T" Party, then the nation's largest trans convention, which they both attended in February 1998. After they raised funds for the International Foundation for Gender Education, Nangeroni asked, "Would you like to dance?" MacKenzie laughed and replied, "I'm too butch for that! Let me buy you a drink." That drink sparked a partnership that would revolutionize the way the world heard—and saw—transgender lives.

Nancy Nangeroni, left, at home with Gordene MacKensie.

Long before they were a power couple of the North Shore, they were navigating their own complex journeys with gender. For Nancy, the road to authenticity was paved with fear, until a crisis forced the issue. After a severe motorcycle accident in 1981, when Nangeroni still presented as male, her roommates, who had been searching for information to contact Nancy's parents, discovered her stash of women's clothes. Nangeroni braced for the end of the friendships. Instead, she found acceptance from her roommates and many others who said, "We still love you." That overwhelming wash of unconditional love didn't just save friendships; it emboldened Nangeroni to step into the light, admitting later, "so much love changed my worldview." A pivotal moment came when she attended Fantasia Fair in Provincetown, MA. There, she felt able to live freely as a woman for the first time, sparking her active involvement in the trans and crossdressing communities.

Gordene MacKensie, left, with Nancy Nangeroni recording GenderVision for Beverly Cable Acccess TV.

For a long time, Nancy's goal was to pass seamlessly as a woman, but over the decades, she has settled into a comfortable visibility, identifying now as trans, non-binary and genderqueer. She never intended to erase the male history that shaped her.

*So much love changed my worldview.*

Gordene, the author of the seminal book *Transgender Nation*, identifies as a non-binary female. Together, they share a deep discontent with the rigid dual gender system that forces expansive human spirits into tiny boxes that must be checked.

Their activism found its voice on the airwaves. In 1995, Nangeroni launched *GenderTalk*, the first radio program on trans topics east of the Mississippi. MacKenzie came on as producer and co-host in 1998. From 2008 to 2009, MacKenzie and Nangeroni co-produced and co-hosted *GenderVision*, an educational cable television program about gender, recorded at the Beverly Cable Access TV studios and distributed nationwide. Through these platforms, they broadcast programming on human and civil rights.

Their integrity was perhaps best illustrated by the night they didn't show up. *GenderTalk* had won a prestigious GLAAD Media Award in 2000. The award was to be presented by

Nancy Nangeroni shows her support for trans people.

Hollywood royalty—Whoopi Goldberg and Elizabeth Taylor. But Nangeroni and MacKenzie had already committed to speaking to a small local trans group that same night. Rather than chase the glitz, they sent volunteers to collect the trophy and kept their promise to the people who needed them most.

However, their work has also touched the darkest parts of the community's history. When Rita Hester was murdered in Allston, MA, in November 1998, the press coverage was horrific, misgendering Rita and effectively "re-assassinating" the victim in print. While MacKenzie worked to correct media coverage, Nangeroni helped lead a vigil on December 4, 1998, to honor Rita's life. That gathering was the precursor to the Transgender Day of Remembrance, a solemn annual observance now held by thousands around the world to honor those lost to anti-trans violence.

After a brief time in Albuquerque, the couple landed back on the North Shore when MacKenzie became chair of the Women's and

Gordene, left, and Nacy at North Shore Pride circa 2014.

Gender Studies Department at Merrimack College, settling into life in North Reading and later Beverly. But they didn't settle down. Nangeroni helped lead the Massachusetts Transgender Political Coalition and, in 2008, worked tirelessly to pass the Beverly Human Rights Ordinance, ensuring protection for all residents, including the trans community.

Today, their focus has shifted to the macro level: restoring democracy. They view the rising tide of hatred not just as a threat to trans rights, but to the social contract itself. Yet, true to their core philosophy, they maintain compassion even for those who oppose them, recognizing that hate is often a learned behavior instilled by upbringing. Their hearts break most for the trans youth asking "Why does everyone hate us?"

To answer them, Nangeroni and MacKenzie keep showing up, proving that while laws are necessary, it is love—unapologetic, visible and persistent—that truly saves the world.

https://www.gendertalk.com/

http://gv.gendertalk.com/

https://www.ifge.org/

https://www.masstpc.org/

# Drag Queen Story Hour

JOHN PAUL RYAN

"You know I'm a lot bigger than you, right? I can knock you out."

The man standing in the doorway of the Second Congregational Church in Boxford wasn't making an idle threat. He was angry, large, and determined to force his way into the Drag Queen Story Hour. But standing in his way was John Paul Ryan.

John, the chair of the Boxford Library Board of Trustees, hadn't planned on being a bouncer that day in 2022. He had simply voted to host a story hour featuring Clara Divine to support the growing number of queer families moving into town. The backlash, however, was swift and vicious. For weeks, John's phone rang with threats. He was heckled in the streets of his own town and received conversion therapy pamphlets in his mail with no return address. The hostility grew so intense that the event had to be moved from the library to the church hall.

On the day of the event, while protesters gathered across the street, John stood at the church entrance, determined to protect the 250 parents and children inside. When the angry man tried to shove past him, throwing John physically into the vestibule, John didn't buckle. Drawing on his background in security, he planted his feet and refused to move until police arrived. "I am not letting hate in," was his resolve. Inside, the children were oblivious to the violence at the door, laughing and enjoying Clara Divine's stories in a safe, joyful space.

The event was a massive success, and the incident galvanized the community, proving that the suburbs were not as quiet as they seemed. In the weeks that followed, queer community members and allies worked together in Topsfield to organize a Tri-Town picnic, uniting Boxford, Topsfield and Middleton. John Paul Ryan, a straight ally who refused to be bullied, witnessed the beginning of a permanent movement for inclusion.

https://www.secondchurchboxford.org/

https://www.boxfordma.gov/157/Library

Trustee Denae Ramos-Pachucki, left, Clara Devine, Trustee John Paul and Jayne Smallman.

# No Place for Hate

KIM DRISCOLL

Long before she was inaugurated as the 73rd Lieutenant Governor of Massachusetts, Kim Driscoll proved her mettle as a fierce queer ally during her tenure as the Mayor of Salem. Her commitment to the city's "No Place for Hate" designation was tested in 2014, when Gordon College requested a religious exemption to allow federal contractors to discriminate based on sexual orientation. Driscoll took a "brave stand," publicly declaring that the city would not renew the college's lease for the historic Old Town Hall if the college maintained policies that excluded inclusivity.

The backlash was immediate and vitriolic. After national right-wing media picked up the story, Driscoll's office was inundated with hateful emails, letters and phone calls. But rather than retreat, Driscoll executed a brilliant pivot that turned the harassment into a windfall for the queer community. As the hate mail piled up, she issued a public pledge: for every hateful message she received that week, she would personally donate five dollars to the North Shore Alliance of LGBTQ+ Youth (NAGLY).

She challenged the public to match her, effectively monetizing the bigotry directed at her administration. The strategy backfired spectacularly on her detractors. In just one week, the campaign raised over $15,000 for NAGLY, with donations pouring in from as far away as Australia. Driscoll's maneuver didn't just silence the trolls; it funded vital youth programming and cemented her legacy as a leader who ensured that in Salem, hatred would be transformed to fuel the very community it sought to harm.

https://www.nagly.org/

https://www.salem.org/blog/salem-massachusetts-is-no-place-for-hate/

While mayor of Salem, Kim Driscoll transformed a flood of hate mail into a huge fundraiser.

# At the Ballot Box

JUDY FLANAGAN KENNEDY

In 2007, when Lynn rolled back bar closing times from 2 a.m. to 1 a.m., City Hall messed with the wrong crowd. Furious at the crackdown on their gathering spaces, the queer community turned last call into a political weapon. They rallied at the bars, ensuring patrons marched directly from their stools to the polls. It was a chaotic "sticker campaign"—queer ally Judith Flanagan Kennedy wasn't even on the ballot—requiring voters to physically paste her name to make it count. In an election decided by exactly 27 votes, that mobilized nightlife undeniably tipped the scales. The establishment tried to shut down the party, but the community stuck together and shut down the mayor instead.

# Kennedy by 27

## Lynn voters elect first female mayor

**LYNN** ◆ Election chart: A11

By THOR JOURGENSEN AND DAVID LISCIO
THE DAILY ITEM

"Who says you can't fight City Hall?" shouted Judith Flanagan Kennedy shortly before 9:30 p.m. Tuesday night as she celebrated her 8,043-8,016 vote win over Mayor Edward J. Clancy Jr.

The win was so close that 45 votes unofficially listed as write-ins for other individuals besides the official candidates could have made the difference for Clancy or Kennedy.

As the city's first woman mayor, the 47-year-old mother of two credited her win to a grassroots group of supporters who knocked on doors in the disperate neighborhoods.

Clancy, who has served as mayor since 2002, spent more than $100,000 on a final election campaign aimed at reversing the second-place finish Kennedy handed him in the Sept. 15 preliminary election.

Despite a heavy advertising campaign and efforts to blanket the city with campaign fliers, Clancy's final election results, precinct by precinct, nearly duplicated his preliminary election finish.

Kennedy scored a strong win in Ward 2, her East Lynn home ward, while Clancy won his West Lynn base in Ward 7. But Ward 3 in East Lynn delivered votes to Kennedy despite ward councilor Darren Cyr's election-eve endorsement of Clancy.

The contestants split precinct wins in Ward 4 and Ward 5 in the city's center while Clancy won all of Ward 6 except Precinct 2.

The city election office reported a 33 percent voter turnout, considered high by mayoral race averages.

The mayor called Kennedy at 9:45 p.m. to congratulate her only minutes after she congratulated her own supporters.

See **MAYOR** PAGE A11

Mayor-elect Judith Flangan Kennedy is surrounded by her supporters at the Franco-American Post after Tuesday's upset win of incumbent Mayor Edward Clancy.

Votes from the queer community may have put Judith Kennedy over the top in 2009.

# Governor's Council

Eileen Duff

When the Transgender Equal Accommodation Bill landed on Governor Charlie Baker's desk in 2016, the political path was anything but clear. Opponents had whipped up fear-mongering rhetoric about public safety, threatening to derail protections for transgender people in public spaces. Eileen Duff, drawing on a lifetime of experience that ranged from hospice chaplaincy to real estate, didn't quarrel to change the Governor's mind; she relied on humanity. In a pivotal, private conversation, she helped cut through

Essex County Registrar, Eileen Duff, at home.

the political noise, appealing directly to Baker's sense of fairness. Her advocacy from her seat on the Governor's Council became a key weight on the scale, helping to secure the signature that guaranteed equal access to public accommodations for transgender citizens across the Commonwealth.

This instinct for bipartisan dialogue wasn't a political calculation; it was her inheritance. Raised in a devout Catholic family in Peabody, Duff grew up with a Democratic father and a Republican mother who viewed the dinner table as a forum for world affairs. The rules of the house were strict but empowering: "If you had an opinion, you had to come up with a solution." That early lesson—that complaints are useless without a plan—became the blueprint for her career, teaching her that progress requires walking into rooms where you might not agree with everyone and finding a way forward.

> *My legacy is who I help on the way, and what they do out there in the world that changes things.*

However, Duff knows firsthand that visibility often comes with a heavy cost. During her 2012 campaign for the Governor's Council, she became the target of vicious, anonymous bullying on the local *Patch* news platform. It was a digital assault fueled by homophobia, designed to silence a queer candidate. But instead of retreating, Duff fought back. She helped the publication recognize the vitriol for what it was—hate speech—and stop printing it. She proved that while a queer candidate might face fire, they don't have to burn.

Her resilience is matched only by her results. On the Governor's Council, she worked alongside Governor Deval Patrick to approve the first pardons in Massachusetts in forty years. Driven by her background in chaplaincy, Duff believed deeply that people are more than their worst mistakes and fought for a system that recognized redemption. Later, as the Register of Deeds for Southern

Essex District, she took on a "dusty," traditional institution and transformed it. In a single year, she diversified the staff more than had been done in the previous four decades, ensuring the face of government actually looked like the community it served.

For Duff, this relentless drive comes from a specifically queer place. She believes that the struggle to be seen gives the queer community a unique superpower: "Our experiences can make us very compassionate to other people's experiences, too." It is this empathy that bridges the gap between a hospice bedside and the State House.

Today, Duff finds her own sanctuary in Gloucester, where she lives with her wife, Jan, and their dogs. But she is never far from the fight. Her definition of legacy isn't about the titles she holds, but about the hands she extends to others. "My legacy is who I help on the way," she says, "and what they do out there in the world that changes things." Her challenge to the North Shore is simple but urgent: Run for office. If you can't run, help someone else run. The door is open, but only if we keep holding it for one another.

https://malegislature.gov/Bills/189/S735

# Live and Let Live

RICHARD TISEI

The reporter's pen was poised, and Richard Tisei took a breath that had been held for decades. "I am gay," he told the *Boston Globe* in 2009. With those three words, the Republican leader stepped out of the comfortable silence of the North Shore suburbs and into history. In that moment, the "live and let live" politician shattered the glass ceiling of his own party, proving that authenticity and conservatism need not be enemies.

Richard Tisei (b. 1962) is deeply rooted in the soil of the North Shore. Raised in Lynnfield and a graduate of Lynnfield High School (1981), he eventually settled in Wakefield. Since 1992, he has been a fixture of the local business community as a realtor, co-owning Northrup Associates in Lynnfield with his partner, Bernie Starr.

Former Senate Minority Leader Richard Tisei.

His political ascent was meteoric. First elected to the Massachusetts House of Representatives in 1984 at the age of 22, he was the youngest

Republican ever to serve. Over 26 years in the legislature, he rose to become the Senate Minority Leader, a testament to his ability to navigate the deep blue waters of Massachusetts politics. His career was defined by a balance of fiscal conservatism and social moderation, and he championed causes such as the Whistleblower Protection Law.

> *I am gay. It is part of who I am, but it is not the only thing I am.*

His 2009 coming out, just before running for Lieutenant Governor alongside Charlie Baker, marked him as a pioneer. Although the ticket narrowly lost, Tisei continued to break barriers. In 2012 and 2014, he ran for Congress in the 6th District; had he won, he would have been the first non-incumbent openly gay Republican elected to Congress. In July 2013, he married Bernie, furthering his visibility as a queer advocate who challenged his party to be more inclusive. As he often noted, "It is part of who I am, but it is not the only thing I am."

# City Council

Coco Alinsug, Dylan Benson, Kyle Davis, Julie Flowers,
Katelyn Holappa, & Tom Sullivan

**Coco Alinsug** The snow was falling so hard you couldn't see the skyline. Coco Alinsug stepped off the plane into the blizzard of February 2002, a gay immigrant from the Philippines shivering in a new world. He had left a political dynasty in Cebu to find a place where he didn't have to hide who he was. He found it not in a palace,

Coco Alinsug at Lynn's Pride Flag raising in 2022.

but in the gritty embrace of Lynn. Twenty years later, the man who arrived in a storm would stand in City Hall as the first openly gay councilor, the snow replaced by the rainbow flag on his desk.

In the Cebu province of the Philippines, the Alinsug name was synonymous with public service for generations. Still, for Coco, the path to political history wasn't paved in his homeland—it was forged in the snow-covered streets of Lynn. Born into a family where his father served as vice mayor and his grandmother as a councilor, Alinsug grew up observing the art of governance firsthand. Yet, as a gay man in a conservative society, he knew his authentic self had to remain hidden behind the curtain of his family's reputation. Seeking the freedom to live openly, he immigrated to the United States, eventually landing in Lynn.

Lynn offered Alinsug something he hadn't found elsewhere: a home. He found sanctuary and friendship at 47 Central, a local queer bar that served as a community hub, and met his future husband, Peter Cipriano, just weeks after arriving. For two decades, Alinsug wove himself into the fabric of the city, organizing events and serving on state committees, but the idea of running for local office seemed daunting. While Lynn had queer councilors in the past, none had served openly. It was Peter who finally pushed him to break the barrier, asking, "If you don't try it, how would we know?"

In 2021, Alinsug took the leap, running for the Ward 3 City Council seat. His campaign wasn't just about policy; it was a test of the city's evolution. When the votes were tallied, the result was a landslide victory that shattered multiple glass ceilings at once. Alinsug didn't just win; he became the first openly gay city councilor in Lynn's history and the first Filipino-American to hold the office.

His election marked a profound shift for the city, proving that a gay immigrant could not only be accepted but also embraced as a leader. Standing in City Hall, where generations of predominantly white leadership had come before him, Alinsug represented a new "Ward 3"—diverse, inclusive and forward-looking. From the political dynasty of Cebu to the council chambers of Lynn, Coco Alinsug's journey proved that while he traveled halfway across the world to find himself, he had to come to Lynn to find his voice.

**Dylan Benson** Dylan Benson made history in 2024 as Gloucester's first openly queer city councilor, but his path to City Hall was paved with resilience rather than political ambition. Raised in public housing by a father struggling with financial hardship, Benson's early battles with poverty and his internal struggle to come out shaped his moral compass. These experiences fueled a relentless drive to advocate for every neighbor left on the margins, from the immigrant community to those facing anti-Semitism.

While his identity is a milestone, his legislative record defines his service. Honoring a family history of military service, Benson counts

Dylan Benson, center, with his campaign team.

his work for veterans as his proudest achievement, successfully implementing tax work-off programs and local options that help aging service members afford to stay in their homes. His advocacy is equally fierce for the queer community; amidst rising national hostility, he initiated a city-wide proclamation explicitly affirming Gloucester's support for transgender residents. For Benson, representation is a tool, not a trophy. He serves with the hope that his visibility will inspire a new generation of queer youth to move from the sidelines to the ballot, ensuring they have a seat at the table where their future is decided.

**Kyle Davis** When a critic sneered, "Tell Kyle when he learns to become a man… maybe he'll have a shot at being elected," Kyle Davis didn't retreat; he won. Elected in 2023, Davis brought a vital,

From left, Jeff Cohen, Chief of Police Lucas Miller, Mayor Dominick Pangallo, city councilors Alice Merkl, Patti Morsillo, Ty Hapworth, Kyle Davis, Cindy Jerzylo, Conrad Prosniewski at North Shore Pride.

missing perspective to the Salem City Council as the body's only renter at the time. He used that voice to challenge predatory brokerage fees in Salem and across the state, a stand he cites as his proudest moment. An openly gay leader who organized the city's last two rainbow crosswalk paintings and fiercely advocates for trans support, Davis proves that true leadership isn't about fitting a mold—it's about breaking them.

**Reverend Julie Flowers** Following the 2016 presidential election, Rev. Julie Flowers looked around the shifting political landscape and realized that, instead of just "making a vague pronouncement that more women should run for office," she needed to be willing to put her own name on the ballot. That decision led to her becoming, according to a widely held belief, the first openly queer member of the Beverly City Council.

One of Flowers' proudest moments came early in her tenure during a contentious statewide battle over transgender protections. While still learning the ropes of municipal government, she introduced a resolution to affirm the rights of trans neighbors against a ballot question seeking to remove them. On the night of the vote, the council chamber was packed with residents, a visual testament to the city's values. "I just felt so proud, looking out," Flowers recalls, realizing the community had shown up to support their vulnerable neighbors rather than letting fear divide them.

Her leadership has since broken significant barriers in local governance. Beverly is

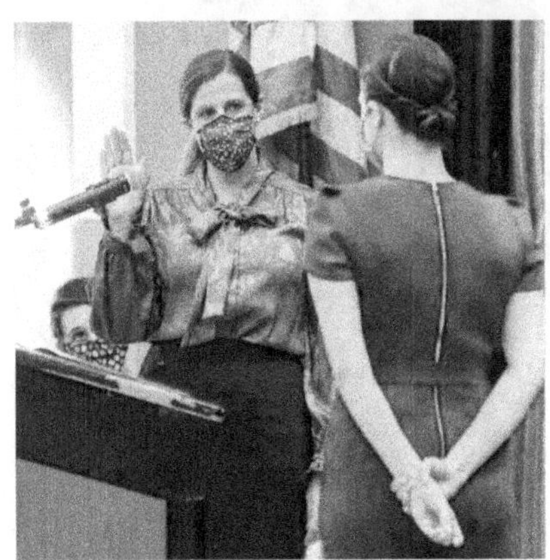

Julie Flowers.

unique in that voters directly elect the City Council President, and Flowers became the first woman to be elected to that role by the people. In this capacity, working alongside the Human Rights Committee, she has championed institutional visibility, including raising the Pride flag and the city's observance of Transgender Day of Remembrance. For Flowers, the goal remains clear: to use the "toolbox" of local government to keep Beverly "growing into the community we're always becoming"—one of safety, welcome and belonging.

**Katelyn Holappa** When Katelyn Holappa stood behind the podium at Salem's Riley Plaza in October 2025 to speak at the "No Kings" protest, she didn't just bring a megaphone; she brought a

Katelyn Holappa.

mirror. Looking out at the Salem crowd—a city famous for its history of persecution—she warned that the fascism of the past wasn't dead, just rebranded. "What do you think they really mean when they say 'Make America Great Again?'" she asked, challenging her neighbors to see the uncomfortable truth: that the systems which once burned witches were now targeting the trans community.

Holappa didn't just shout from the outside; she stepped inside to change the machinery itself. A software development manager and Eagle Scout, she ran for Salem's Ward 6 city council seat not to be a symbol, but to fix the sidewalks and the systems. In a landslide victory that shattered the "cement ceiling" of local politics, she became the first openly transgender City Councilor on the North Shore. For Holappa, the fight against rising authoritarianism isn't just about protests; it's about showing up to the boring meetings, balancing the budget and proving that a trans woman belongs at the head of the table where the decisions are made.

**Tom Sullivan** Growing up gay in Haverhill in the 1960s was tough, but Attorney Tom Sullivan is proud that he finally had the "balls" to come out in 2001 and live honestly. That courage, paired with a lifetime of service, has made him a political powerhouse in his hometown. Sullivan built his foundation at the Massachusetts State House, starting as a Legislative Page in 1981 and rising to become a Legislative Aide and eventually Chief of Staff to a State Senator. While mastering the intricacies of state and local government, he also earned three degrees, including his law degree, from Suffolk University.

In 2012, Sullivan was elected to the City Council, likely becoming the first openly queer city councilor on the North Shore. The community's trust in him is absolute; by 2024, he was the city's second top vote-getter and was chosen by his colleagues to serve as Council President for the 2024–2025 term.

Sullivan's support for the queer community has been both practical and profound. When young organizers sought to launch the first Haverhill Pride parade in June 2025, they had the vision but needed navigational help. Sullivan stepped in, drawing on a deep family legacy of logistics. His father, the late John T. Sullivan, along with veterans from Lorraine Post 29 VFW, had organized the first annual VFW Santa Parade in 1964. Upon his father's passing in 1985, Sullivan joined the committee, serving as its Chair from 1986 to 2001 and remaining a member today. Leveraging decades of experience with traffic logistics and city approvals, he ensured the Pride Parade became a reality.

Tom Sullivan and his sister Sheila at the 2025 Haverhill Pride.

Beyond the parade, Sullivan has coordinated the annual Pride Flag Raising Ceremony at City Hall for the past several years. For Sullivan— now the grandfather of a seven-month-old—his sexuality was never a campaign issue. To the voters of Haverhill, his lifelong commitment always spoke louder.

# School Committee

Tiffany Magnolia, Brenda Ortiz McGrath & Tristan Smith

**Tiffany Magnolia** The school board meeting in 2023 was polite, bureaucratic and stagnant—until Tiffany Magnolia spoke up. She hadn't run for office to approve budgets; she had run to protect the kid she used to be. Channeling her past as a punk-rock activist in D.C., she took aim at the Lynn school district's sexist dress code and the lack of protections for trans students. She didn't ask for permission; she demanded change, shattering the "straight" facade she had maintained for years to become the fiercely visible champion that Lynn's queer youth had been waiting for.

For years, Tiffany Magnolia lived a quiet double life in Lynn. To her colleagues at North Shore Community College, where she has taught for two decades and directs the Honors Program, she was a fierce advocate and union president. But at home, her reality was more complex. She was married to a man, Rex, whom she had supported through a gender transition years earlier. To the outside world, they were a straight couple, a perception Magnolia allowed to persist to protect her husband's privacy. But after years of silence, the former punk rocker and ACT UP activist from D.C. decided she could no longer leave her identity at the door.

Magnolia's journey to the Lynn School Committee began far from the North Shore, in a chaotic childhood split between Florida and Virginia, marked by a struggle to survive a schizophrenic mother and strict religious grandparents. She found her salvation not in conformity, but in the queer activism of the late 80s and early 90s, delivering Meals on Wheels to AIDS patients when few others would. That fire for justice followed her through a Ph.D. at Tufts and eventually to Lynn in 2004.

*She didn't ask for permission; she demanded change.*

When she decided to run for the School Committee in 2021, Magnolia made a conscious choice to run as an openly queer candidate, shattering the "straight" facade she had maintained. Despite backlash and advice to tone it down, she won, becoming the committee's first openly queer member. Once elected, she didn't just fill a seat; she shook the table. She led the charge to gut the district's sexist dress code, fought for gender-neutral graduation

Tiffany Magnolia at Lynn's flag raising in 2022.

gowns and became a vocal defender of trans students, ensuring they had the protections she wished she'd had growing up.

Magnolia was not re-elected. Today, Magnolia describes progress not as a straight line, but as concentric circles that expand and contract.

Interview.

Whether in her classroom at North Shore Community College or on the political stage, she remains a tireless force for that expansion, proving that the most powerful thing a leader can be is authentically, unapologetically themselves.


**Brenda Ortiz McGrath** "You're never going to make it."

The words hung in the air of the guidance counselor's office. Across the desk sat teenage Brenda Ortiz McGrath, a girl from the Waltham projects who had been pigeonholed into the high school's lowest academic track. The verdict was cold and absolute: don't apply to a four-year college; don't dream beyond your station. That counselor, however, didn't just underestimate her; they fueled her. Ortiz McGrath didn't just go to college; she returned to that very same high school building years later—not as the student listed for failure, but as the principal running the school.

Ortiz McGrath's career has been defined by a relentless drive to dismantle the barriers that once blocked her own path. She has become a nationally recognized educational leader and social worker, building systems that uplift marginalized communities across Massachusetts. In 2021, while leading in Waltham, she took on a rigid tradition: graduation gowns were color-coded, white for girls and red for boys. For her transgender and non-binary students, this wasn't a celebration; it was a public crisis of identity. Despite warnings that the community would push back, Ortiz McGrath refused to fold. She unified the class in single red gowns, transforming a moment of alienation into one of belonging. "I had several transgender students," she said, "and honoring their identities was critically important."

*We have to be unapologetic about who we are.*
*That is our truth.*

Now, she brings that survivor's grit to the North Shore as the only openly queer member of the Lynn School Committee and a district administrator in Chelsea. A proud Latina and mother, she understands that academic success is impossible if a child is in survival mode. This is why she is a fierce champion for Social-Emotional Learning (SEL). For Ortiz McGrath, this isn't just educational jargon; SEL builds emotional awareness, connection and life skills—the very infrastructure that vulnerable kids need to thrive. She has spent years working to ensure that no student falls through the cracks, as she almost did.

Sophia, Jane, Brenda Ortiz McGrath and Jaylene.

Living openly with her wife, Jane, and their two daughters, Ortiz McGrath models the one lesson she wants every Lynn student to learn: "We have to be unapologetic about who we are. That is our truth." Brenda Ortiz McGrath is no longer asking for permission to belong; she is the one holding the door open for the next generation.

**Tristan Smith** When the votes were tallied for the 2025 Lynn School Committee election, Tristan Smith wasn't just on the list— he was the top vote-getter. It was a resounding validation for a candidate who had made a bold choice: to run entirely as himself. During Pride Month, in the heat of the campaign, Smith made a conscious decision to come out publicly on social media. As possibly the first out bisexual male School Committee member on the North Shore, he knew that representation wasn't just a buzzword; it was a lifeline.

*We're coaching the next generation of young leaders.*

The response from voters was overwhelmingly positive, proving that authenticity resonates. For Smith, a lawyer and former instructor at North Shore Community College, lived experience is a vital policy tool. He ran on the belief that schools must be sanctuaries where students feel seen. His priority is to implement policies that empower teachers and staff to be "trusted adults"— ensuring that when a student gathers the courage to share their truth, they are met with support, knowledge and safety.

This philosophy of "seeing" the individual extends to the track at St. Mary's in Lynn, where he coaches. One of his proudest moments didn't come from a trophy, but from a letter to the editor written by a former student-athlete now attending Harvard. The student didn't write about winning races; he wrote about how Coach Smith saw him as a whole person, not just a runner. That connection is the heart of Smith's work. Whether in the courtroom or on the field, his mission is the same. As he puts it, "We're coaching the next generation of young leaders." In Tristan Smith, Lynn's youth have found a leader who is proudly, unapologetically one of them.

Tristan Smith.

# Hope for the Future

HOPE WATT-BUCCI

When Hope Watt-Bucci looked across the North Shore fifteen years ago, she saw a community living in the shadow of silence. It was a time when hate crimes were ticking upward, and the vibrant queer life of Boston felt a world away. The turning point came one day on the street, when a group of young girls hurled the slur "faggot" at her. That moment of stinging intolerance, coupled with witnessing a shocking anti-gay incident at a local restaurant where patrons

Hope Watt-Bucci on the stage at North Shore Pride in 2025.

harassed an elderly gay couple, made her realize that safety couldn't be granted; it had to be claimed. She and the original founding North Shore Pride Board members organized the first North Shore Pride Parade and Festival in 2012. Their grassroots vision has exploded into a massive celebration, drawing 40,000 marchers to the historic streets of Salem in 2025.

Raised in Manchester-by-the-Sea, Watt-Bucci's life has been heavily defined by service. She is an active-duty veteran of the United States Army and made local history as the first female Commander of the Manchester-by-the-Sea American Legion Post.

Today, her impact extends far beyond a single weekend in June. Watt-Bucci helped build and facilitates the Rainbow Coalition uniting organizers across small North Shore towns, ensuring queer eevent organizers from Lynn to Topsfield and from Amesbury to Lawrence have visible support networks. Recently honored with a

Hope Watt-Bucci, right, with members of OUTVETS, a Massachusetts LGBTQ+ Veterans organization marching in the St. Patrick's Day Parade in East Boston.

Martin Luther King, Jr. Leadership Award from Salem State University "for outstanding and significant contributions to the causes of freedom, justice, peace and equality", Watt-Bucci —who also holds a Ph.D. in Law and Policy—remains on the front lines. In late 2024, she rallied crowds in Salem to publicly defend the rights of transgender youth against political attacks, demanding equity and inclusion.

Alongside her wife, Lisa, Watt-Bucci continues to live, work, and organize locally. She is a living testament that true heroes don't just fight for a place in the community—they build a bigger table for everyone else.

North Shore Pride board members providing resources in the community. In the center is Stonewall Survivor and NSP Award recipient, Denis Castleton. Hope Watt-Bucci, center right. Lisa Watt-Bucci, centr left.

# The Mayor's Liaison

Naming a university building usually requires a massive donation. Michael Corley did it with a letter to the editor and tenacious advocacy. Arriving in Salem from Florida in 2019 to support his grandmother, Corley noticed that Salem State University's campus honored almost exclusively white figures. As a Black gay man completing his media and communication degree during the isolation of the pandemic, he refused to let that erasure stand. He spearheaded a campaign challenging the Board of Trustees, resulting in the university's newest building being named for Charlotte Forten, the school's first African American graduate and a celebrated abolitionist.

His advocacy at the university extended beyond names on buildings. Corley also worked with University Leadership and The Massachusetts Tribe to help Salem State develop its first land acknowledgment, while simultaneously creating

Michael Corley, left, and Salem Mayor Dominick Pangallo at North Shore Pride.

and endowing a scholarship to help cover room and board for those who identify as Indigenous.

That drive to amplify marginalized voices now defines Corley's work as the LGBTQIA+ liaison in the Salem Mayor's office. He has moved beyond symbolic gestures to institutionalize equity, developing specific LGBTQ+ training for city employees and helping to lead an Employee Resource Group to foster community within the municipal workforce. He is also expanding the city's definition of inclusion by leading efforts to adopt a gender-neutral dress code and working to elevate the often-overlooked intersex community, with plans to fly the intersex flag at City Hall in October.

Despite his growing influence—including earning a Master's in Public Administration and being asked to deliver the student commencement speech at SSU in 2023—Corley remains grounded in personal connection. He volunteers as a mentor with Jewish Big Brothers Big Sisters, a role that challenges him to look outside his own experience. For Corley, whether he is shaping city policy or spending a weekend afternoon with his mentee, the mission is the same: "Every day there are new ways to help people."

https://www.salemma.gov/426/LGBTQIA-Liaison

https://www.salemstate.edu/LandAcknowledgement

Michael Corley at North Shore Pride.

# Resolve

OLIVIA WERTH

When the political winds shifted, threatening to blow the hard-won rights of transgender people back into the dark, Olivia Werth didn't seek shelter; she built a fortress. In April 2025, Werth stood at the center of a historic victory in Salem, spearheading the effort to pass a City Council resolution declaring Salem a sanctuary for the transgender and gender non-conforming community. While national headlines debated the existence of transgender people, Werth's advocacy ensured that Salem would legally commit to protecting gender-affirming healthcare and ensuring safety in schools, turning a city famous for its past persecution into a modern beacon of refuge.

But Werth knew that laws alone cannot comfort a community under siege. In the heat of the 2024 election season, as anti-trans rhetoric spiked nationwide, she spotted a critical gap in the local landscape: there were no in-person support groups for trans adults. Refusing to let her neighbors face the hostility alone, she founded North Shore Trans Support that June. What began as a necessary response to political attacks has blossomed into a bi-weekly lifeline where members find consistency and care. For the regulars who gather there, Werth hasn't just organized a meeting; she has built a place where they can finally feel at home. Werth also volunteers at NAGLY to support trans youth.

Interview.

Her activism spills out from the meeting room into art and ink. As the creator of *Prismatic*, a queer zine, she captures the vibrant, unpolished reality of queer life on the North Shore. Drawing from her own journey—from a childhood in Iowa where identity was often shrouded in silence, to her life in Lynn—she uses the zine to amplify voices that might otherwise be lost. Whether she is drafting municipal policy, facilitating a support circle, or stapling together pages of queer art, Werth is a builder, proving that safety is constructed through laws, stories and the spaces we make for one another.

https://www.facebook.com/groups/992320235869986/

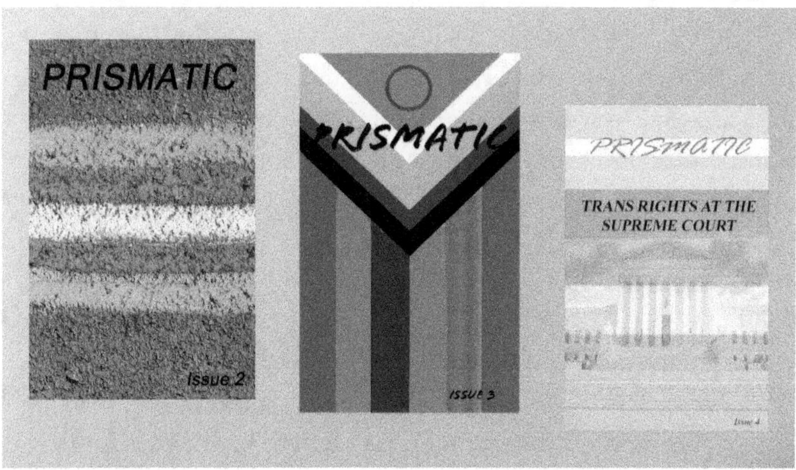


Prismatic zine.

# Political Advisor

CHRIS SICURANZA

"That's all nine! A clean sweep!" Chris Sicuranza shouted over the roar of the crowd at Rockafellas. It was election night 2015 in Salem, and the progressive coalition he supported had secured a massive victory, with every single candidate he worked with winning their seat. The win validated Chris's "Salem First" strategy, which eschewed the old guard's backroom deals in favor of voter registration efforts, a strong Facebook strategy and the use of other social media to wake a sleeping electorate.

For Sicuranza, this political openness was deeply personal. His own journey to authenticity began not with a press release, but with liquid courage. Drunk and terrified at twenty-one, he had finally asked his friends, "What if I were a man who wanted to sleep with other men?" Their casual willingness to accept him gave him the strength to live out loud. This culminated in 2018, when he and his husband, Francesco, were married by the Mayor of Gloucester—a historic ceremony recognized by the Secretary of State as the first mayor-officiated same-sex wedding officiated by a mayor in a City Hall auditorium in the Commonwealth.

Sicuranza turned that visibility into action. His "Go Out Loud" events promotion team became the premier sponsor of North Shore Pride for years. Yet, despite his progressive credentials, he fears that a new generation is being "seduced" by false narratives and rigid labels, choosing to cancel others rather than engaging in the messy, necessary work of finding common ground. For Sicuranza, the "clean sweep" wasn't about silencing the opposition, but about opening the doors wide enough for everyone to have a voice in the conversation.

Chris Sicuranza, right, marches with Go Out Loud at North Shore Pride in 2014.

# Christian Nationalism

The holiest ground Reverend Donna Spencer Collins ever stood upon was not the altar of a cathedral, but the tacky dance floor of a queer bar in Lynn. Raised in a devout Irish Catholic family, she had been warned that the people inside 47 Central were "the scum of the earth." Yet, in the shadows of the nightlife, she found the light that was missing from Sunday services. "You come to find out there's more love and compassion and empathy and caring there," she realized. "It was the best church I'd ever been to, to be honest."

Reverend Donna Spencer Collins.

Now serving as the senior reverend at Groveland, MA, Congregational Church, Collins sees a terrifying darkness gathering on the horizon—not from the outcasts she once feared, but from within the church itself. She is sounding the alarm against the rising tide of "Christian Nationalism," a movement she identifies as a hijacking of faith for political domination. In her 2025 manifesto, *Thus Says the Lord: NOT THIS: A Faithful*

*Rebuke of Christian Nationalism and Justice for All*, she exposes the hypocrisy of a theology that wraps authoritarianism in the American flag and justifies it with the Cross.

With prophetic fire, Collins warns that this "spiritual gaslighting" is not just a difference of opinion; it is an existential threat to democracy and human dignity. As rights are clawed back and hate is sanctified from the pulpit, she stands in the breach, reminding her flock that the true enemies of the gospel are those who use God's name to build an empire of exclusion.

https://www.grovelanducc.org/

Collins, Donna J. S. Thus Says the Lord: NOT THIS: A Faithful Rebuke of Christian Nationalism and Justice for All.

Coco Alinsug, left, with T Nash, Sunil Gulab, Kirsten Freni, and Reverend Donna Spencer Collins.

# EIGHT

## Firsts & the Famous

For centuries, the queer history of the North Shore was written in invisible ink—stories of survival whispered in private rooms. But in the modern era, that ink has turned into neon. This section celebrates the "Firsts and the Famous," a generation of trailblazers who didn't just step out of the closet; they stepped onto the world stage and commanded the spotlight. This is the era where the

margins moved to the center, and the North Shore became a launchpad for history.

We stand at the pinnacle of political power with Maura Healey. When she took the oath as the first openly lesbian governor in American history, she proved that a daughter of the North Shore could shatter the ultimate lavender ceiling. But the history makers are everywhere. We celebrate Rashida Ellis, the world champion boxer from Lynn who turned grit into gold, and Alex Newell, the Tony Award-winning powerhouse who brought non-binary joy to Broadway. We honor the global grace of Miss Trans Global, proving that beauty knows no binary.

Yet, we also examine the private price of public glory. We trace the journey of Jonathan Knight, who navigated the screaming crowds of New Kids on the Block fame while holding his truth close, eventually finding peace on a quiet farm in Essex. From the first couples to secure marriage licenses to the firefighters protecting our cities, these heroes remind us that true power isn't just about making headlines—it's about making a difference.

# Our Governor

Before Maura Healey even took her first breath, her legacy was already deeply rooted in the rocky earth of the North Shore. Because she was scheduled to be born at a naval hospital in Maryland, her grandparents worried she would be robbed of beginning her life in her home state. Refusing to let geography sever that birthright, her grandmother, Dorothy, dug up a small bag of dirt from a woodlot on Middle Road in Byfield, caught a flight to Maryland, and secretly placed it under the hospital delivery table. She ensured her granddaughter's life would officially begin over North Shore soil.

Governor Maura Healey at the 2025 State House Pride celebration.

That fierce, uncompromising dedication to her home is a family tradition spanning more than three centuries. Healey descends from a lineage of fighters and laborers. On her father's side, her great-grandparents settled in Newburyport after emigrating from Ireland, and her father, Jerry, captained the football and baseball teams at Newburyport High School. Her grandmother, Dorothy M. Burton, met Healey's grandfather on the Gloucester fishing docks. They raised Healey's mother, Tracy, on Chapel Street in Newburyport. Healey even had a great-great-grandfather who, at just 16, convinced his father to sign a permission slip so he could fight for the Union in the Civil War.

Healey honors these roots not just in memory, but also in presence. She was there to march in the very first Newburyport Pride parade, walking the streets her family helped build, affirming that the North Shore is a place where history and progress march side by side.

Governor Maura Healey, Center, at Newburyport's first Flag Raising with board members and volunteers.

It is from this deep, gritty, blue-collar lineage that Healey built a historic career of unapologetic resistance. When she won the gubernatorial race in 2022, she didn't just win an election; she shattered a lavender ceiling that had held firm for centuries, becoming the first out lesbian governor elected in United States history. For the LGBTQ+ community, her victory was a monumental triumph of representation. Healey recognized the profound emotional weight of her win, noting that queer youth across the country can now look at the highest levels of government and know with absolute certainty that they belong there. "I am proud of who I am," she has stated, emphasizing that children desperately need to know they are loved, seen, and celebrated for exactly who they are.

> *I wouldn't be here as the country's first lesbian governor if it weren't for all of the people who went before me.*

She intimately understands the terrifying, liberating journey of coming out. While she started pondering her sexuality during summers working as a waitress at the Hampton Beach Casino Ballroom, the true revelation came later. After playing professional basketball in Austria for two years, Healey returned to the United States and finally found the courage to come out to her former college roommate and teammate, Liz Resnick. With her voice cracking through tears, she told her friend she had something to say—only to experience the profound, beautiful relief of having Resnick immediately come out to her in return.

A relentless fight for equality has defined every step of Healey's time in public office. As the Civil Rights Chief in the Massachusetts Attorney General's Office, she wielded the law as a shield for the vulnerable, spearheading the nation's first successful challenge to the Defense of Marriage Act (DOMA) and helping dismantle the federal law that denied rights to same-sex couples. After being elected as the country's first openly LGBTQ+ state attorney general in 2014, she stood on the front lines against a rising tide of anti-LGBTQ+ legislation.

Now, as Governor, she uses her immense platform to champion further protections. She is actively fighting to adopt gender-neutral markers on official documents, mandate inclusive education, and ban the archaic LGBTQ+ "panic" defense—a shameful, horrific legal loophole used to excuse and minimize violent hate crimes by claiming an attacker was simply "provoked" by the discovery of a victim's sexual orientation or gender identity. In an era where hundreds of anti-LGBTQ+ bills are weaponized nationwide, she has offered a fierce, unwavering counter-narrative to the hostility. "You are safe in Massachusetts," she boldly promised the community. Knowing the long, brutal road it took to make that promise a reality, Healey acknowledges her place in a much larger, beautiful dynasty: "I wouldn't be here as the country's first lesbian governor if it weren't for all of the people who went before me."

https://www.mass.gov/orgs/governor-maura-healey-and-lt-governor-kim-driscoll

# Marriage Equality

MARCIA HAMS & SUSAN SHEPHERD

**Marriage Equality** May 17, 2004, marked a monumental turning point in American history and while the national spotlight focused on Cambridge, the heart of the victory beat strongly in Lynn. That midnight, Marcia Hams and Susan Shepherd became the first same-sex couple in the United States to receive a marriage license officially. Though the paperwork was filed in Cambridge, their resilience and spirit were forged on the North Shore.

Marcia Hams, center, and Susan Shepherd received the first same-sex marriage license in the United States, shown here with their son Peter at their one year anniversary.

Interview.

Hams and Shepherd's story is a quintessential Lynn narrative. They met amidst the industrial clamor of the General Electric River Works, two women from different worlds—Hams from Michigan and Shepherd from a Polish enclave in South Boston—united by labor activism. As union stewards, they fought tirelessly for women's rights and fair treatment on the factory floor. Hams and her fellow organizers in the Women's Committee fought for and won equal wages for women at GE. For over a decade, Hams and Shepherd made Lynn their home, raising their son Peter in a city they loved for its unpretentious grit and diversity. Their journey from the GE plant to the center of a national civil rights storm was paved with the same determination they used to organize workers.

The road to that midnight celebration was long, stretching from the restrictive Defense of Marriage Act in 1996 through the hard-won battle in the Massachusetts Supreme Judicial Court in 2003.

Jeff, center, and Steve exchange vows at Lynn's first same-sex wedding, which took place on Lynn Beach.

When the barriers finally fell, the joy reverberated throughout Lynn as well. At City Hall, Emily Sherwood stood proudly to receive one of the city's first local licenses, while a mother in the crowd lifted her child to witness the moment, whispering that they were watching history unfold.

> *It was just a wonderful thing to happen, and there were 200 other couples there. We're all lined up... it was a party.*

The celebration culminated on the sands of Lynn Beach, where the community gathered for the city's first same-sex marriage ceremony. There, with the Atlantic Ocean as their backdrop, Margot Abels and her wife, Bridget McGuiness, joined Steve Harrington and his partner, Jeff, to exchange vows. It was a profound declaration of love and legitimacy, foreshadowing the eventual US Supreme Court victory in 2015 that would finally bring marriage equality to the entire nation. From the factory floor to the shoreline, these North Shore pioneers proved that love, backed by the courage to fight for it, eventually wins.

**Comparable Worth** In 1976, the General Electric River Works in Lynn was an industrial fortress of 30,000 workers where lucrative skilled trades were the exclusive domain of men. Women were sequestered in satellite plants, often paid less for complex assembly than men were for sweeping floors. Enter Marcia Hams, a self-described "Cambridge dyke" who started in the gritty "scrap house" looking for a fight.

Hams quickly realized the pay scales were rigged. When the Equal Employment Opportunity Commission brought the "Krikorian suit" against GE for discrimination, the union, IUE Local 201, was initially named as a defendant. Knowing they couldn't rely on the old guard, Hams and the Women's Committee took a radical step: they hired their own lawyer, Nancy Gertner, to intervene independently.

This high-stakes maneuver forced the company to face "comparable worth"—the idea that labor is valued by skill, not gender. Their victorious out-of-court settlement was a watershed moment. The settlement secured back pay and permanently flung open the doors to high-skilled training programs. Marcia Hams came to Lynn to organize, and by the time she was done, she and her union sisters had remade the rules.

Kahn, Karen, and Patricia A. Gozemba with photographs by Marilyn Humphries, Courting Equality: A Documentary History of America's First Legal Same-Sex Marriages.

Gertner, Nancy. "Thoughts on Comparable Worth Litigation and Organizational Strategies." University of Michigan Journal of Law Reform.

Susan Shepherd, right, operates a lathe as part of the apprentice program at General Electric in Lynn, MA.

# World Champion

In the schoolyards of Lynn, Massachusetts, Rashida Ellis didn't start fights—she finished them. Her father, Ronald, realizing that her scrappy energy needed more discipline to match its intensity, took away her football—her first favorite sport—and steered her toward the boxing ring at age 10. It was there, amidst the rhythmic thud of heavy bags at Private Jewels Fitness, that a champion began to take shape.

Born into a family where fighting was practically a love language— her brothers Rashidi and Ronald were also pros in the sport– Rashida, a lesbian, didn't just inherit a legacy; she fought to redefine it. She carved a path through the amateur ranks with a style that was equal parts flash and ferocity, adopting the mantra: "I don't do 'easy';

Rashida Ellis.

I make things happen." That determination carried her all the way to the 2020 Tokyo Olympics, a dream she had held for years.

*I don't do 'easy'; I make things happen.*


But the Olympic dream hit a harsh reality in Tokyo when she lost in the Round of 16 to Great Britain's Caroline Dubois, leaving the games without a medal. For a fighter from Lynn, that heartbreak was just fuel. She returned to the gym with a renewed focus, setting her sights on the 2022 IBA Women's World Boxing Championships in Istanbul. Her redemption came in the gold medal bout against her arch-rival, Beatriz Ferreira of Brazil—a woman who had beaten her three times prior. Battling through a grueling 3-2 split decision, Ellis secured the victory. When her hand was raised, she became the first American woman to win a world title in the lightweight division since 2016. From the blacktop of Lynn, where she defended her classmates to the world stage where she defended her country's honor, Rashida Ellis proved that the most important fight isn't the one you lose—it's the one you come back to win.

https://www.youtube.com/watch?v=2dGEyUfyJHQ

# Tony Award

ALEX NEWELL

Inside the Zion Baptist Church in Lynn, a six-year-old child stood before the congregation, took a breath and let out a sound that seemed too big for such a small body. It was Christmas as Alex Newell belted out "O Holy Night." The sheer power of that voice didn't just fill the room; it shook the rafters. But the joy of that moment was intertwined with profound loss. Just that same year, Alex's father, a deacon at the church, had passed away from cancer. Raised by a single mother who became both anchor and champion, Alex learned early that resilience wasn't just about surviving—it was about singing louder than the silence left behind.

That voice would not stay contained in Lynn for long. While attending Bishop Fenwick High School, Alex uploaded an audition video for *The Glee Project* to YouTube. It was a long shot that turned into a lightning strike. The world watched as the kid from the North Shore fought for a spot on national

Alex Newell.

television, eventually landing the groundbreaking role of Unique Adams on *Glee*.

For the first time, millions of viewers saw a black, transgender teenager on primetime TV, portrayed with dignity and ferocity by a performer who was living their own truth in real-time. Newell wasn't just playing a character; they were carving out space for an entire community that had been kept in the wings.

But Broadway was Alex's ultimate dream, and the road there was paved with acclaim. After a standout run in *Once on This Island*, Alex took on the role of Lulu in the musical *Shucked*. As the whiskey-distilling, no-nonsense character, Alex brought the house down nightly with the showstopping number "Independently Owned." The performance was undeniable, a force of nature that demanded recognition.

On a warm June night in 2023, Alex Newell made history. When the envelope was opened at the 76th Tony Awards, the name read out was the kid from Lynn. In that moment, Alex became the first openly non-binary actor to win a Tony Award. Taking the stage in a shimmering gold gown, Alex looked out at the industry elite and delivered a speech that echoed all the way back to the pews of Zion Baptist. "I should not be up here as a queer, non-binary, fat, Black little baby from Massachusetts," Alex declared through tears. "And to anyone that thinks that they can't do it, I'm going to look you dead in your face that you can do anything you put your mind to." It was a victory not just for a performer, but for every "little baby" from Lynn waiting for their turn to be seen.

https://www.youtube.com/watch?v=VlsSm36RhfM

# Witness to History

MARILYN HUMPHRIES

A cool October breeze swept across the National Mall in 1979 as Marilyn Humphries stood at the base of the Washington Monument, looking out over a sea of 75,000 people. It was the first "National March on Washington for Lesbian and Gay Rights," a kaleidoscope of energy and defiance that Marilyn was there to document. As she took in the sheer scale of the moment, a fellow attendee handed her a copy of *The Guardian*. Marilyn looked down and was shocked to see her own face staring back at her. There

Pat Gozemba, left, with Marilyn Humphries circa late 1970s.

she was, alongside her friend Pat Gozemba, splashed across the cover in a photo from a recent protest at the Seabrook Nuclear Plant in New Hampshire.

For a woman who describes herself as shy, it was a jarring moment. Marilyn has never sought the spotlight; she prefers to remain behind the lens, watchful to capture the perfect moment. The true joy of photography, she insists, is not in being seen, but in the seeing—capturing the faces of those brave enough to stand up. "Even though all these other people are doing it, in the larger scheme of things, they're exceptional for doing it," she says. "That's where the joy is for me." For decades, she has been the eyes of the movement, a tireless witness to history who understands that if an event isn't documented, it risks being erased.

That camera became her passport to the front lines. Working for small press papers like *Gay Community News, Sojourner: The*

Ralph Sweeney, left, with Tom Carico and Marilyn Humphries, at Boston Pride in 1977.

*Women's Forum, Bay Windows, The Boston Phoenix* and *South End News* was, as Marilyn describes it, "a real gift." At a time when major outlets like *The Boston Globe* often ignored the nuances of queer life and social justice movements, the alternative press provided essential coverage. These credentials gave Marilyn access to people and situations she otherwise never would have witnessed, allowing her to build a portfolio of photos, some of which would eventually appear in *The New York Times* and *Business Week*.

Her dedication to the craft is legendary. At Boston Pride, she would shoot one location, then furiously bicycle to the next to beat the parade, while a second crew wrestled a ladder through the crowds to get her the perfect overhead shot. For years, she worked full-time jobs just to support her passion for documenting the struggle. As a founding member of the North Shore Gay Alliance in 1978, she didn't just observe the community; she helped build it. From the women's movement to welfare rights, from war protests to the labor movement, from the AIDS crisis to environmental justice, Marilyn has been there to record it all.

1987 candlelight vigil at the Reflecting Pool in Washington, D.C. Photo by Marilyn Humphries.

Being a witness means documenting the full spectrum of humanity, from the grotesque to the sublime. One of her most haunting images was taken at a Ku Klux Klan rally in Connecticut; in the center of the robed figures stands a young child brought by their parents to join the hate. It was a stark, undeniable document of exactly how prejudice is transmitted from one generation to the next.

In contrast, her favorite image captures the transcendent power of community. During the 1987 March on Washington, she photographed a candlelight vigil at the Reflecting Pool. As the sun set, thousands of hands raised flames against the darkness, the light reflecting off the water in a visual testament to a people holding up the light for one another.

Today, Marilyn continues to document the resistance with the same urgency she felt in 1979. She is frequently found on the streets photographing "No Kings" and other anti-Trump rallies, persisting even as mainstream newspapers turn away because the protests are "no longer new." But for Marilyn Humphries, the news cycle is irrelevant. She photographs because she knows that history is happening right now, and she refuses to let it pass unseen.

https://www.flickr.com/photos/mhimages/

Pat Gozemba, left, with Fran Collins at
Fran's Place. Photo by Marilyn Humphries.

# Renaissance Man

JOHN ARCHER

As the yacht *Trump Princess* sliced mightily through the swells of Boston Harbor, John Archer, Joan Kennedy and Donald Trump sat sipping martinis. Lots of martinis. That image—decadent and strange—is the polar opposite of where you typically find the progressive and liberal John Archer. You are far more likely to find him in a boardroom, a garden,  on stage. or volunteering for his many charities.

Although he has run Archer Insurance in Beverly for 53 years, Archer describes himself as a "professional volunteer," dedicating half his life to the non-profit world. In 1980, following the

John Archer singing at his home in Davers, MA.

heartbreaking death of his mother, he co-founded Hospice of the North Shore with Paul Lanzikos. Now known as Care Dimensions, it has grown from a grassroots effort to an organization with 500 employees. His philanthropic footprint is massive: he served as chairman of the board of the Visiting Nurse Association of the North Shore for 30 years, founded the River House homeless shelter in Beverly, and chaired a cancer walk that raised one million dollars in a single day.

But Archer is also a Renaissance man of the arts. He serves as president of both the Danvers Art Association and the Essex County Horticultural Organization. He teaches dance, drawing and literature, and has commanded the stage at the Marblehead Little Theater as Henry Higgins and Captain Von Trapp. Long out as an openly gay man, he founded the North Shore Men group with Michael Toby.

For decades, his social orbit included nights at the Boston Symphony Orchestra with his dear friend Joan Kennedy and his late partner, *Boston Globe* music critic Richard Dyer. Now 75, Archer is a self-proclaimed dinosaur who refuses to own a cell phone. Yet, he remains the center of the community, throwing open the doors of his historic home to host galas for NAGLY, blending his love for a good party with his relentless drive to do good.

https://lifebridgenorthshore.org/locations/river-house/

Peter Konrad, left, with John Archer, rear, and Jack Armitage.

# Miss Trans Global

"You have to go as a girl!" her friends insisted as Chelsea Page Moses prepared for her first visit to a club called Peanuts in Los Angeles. She arrived looking like a disco-era Donna Summer, stepping into a world that would help define her.

Though she always felt different, it was at fashion college in Los Angeles that she learned the language of her identity, finding her tribe at Club Arena and the ballroom "House of Slander." She took her first hormones at age 19, a decision she speaks of with absolute clarity: "Chelsea saved my life." She navigated her transition with grace, living as a woman for 34 years.

For a long time, Moses passed at her healthcare job. When she finally revealed her trans history, she was terrified, yet she found that her co-workers offered a level of support that sometimes exceeded what she found even within the trans community.

Moses started a business to provide concierge home healthcare services.

Moses competed in and won state, national and international pageants. Now, holding the worldwide title of "Miss Trans Global Diamond," Moses has moved from blending in to standing out. She uses her crown to champion visibility, giving aspirational talks that prove a trans life is a life of dignity. Guided by faith, she insists that

God answers her prayers. She lives by a mantra as elegant as her runway walk: "Be kind, it costs you nothing."

https://misstransglobal.com/

Chelsea Page Moses, Miss Trans Golbal Diamond.

# Firefighter

ALISHIA OUELLETTE

"Someone found your trans profile on the internet and is spreading it around the firehouse." When Alishia "Ali" Ouellette received that terrifying text message from a firefighter friend in 2003, she faced a choice: hide or stand her ground. At the time, transgender people had no employment protections in Massachusetts, meaning Ouellette could have easily lost her livelihood and pension. Instead, she transitioned on the job at the Danvers Fire Department, becoming likely the first out trans firefighter in New England.

Born in 1954, Ouellette had always been a survivor. She hated high school, so she joined the Navy, where she earned her GED. She narrowly missed deployment to Vietnam in 1972 and was stationed on a destroyer in the Middle East. Decades later, working for the Danvers Fire Department, that toughness served her well. While she had the support of her captain and friends, she endured quiet hostility from colleagues who avoided working with her. The town's administration, fearful of lawsuits, issued legal warnings that left many city employees resentful and walking on eggshells.

Despite the tension, Ali's dedication never wavered. In 2007, following her response to a chemical plant explosion, she accepted the Governor's "Firefighter of the Year Fire Marshal Award." With her long hair flowing and wearing the female uniform's cross tie, she was undeniable proof that courage has no gender. Now retired after 22 years of combined service, Ouellette considers her proudest achievement her time as a youth advisor at NAGLY. A fierce activist, she served on the Massachusetts Commission for LGBTQ Youth and worked with the Mass Transgender Political Coalition. She guided young people to Native American powwows and the State House, empowering them to fight for marriage equality, trans rights and anti-bullying laws, ensuring her legacy cleared the path for others.

https://www.mass.gov/orgs/massachusetts-commission-on-lgbtq-youth

https://www.masstpc.org/

Alishia Ouellette.

# Three of Us

DENAE RAMOS-PACHUCKI

The photographer was ready, but Denae Ramos-Pachucki was nervous. It was the dawn of the new millennium at Lynn English High, and the Gay-Straight Alliance had only three members. But when the call went out for the club photo, the doors opened, and students kept coming. Allies, friends and athletes—they crowded into the frame, shoulder to shoulder. When the shutter clicked, it captured more than a club; it captured a revolution, freezing in time the moment when a lonely fight became a collective stand.

Denae Ramos-Pachucki.

Ramos-Pachucki grew up in Lynn's Highlands neighborhood, where toughness and tenderness lived side by side. Five stolen bikes and a street full of families from around the world taught her early that life wasn't simple — but people were worth understanding. "You really get to understand people on a deeper level that you can't teach," she says. That instinct became her compass.

Interview.

By the time she graduated from Lynn English High School in 2000, Ramos-Pachucki had already helped shift the culture of her school. At 14, she came out — a courageous act in the mid-1990s — and soon helped found the school's first Gay–Straight Alliance.

Ramos-Pachucki found courage and community beyond school, too. At NAGLY, she stepped into a world where queerness was normal and celebrated. At Girls Inc. of Lynn, she worked on the Teen Line, learning to listen, comfort and advocate for other teens. Mentors like Beth Anderson introduced her to feminism and the idea that authenticity was a form of strength. "It just felt so cool to be somewhere that encouraged us to love ourselves," she says.

*It wasn't just a club photo; it was a revolution in the yearbook.*

Her personal life reinforced that lesson. Her father's own coming out — and the compassion that followed — taught her the cost of pretending and the relief of truth. When a close friend died suddenly, she made a quiet vow: life was too short not to live fully.

After high school, Ramos-Pachucki attended North Shore Community College and UMass Boston while working full-time. She once drove to Washington, D.C. on a whim to protest the Iraq War, but her long-term calling emerged in helping people rebuild their lives. Today, as a Career Counselor for Mass Ability, she supports individuals with disabilities or mental health challenges as they return to work and rediscover confidence. "It's those joyful moments," she says. "When someone gets a job or starts a new chapter — that's what keeps me hopeful."

Though she's seen rights eroded and old prejudices resurface, Ramos-Pachucki's optimism endures, fueled by the openness she sees in young people. "They just say, 'Live your life.' They're the ones who'll make change."

Ramos-Pachucki's philosophy is simple, shaped by Lynn, activism and hard-won empathy: "Treat others the way you want to be treated. Don't be an asshole."

She has spent her life living exactly that — building bridges with resilience, humor and unapologetic truth.

https://www.unitedlynnpride.com/images/denae-ramos-pachucki?pgid=lrxtpv0f-2000-lynn-english-high-school-gay-straight-alliance_1

https://www.girlsincbl.org/

https://www.nagly.org/

# New Kids

Jonathan Knight

There was a time when Jonathan Knight couldn't hear himself think over the screams of 30,000 fans. As the "shy one" of the famous boy band, New Kids on the Block (NKOTB), the teenage heartthrob lived a life millions envied but which secretly terrified him. Crippling anxiety and panic attacks eventually forced him to walk away from the spotlight in 1994, seeking refuge in a world far removed from arenas: the quiet, historic landscapes of New England.

He traded choreography for carpentry, discovering a deep passion for saving old homes. Now a seasoned preservationist who has renovated over 200 houses, Knight has turned his second act into the hit HGTV show Farmhouse Fixer. Unlike the "tear-down" culture of modern development, Knight meticulously restores centuries-old farmhouses, ensuring their stories survive for future generations.

His personal sanctuary is a farm in Essex, Massachusetts, where he lives with his husband, Harley Rodriguez. While his sexuality was once a topic of tabloid speculation—famously making headlines when fellow 80s icon Tiffany accidentally "outed" him in 2011—Knight clarified that he had never hidden who he was. "I have never hidden the fact that I am gay," he wrote at the time, explaining that he simply chose not to exploit his private life for a magazine cover. Today, Knight balances touring with NKOTB and his life in Essex, standing as a quiet yet powerful example of resilience, proving that one can survive the storm of fame to build an authentic, grounded life of peace.

Jonathan Knight, second from the right, with New Kids on the Block.

# NINE

## Queer Folks

2000 -Present

While history often spotlights the trailblazers who shatter glass ceilings or command the world stage, the true fabric of a community is woven by those who show up, day after day, in the quiet corners of ordinary life. Section Nine turns the lens away from the podium and toward the street level, celebrating the "everyday heroes" who are redefining what it means to be queer on the North Shore in the new millennium.

This is the era of the storyteller, the healer and the neighbor. In these pages, we meet journalists like Cristela Guerra and curators like Doneeca Thurston-Chavez, who are doing the essential work of ensuring our stories are not just told, but preserved with dignity. We witness the quiet revolution of mental health professionals like Jay Nakhai, who are building new frameworks of care for a generation that refuses to be pathologized. We celebrate artists like Sunil Gulab, who teach us to see the miraculous in the mundane, and role models like Kelci Desruisseaux, who are becoming the mentors they once needed.

These are not figures seeking fame; they are seekers of connection. They remind us that while laws are changed in statehouses, culture is changed in living rooms, therapy offices, and art galleries. This section honors the profound impact of simply living authentically—unapologetically and visibly—proving that the most powerful form of activism is often the act of being yourself.

# Empathy

CRISTELA GUERRA

In 2018, Cristela Guerra moved into an apartment in Lynn that was more than just a home; it was a reclamation of history. The building stood on the former site of Fran's Place, the North Shore's legendary queer bar. Living in the footprint of that sanctuary, Guerra didn't just inhabit the space—she excavated it. Her reporting on the bar's closure became the catalyst for uncovering a seminal paper by Pat Gozemba and Janet Kahn about lesbians gathering at the Light House Café in the 1950s, opening a rich vein of research that proved foundational for the award-winning queer Lynn history project, *Through A Rainbow Lens*.

A queer Panamanian journalist and 2024 Nieman Fellow at Harvard, Guerra has made it her mission to document stories from the diaspora with a fierce commitment to joy. She rejects the flat, tragedy-laden narratives often assigned to queer lives, insisting instead on a more abundant way of viewing this identity. This profound empathy allowed her to connect with the family of Rita Hester, whose murder

Cristela Guerra.

inspired the Transgender Day of Remembrance; where others saw only a headline, Guerra saw a human being, earning the family's trust to tell Rita's story with the dignity it deserved.

She cites her podcast episode for Latino USA about the Panama Canal as her proudest piece of journalism. Produced during a tense geopolitical moment when President Trump threatened to invade the country, the story allowed her to reclaim her own family's narrative and the history of her homeland with unshakeable dignity.

> *I can be proud to live here and also be authentically Panamanian and be authentically queer.*

Yet, it is Lynn that holds a sacred place in her own history. It was here, she reflects, that "I built myself," creating the life she truly wanted. Standing between the dense, green embrace of the = and the vast, open Atlantic, the landscape whispered to her of Panama. This specific proximity of forest and ocean grounded her, offering a profound sense of belonging that transcended borders. For a queer

Cristela Guerra, right, with an American soldier in 1989.

nonbinary lesbian navigating the complexities of the diaspora, finding that physical and spiritual resonance was a revelation—tangible proof that she did not need to assimilate to be whole. She realized, "I can be proud to live here and also be authentically Panamanian and be authentically queer."

Interview.

Until very recently, she worked for nearly seven years as a senior arts and culture reporter for WBUR. Now she brings her fire to her current role as a Regional Manager for Report for America and its mission to uplift local newsrooms. She guides 35 reporters placed in newsrooms where  they are needed, such as news deserts and covering necessary beats. Her pride is palpable, whether she is producing a podcast episode that reclaims the narrative of her homeland or marching in the North Shore Pride Parade with RAW Art Works. For Guerra, journalism is an act of preservation—a way to prove that it's not all oppressive; it's not all terrifying. Some of it is just us being ourselves. She writes to ensure that future generations understand not just how this community survived, but how it thrived.

https://www.latinousa.org/2025/02/23/panamacanal/

https://www.wbur.org/news/2020/07/15/two-decades-after-her-death-rita-

https://www.wbur.org/news/2025/06/12/pride-queer-immigrant-boston-

https://www.wbur.org/news/2024/11/06/indigenous-artist-jeffrey-gibson-

https://www.wbur.org/news/2021/09/20/artery-25-bashezo

# Curator

When visitors walked into the Lynn Museum & Arts Center and saw the giant pink triangle from Fran's Place—a relic of a bygone local queer bar—their faces didn't just smile; they lit up with the shock of recognition. For Executive Director Doneeca Thurston-Chavez, that illumination is the entire point. She is not just preserving history; she is ensuring that every resident of Lynn sees themselves reflected in it.

Doneeca Thurston-Chavez.

Born and raised in Lynn to a Bahamian father and a mother whose family has lived in the city for generations, Doneeca embodies an intersectionality that the museum field desperately lacks. As a mixed-race woman who began identifying as queer in her mid-20s after years of grappling with her identity, she knows the isolation of looking at cultural leadership and seeing no one who looks like you. She has turned that personal journey into a professional purpose.

A fearless "can-do" spirit defines her leadership style. When Project Director Jim Moser approached her about an exhibit on Lynn's queer history, he hesitated, warning, "We did not budget for that." Doneeca didn't blink. "We can do it," she insisted. "Don't worry, we have a great team." That confidence paved the way for "*Through a Rainbow Lens*, a landmark exhibit that celebrated the city's queer legacy.

Her path to the director's chair was almost fateful—a chance meeting at the Lobster Shanty with outgoing director Drew Russo led her back to the institution where she had volunteered in college. Taking the helm six years ago, she navigated the museum through the whiplash of COVID-19 closures and reopenings. Today, she extends her influence as the VP of the Massachusetts Museum Association and as a board member of the Essex County Community Foundation, the Essex National Heritage Area, and MASSCreative. By hosting annual exhibits of local queer artists, Doneeca Thurston-Chavez ensures that the museum doors in Lynn are open to everyone.

https://lynnmuseum.org/

https://througharainbowlens.vrticalmedia.digital/

https://www.unitedlynnpride.com/lgbtqhistory

# Seeing Things Differently

SUNIL GULAB

One in 400 trillion. That is the probability that any single individual exists. For Sunil Gulab, this isn't just a statistic; it is proof that every person is exactly who they are meant to be. If we view ourselves and others as miracles, kindness becomes the only logical response.

This philosophy defines Gulab's life as an artist. Whether working in paint, charcoal, black-and-white photography, or ceramics, he looks beyond the obvious to find the extraordinary. In a still life, he doesn't just see fruit; he sees the negative spaces between objects and the vibrating values of light and dark. His creativity is boundless and unconventional—he has painted landscapes using a piece of broccoli to capture the perfect texture of foliage and baked focaccia bread that resembles a Van Gogh sunflower, using peppers and olives.

This artistic freedom stands in stark contrast to his early years in Zimbabwe, where he navigated the rigid structures of apartheid and the internal pressure to be the "perfect son." It was only when he moved to Lynn that he found his true canvas. The pub at 47 Central became his sanctuary. It was more than a bar; it was a place where the weight of hiding his authentic self finally lifted. There, he found safety and a chosen family, realizing that his identity was not something to hide, but a miracle to be celebrated.

Today, Gulab pours that sense of wonder back into the community by volunteering with the Goldfish Pond Association and the Lynn Cultural Council. His proudest creation, however, wasn't on a canvas, but in an act of logistical love. He once shipped ten massive

Painting by Sunil Gulab.

Interview.

Gateway computer boxes filled with 3,000 collected toys back to Zimbabwe. Word spread, and children traveled from surrounding villages, lining up for hours just to receive a simple doll or plastic figure—their first toy, and a tangible reminder that they, too, are miracles.

https://massculturalcouncil.org/local-council/lynn/

https://www.unitedlynnpride.com/interviews/sunil-gulab

https://goldfishpond.org/

Sunil Gulab, right, on the Fenway float at Boston Pride.

# Storyteller

ELLYN RUTHSTROM

"I get to inspire others to come into their stories." For Ellyn Ruthstrom, this isn't just a job description; it is a life's mission. As the Executive Director of SpeakOUT Boston, she acts as a bridge for the queer community, helping individuals find their voices and fostering understanding through the power of personal storytelling.

Born in 1959, Ruthstrom spent her early childhood in Beverly, MA, and Connecticut. She has been a feminist since age 13, but her journey to her full identity took a more winding path. It wasn't until she turned thirty, after moving to the queer-positive feminist haven of Northampton, Massachusetts, that she "came out in force." Today, she identifies as both bisexual and queer, explaining, "I don't let the barriers of sex or gender inhibit my attraction to people," and "I see all the many identities united under the queer community."

Ellyn Ruthstrom, center, at the roundtable on bisexual issues at the Obama White House in 2013.

Ruthstrom has long championed the "B" in LGBTQ+, noting that while bisexuals statistically make up the largest component of the queer community, they often face erasure. During her tenure as president of the Bisexual Resource Center, she fought to change that. In a historic milestone, she co-organized a roundtable on bisexual issues at the Obama White House in 2013. The event brought together bisexual leaders from across the country to meet with government agencies, putting a human face on the community's specific health and policy needs. That gathering sparked the creation of Bisexual Health Awareness Month, now celebrated every March.

Her advocacy continues with SpeakOUT Boston, the nation's oldest queer speakers bureau, which celebrated its 50th anniversary in 2022. Ruthstrom began as a volunteer speaker in 2008 and now leads the organization, coordinating 75 speakers who deliver nearly 100 engagements a year to schools, faith communities and businesses. Whether tabling at North Shore Pride or facilitating a panel, Ruthstrom is proudest of the daily work of connection— helping others stand in their truth, just as she found hers in Northampton years ago.

https://www.speakoutboston.org/

https://biresource.org/

Ellyn Ruthstrom, second from left, with a group
of SpeakOUT panelists at a Pride event in 2025.

# Good Therapy

Jay Nakhai, LICSW

"They are terrified. They are anxious, and they are scared." Jay Nakhai does not mince words when describing the young patients left in limbo when major Boston hospitals abruptly paused gender-affirming care for those under 19. While the institutions pulled back, Nakhai's practice, Aeon Counseling and Consulting, stepped up to handle the overflow, providing a critical lifeline to vulnerable youth when they needed it most.

Born in Houston in 1987 to a Cuban mother and a Persian father, Nakhai's journey to becoming a "mental health disruptor" was fueled by a refusal to be diminished. Early in her career, she grew tired of the disrespect in health centers where colleagues wouldn't use her name, dismissing her simply as "the Spanish therapist." She knew she could do better. Ten years ago, she launched Aeon to offer something different: concierge, boutique, holistic healing practiced through a trauma-informed, family-centered lens. Her goal was to

Jay Nakhai, LICSW.

create "corrective experiences" in a broken healthcare system. Today, Aeon employs 20 therapists, and Nakhai has personally consulted to help open 32 new practices, building the infrastructure for a more inclusive future.

Her professional revolution mirrors a personal one. Nakhai, who identifies as a non-binary human being, found freedom in the realization that gender is often just conditioning. It wasn't until meeting a "beautiful non-binary person" named Nora that the pieces fell into place. Nora taught her about the concept of being an "egg"—someone unaware of their trans identity waiting to crack open. One day, Nakhai called Nora in tears, the realization hitting home: "I think I've been non-binary this whole time. I just didn't have the language." Now, fully embracing that truth, Nakhai stands as a powerful testament that whether building a business or building a self, living authentically is the ultimate form of freedom.

https://getaeonhelp.com/

Jay Nakhai, LICSW, left, with Nita Akoh.

# A Future is Possible

TONY TRAN

Queers everywhere! Tony had never seen such a crowd, and it was fabulous. "I belong." That realization hit Tony Tran like a physical wave during his first Boston Pride march. As a high school senior, he had traveled into the city with members of the Lynn English High School Gay Straight Alliance, wearing black "battle paint" streaks to defy stereotypes. But as he marched on, the rain began to fall, washing the paint down his cheeks, and the defiance melted into pure, unadulterated joy. Surrounded by electric queerness on all sides, someone handed him a massive rainbow flag. As he "twirled like never before", he saw that a future was possible for him—a future he thought was impossible.

That moment of belonging stood in stark contrast to his childhood. Born in Salem in 1993 and raised in Lynn from the age of six, Tony grew up in a loving but conservative Vietnamese household. His parents, refugees who arrived in the U.S. in 1987, built a stable life, but Tony navigated his identity in silence. He had no map for being both

Tony Tran at Boston Pride, 2011.

Vietnamese and gay; there were no role models to look to, no mentors who looked like him. He often felt he was merely surviving, unable to imagine a life where he could be his whole self.

Today, Tran is the role model he once searched for. Now an academic advisor at Brandeis University, he has replaced the isolation of his youth with a "community of care." He champions queer joy in his hometown, hosting high-energy Pride Zumbathons at the Lynn YMCA. A recent trip to Vietnam further cemented his sense of self; while respectful of his parents' wishes with extended family, he walked through the city with his head held high. From a boy searching for a reflection to a proud "Queer Vietnamese American Lynner," Tony now lives surrounded by the very love he once thought was out of reach.

Tony Tran.

# Role Model

KELCI DESRUISSEAUX

"I became the person that I wanted to look up to." For Kelci Desruisseaux, this isn't just a statement of pride; it is a victory over a childhood defined by silence. Growing up with a Haitian father and a Southern Baptist mother, Kelci navigated a landscape void of queer role models. There were no mentors, only a deep, isolating shame. Yet, when her parents learned she had a girlfriend, she found unexpected grace and support—a foundation of gratitude she now builds upon.

Today, Desruisseaux is the role model she once desperately needed. Armed with an MBA, she dedicated herself to the Family Resource Center at Centerboard, where she became a lifeline for queer youth. She ran a weekly teen group and helped families navigate critical resources like housing, ensuring that the next generation wouldn't have to walk alone. As a founding board member of United Lynn Pride, she helped carve out a permanent space for celebration in her city.

However, her hope is tempered by reality. Raised by immigrant parents who sang the praises of American freedom, Kelci believed the Supreme Court's legalization of same-sex marriage marked a permanent victory. Now, watching the harsh treatment of trans individuals and immigrants, she feels a sickening slide backward. "We must see others as human," she insists.

Despite the political shadows, Kelci presses forward. In August 2026, she will marry her partner, Lucy, a personal triumph of joy over despair. She has moved from a place of shame to one of power, standing tall as the leader she always sought.

https://www.centerboard.org/frc

Kelci Desruisseaux, right, working for the Family Resource Center, picking up food to make kits for families.

# TEN

## Join Us

For generations, the queer experience on the North Shore was often defined by the singular pronoun "I." *I am the only one. I am alone.* But at this point in our history, that pronoun shifts to a triumphant, collective "We." This section chronicles the era where the community stopped hiding in the shadows and started building its own infrastructure of joy, support and belonging.

The transformation began with the most vulnerable among us. In a church attic in Salem, visionaries like Lisa Goldblatt Grace and Tim Hegan founded NAGLY (North Shore Alliance of LGBTQ+ Youth), replacing the silence of isolation with a lifeline of connection for a new generation. But the circle of care did not stop with the young. We also honor "Over the Rainbow," the group that ensured our elders—the pioneers who survived the hardest decades—found dignity and companionship in their golden years.

This history is not just about crises; it is about the radical act of having fun. It is about the "Blush Bowling Beauties" claiming the lanes, the "Queer Gears" hitting the road on two wheels, and the faithful reclaiming their place in the pews. It is the story of how we moved from merely surviving to thriving, weaving a social fabric so strong that no one on the North Shore ever needs to feel like a "glitch" again. We found our people, and in doing so, we found our home.

# Queer Youth

**BE YOU** The rainbow flag snapped against the bright blue sky as Evan Collis Puro grabbed a handful of streamers, dancing around the flagpole on the freshly cut lawn of St. Stephen's Episcopal Church in Lynn. It was a scene of pure, unadulterated joy: a bouncy house, pulsating music and crafts filling the air for the city's first Youth Pride celebration. For Evan, whose journey began with an accidental online outing, this wasn't just a party—it was liberation.

He watched with wonder as the adults, led by Jason Cruz and Daniel Bell, enthusiastically embraced his reality. They decorated the church not with judgment, but with rainbow flags, a "Brown Jesus," and colorful androgynous cut-out figures that told him he didn't just exist—he belonged. Launched in October 2015, the "BE YOU" ministry began as a quiet refuge for dinner and prayer but quickly transformed into a roaring engine for justice. Here, Collis Puro found the confidence to explore his queer identity, evolving from a participant into a mentor who led a group at his high school. It was this foundation that supported him as he navigated his social and medical transition at eighteen.

The group's activism peaked when they constructed the "Rainbow House" on the church's front lawn. This wasn't merely an art project; it was a provocative sanctuary designed to force the city to look at the invisible crisis of homeless queer youth. It stood as a physical testament to the children who had nowhere else to go, demanding safety in a world that often offered none.

Their demand for visibility expanded beyond Lynn when the group traveled to Boston to march in the Massachusetts Youth Pride Parade in 2015. For a brief, shining era, they occupied the streets and the pews with equal confidence. Although "BE YOU" formally concluded in June 2017, its legacy did not fade when the doors closed. It gave Collis Puro the courage to live authentically and left a permanent mark on the congregation. The streamers may have eventually come down, but the space they carved out remained, proving that a church could be more than a sanctuary; it could be a fortress of radical love, powerful enough to shatter the silence and save a life.

https://www.youtube.com/watch?v=ROen3uCVMck

BE YOU built a "Rainbow House" in 2016 to call attention to unhoused youth, especially queer youth. Dan Bell left rear.

**NAGLY** In the early 1990s, the North Shore offered little sanctuary for teenagers trying to decode the language of their own hearts. For queer youth, the region was often a landscape of silence, where the lack of visible role models or safe gathering spaces turned isolation into a physical weight. Lisa Goldblatt Grace, a professional working with high-risk youth, saw this void not just as a social problem, but as a public health emergency. Driven by the simple truth that the difference between despair and thriving often comes down to belonging, she founded the North Shore Alliance of LGBTQ+ Youth (NAGLY).

It began quietly, a lifeline huddled in a church attic for just three hours a week. The organization's survival in those fragile early years demanded fierce advocacy and structural fortitude. Stalwarts like Tim Hegan took the baton from Lisa, ensuring those attic doors stayed open when resources were scarce. Director Jack Vondras trained youth leaders and built the group from three youths to more than sixty.

The transformational impact of this early era is mirrored in the story of Abe Rybeck. A high school dropout living in Dorchester with his two mothers, Rybeck found NAGLY on AOL Instant Messenger at age seventeen. He traveled by train to the church attic, where he found not just a meeting, but a future. Executive Director Jack Vondras greeted him not with pleasantries, but with the demanding question,

Tim Hegan, left, with Lisa Goldblatt Grace.

Tim Hegan, left, and Marilyn Cairns receive an award for NAGLY from  Lt. Gov. Paul Cellucci

NAGLY members in front of their center after receiving a $100,000 grant from the Cummings Foundation.

"Have you gotten your GED yet?" That tough love pushed Rybeck to succeed. He eventually organized the group's first field trip to Six Flags—combining his love for roller coasters with his new community—and in 2009, Coco Alinsug called to tell him he had been voted in as the first youth board member. Rybeck, who wrote the organization's first handbook, has since earned a Master's degree from Brandeis, a testament to the hope he found in that attic.

As the organization grew, new leadership emerged to guide it through critical transitions. In 2006, Kirsten Freni joined NAGLY, initially expecting her volunteerism to be a brief stint; instead, she "met the kids, fell in love, and never left," beginning a twenty-year tenure on the board of directors. Coco Alinsug also stepped forward as an early executive director, working to weave the organization into the wider fabric of the community and championing the expansion of support systems in schools. Alongside the leadership, dedicated staff like Ali Ouelette spearheaded outreach, conducting sensitivity training for Gay-Straight Alliances (GSAs), police and court officers. To ensure the youth understood their history and rights, the team organized educational field trips to Ogunquit and

NAGLY marching at 2012 Boston Pride.

Provincetown and even visited Beacon Hill to put a human face to queer youth for legislators.

The year 2014 marked a massive turning point: NAGLY officially incorporated, shifting from a grassroots collective to a formal institution. It was a busy year fueled by community support; the organization raised tens of thousands of dollars through Salem Mayor Kim Driscoll's "No Place for Hate" challenge. Additionally, with the help of Tan Pham, they secured a transformative $80,000 grant from TripAdvisor.

This momentum led to the organization's physical transformation, arriving with a secret plan hatched by Executive Director Steve Harrington. One evening, instead of their usual meeting, Harrington led a group of twenty-five confused teenagers on a "secret field trip" through Salem. They whispered among themselves, convinced they were heading to the movies. They were wrong. They were going home. When Harrington threw open the double doors in the Witch City Mall to reveal a cavernous, empty space with "Welcome Home" taped to the wall, the reaction was

NAGLY.

electric. The kids didn't just walk in; they sprinted, claiming every inch of the hallways.

Fueled by the TripAdvisor grant and sheer grit, Harrington and his husband had scoured the city to find this location, furnishing it with corporate auction finds and rescuing folding chairs with a U-Haul. The move was made possible by mall owner Brett Marley, who offered a break on the rent as a way of giving back to the community, while Police Chief Paul Tucker ensured the new public-facing space remained protected. This move turned NAGLY into a visible cultural institution. Leaders like Kirsten Freni, who had become board president, viewed this new space not just as a clubhouse, but as a necessary refuge for marginalized youth—a place to learn queer history and forge the resilience needed to navigate a heteronormative world.

The true measure of this home is found in the lives of the youth who walked through those doors and never left. Jillian Lamy began coming to NAGLY in 2003, starting a twenty-two-year journey that

NAGLY at Boston Pride. Kirsten Freni, center.

mirrors the organization's own growth. She progressed from a youth participant to a peer advisor, then an adult advisor, and eventually became the youngest member of the Board of Directors. Lamy established a humble clothing swap, a project that blossomed into the "Boutique," a permanent resource offering free, gender-affirming clothing to anyone in need. For Lamy, who found lifelong mentors and friends within these walls, NAGLY was more than a center; it was a "second family" that quite literally saved lives.

To sustain this growing "second family," the organization focused on financial longevity. In 2017, NAGLY hosted its first "Red Party," a Valentine's Day event that evolved into a major annual fundraiser. By 2019, the organization secured its first grant from the Cummings

Kirsten Freni, left, with Bill and Joyce Cummings of the Cummings Foundation and Steve Harrington.

Foundation—$100,000 over five years—based on the dedicated work of Freni, Margot Abels and Steve Harrington.

As the organization matured, the leadership torch eventually passed. In 2023, Peter Konrad became chairperson of the board, following Freni's two-decade tenure. Working with the board, Konrad secured a second, pivotal grant from the Cummings Foundation in 2025—this time for $400,000 over ten years—fueling the expectation that NAGLY will expand its reach on the North Shore.

Today, under the leadership of program director Tony Leone and Executive Director James Giessler, the once-empty shell of a building is one of the largest queer youth centers in the country. The facility features a library with thousands of queer titles, a full kitchen for life-skills workshops and Lamy's bustling Boutique. It hosts everything from Dungeons & Dragons clubs to critical mental health counseling. What began as a fragile flame in a church attic has become a powerful beacon on the North Shore, proving that when you give queer youth the space to exist authentically, they do not just survive—they thrive.

https://www.nagly.org/

https://www.cummingsfoundation.org/

# Keeping the Faith

Rabbi Alison Adler, Rev. Joe Amico, Rev. Andre Bennett, Rev. Wendy Fitting, Rev. Julie Flowers, Brian Liberge, Rev. Chisei Majeau, Rev. Canon Greg Perez & Rev. Donna Spencer Collins

**Rabbi Alison Adler** "Of course you can! Why are you even asking?"

When Rabbi Alison Adler asked her board at Temple B'nai Abraham if they could fly the Pride flag year-round, she expected a debate. Instead, she got a mandate. It was a profound shift from fifteen years ago, when Rabbi Alison first arrived in Beverly as the congregation's spiritual leader and pastoral counselor. Back then, there were no openly queer households. Today, there are close to twenty households, a testament to the safe harbor she has built.

She isn't doing this work alone. Emma Mair, the only out queer professional Jewish staff member on the North Shore, joins her. Their partnership illustrates a powerful generational evolution. Rabbi Alison remembers the silence of the 1980s, when Jewish seminarians studying to become rabbis or cantors stayed closeted to survive. Emma, conversely, notes that today, nearly half of non-Orthodox rabbinical students are queer.

Together, they are dusting off ancient texts to reveal a theology of inclusion. Rabbi Alison teaches that Jewish scripture isn't binary but actually acknowledges eight distinct sexes. This wisdom shapes their liturgy: "Bar" and "Bat Mitzvah" have become the gender-neutral "B Mitzvah," and the traditional call of "son or daughter of" is now the inclusive "from the house of."

This welcome isn't just theoretical. It is lived out in interfaith Pride services, in marching banners held high and in the ritual bath where Rabbi Alison has performed conversions for trans and non-binary congregants. It is a partnership of ally and advocate—Rabbi Alison, the devoted supporter, and Emma, the queer leader whose own wedding Rabbi Alison officiated—working together to ensure that in this house, everyone belongs.

https://tbabeverly.org/

Kelly Mair, left, Rabbi Alison Adler and Emma Mair.

**Reverend Joe Amico** When Reverend Joe Amico arrived at Tabernacle Church in Salem in 2014, he faced a peculiar paradox. The wider community whispered that the congregation was anti-queer, a reputation born from a painful chapter in the church's history. A previous pastor had preached an Easter sermon comparing the transgender experience to the resurrection of Christ. The message was so controversial within the pews that it caused a schism, leading to the pastor's departure and a fractured congregation. Outsiders assumed those who remained were hostile to the queer community. They were wrong. Their rebuttal to that reputation was definitive: they called Joe, an openly gay man and seasoned addiction counselor, to be their shepherd.

Under Rev. Joe's leadership, Tabernacle has become a fortress of visible inclusivity. The church's rainbow doors, installed annually for Pride and remaining until World AIDS Day, serve as a landmark of unconditional welcome. When vandals defaced them with hate speech, the attack only strengthened local resolve, inspiring neighboring churches to hoist their own Pride flags in solidarity.

Reverend Joe Amico, leftt, at 2024 North Shore Pride.

Beyond symbols, the congregation acts. They previously hosted the North Shore Pride Interfaith Service and currently sponsor an annual World AIDS Day concert, donating all proceeds to NAGLY to support queer youth. Joe himself, a bi-vocational minister who helped establish the first LGBTQ+ psychiatric unit in New England, has been honored as one of North Shore Pride's "Fabulous Five" and a recipient of their Community Service Award. Far from the rumors of the past, Rev. Joe and his flock stand as unwavering pillars of love on the North Shore.

https://tabernaclechurch.org/


**Reverend Andre Bennett** "Be open to love. Love is colorless. Love is genderless. Love often comes from the least expected area."

These words, spoken by a close female friend during a pilgrimage in Washington D.C., dismantled a lifetime of armor. Walking among the monuments, Reverend Andre Bennett felt a profound shift. He wasn't thinking of the woman speaking, but of his best friend back home, Linwood Wilson. The truth settled in: "I've been the happiest I've been when we're together." He decided then to stop fighting and simply allow their connection to blossom.

For Rev. Andre, the Pastor of Youth & Young Adults at Zion Baptist Church in Lynn, MA, this personal awakening demanded a painful professional reckoning. A Jamaican immigrant who followed his wife's teaching career to the U.S., he had built a formidable life, earning three Ph. D.s and raising four children. But he also carried the weight of his past sermons—years of preaching "hell, fire and brimstone" against the queer community.

The realization of his love for Linwood, combined with the grace shown to him by a lesbian couple who befriended him, broke his heart in the necessary way. He made a solemn vow: "to work as long as I can, and as hard as I can, to repair whatever harm I did to the community."

Today, Rev. Andre navigates the complexities of the Black church, where queer advocacy is often pushed to the margins by other urgent survival issues. A private man who refuses strict labels, he lives with radical honesty. Whether serving on the board of the Zen Center North Shore or organizing with the Mass Communities Action Network, the Essex County Community Organization (ECCO) and United Interfaith Action, his ministry is now defined by penance and progress. He is proudest to see his own son actively work to be different in the world, embracing a deep understanding

Reverend Andre Bennett, left.

of the issues and an intentionality to avoid becoming a statistic. Rev. Andre is driven by a determination to heal the very spirits he once condemned.

https://www.zionbaptistlynnma.org/

**Reverend Wendy Fitting** When Reverend Wendy Fitting arrived at the Unitarian Universalist Church of Gloucester in August 1989, the doors were barred with a "No Trespassing" sign—a stark welcome for the first female and first openly lesbian minister on Cape Ann. She was stepping into a pulpit steeped in rebellion, the historic site where early Universalists once defied a Puritan theocracy to demand the separation of church and state. Now, it was her turn to defy the silence.

Her start was a trial by fire. A denominational official outed her to the board during the hiring process. Yet Rev. Wendy refused to retreat into the closet. She discovered that "being honest worked out really well," choosing to build trust rather than push politics. She inherited a historic structure that was physically crumbling, but she didn't fix it alone. She rallied a tiny, mighty congregation who launched multiple capital campaigns, raising the funds to rebuild their spiritual home stone by stone.

Her courage reached its crescendo in 1994. Long before marriage equality was legal, Rev. Wendy officiated the union of Peter Stickle and John Bumstead. In a blue-collar, largely Catholic fishing port, locals braced for a spectacle, expecting a campy display of "flaunting." Instead, they witnessed transcendent dignity—a strictly formal ceremony filled with music from Boston Symphony Orchestra players. The church members, initially nervous, were overwhelmed not by scandal, but by profound pride. When Rev. Wendy retired in 2013, she left behind a thriving congregation and a fully restored sanctuary, proving that the holiest foundation is authenticity.

https://www.gloucesteruu.org/


**Reverend Julie Flowers** Julie Flowers rose from the chancel steps of the First Baptist Church in Beverly, her hands trembling slightly under the weight of fifty manila envelopes. Inside each was a declaration of truth that she had been explicitly warned against sending. It was 2008, and she was standing at a precipice. Colleagues had urged her to sanitize her ordination papers, to remove the section about being lesbian, or risk losing everything. She refused. Walking out of the sanctuary she had known since childhood, she marched down Cabot Street to the blue mailbox. With a heart pounding in rhythm with her determination, she opened the lid and let the envelopes fall into the dark—a terrified, defiant act of letting go that brought with it a sudden, deep peace. Honesty was the only path she could walk.

That single moment of bravery set a historic precedent, making Flowers the first openly lesbian candidate to be ordained within the American Baptist Churches of Massachusetts. The road was bruising; her application sparked a contentious debate that ended in a razor-thin 24 -20 vote. At her ordination, she answered that narrow margin with a visual roar: a "Shower of Stoles" draped over the pews, fifty liturgical garments representing the countless clergy who had been silenced, denied, or defrocked for loving who they loved.

Her courage kicked the door open for others, transforming First Baptist into a beacon of radical welcome. While the church had officially become a welcoming congregation in 1997, placing it on the cutting edge, it has flourished under Flowers' leadership. Today, nearly 20 percent of the congregation identifies as queer. Flowers, who first realized she was lesbian while falling in love with her best friend at Wellesley College, now leads "The Plus Club," a monthly fellowship ensuring that the sanctuary remains a place where no one ever has to hide to be holy.

https://www.fbcbeverly.org/

**Brian Liberge** When the Sisters of Perpetual Indulgence arrive, the first thing you notice is the striking white-face makeup; the second is the overwhelming sense of joy. They are a modern order of nuns comprising people of all genders, sexualities and spiritualities, dedicated to community service and using "irreverent wit to expose the forces of bigotry." Their mission is simple but profound: to expiate stigmatic guilt and promulgate universal joy.

While the Boston house of the Sisters is based in the capital, their ministry frequently crosses the county line, driven by members like Sister Brother Freddie Anne Willing. In daily life, he is Brian Liberge, a Lynn resident whose drag name is a playful pun on

Sister Brother Freddie Anne Willing and Sister Stella Tension-hör.

"Ready and Willing." He ensures the order is a visible, benevolent force on the North Shore. The Sisters are a staple at North Shore Pride, support queer youth at NAGLY and work with the Survivor program in Salem. In 2024, the Sisters deepened this local connection by officially "sainting" the community of St. Stephen's Memorial Episcopal Church in Lynn as "Saint Stevie Lynn the Weaver," recognizing the church's vital role in weaving together the diverse threads of the community.

https://www.thebostonsisters.org/

**Reverend Chisei Majeau** "What makes the program Zen, and what makes it queer?" That is the koan at the heart of Rev. Chisei Majeau's work. For Rev. Chisei, an ordained Zen priest who identifies as agender, asexual and aromantic, the answer lies in creating a sanctuary. In the Spring of 2025, amidst a political climate they felt was growing increasingly hostile, Rev. Chisei helped launch "Queer Zen" at the Zen Center North Shore. The goal was simple but profound: to offer a refuge where practitioners didn't have to

Zen Center North Shore members at 2025 North Shore Pride. Jim Moser, left, Rev. Chisei Stephanie Majeau, Kenho Emily Dashawetz, Seitetsu Kate Farrington and Rev. Myozen Joan Amaral.

"perform queerness" or educate others, but could simply be themselves in safety.

Zen Center North Shore's founder and guiding teacher, Rev. Joan Amaral, modeled the initiative after long-standing programs in San Francisco. The gatherings are designed to be accessible to everyone, regardless of experience. Instruction is always provided for newcomers, ensuring that those brand new to the practice feel just as welcome as seasoned practitioners. The practice includes Zazen (seated meditation) and Kinhin (slow walking meditation) followed by open sharing. The group meets in the Center's new dedicated practice center in Amesbury. For Rev. Chisei, growth isn't measured by filling seats, but by the depth of each person's journey, held in a space where the silence of the cushion meets the authentic truth of identity.

https://www.zencenternorthshore.org/

Reverend Canon Greg Perez, left, with his husband, Doug Flores.

**Reverend Canon Greg Perez** As Reverend Greg Perez raised his hands to bless the potluck dinner in the gaily decorated hall of St. Stephen's in June 2023, the moment held a weight far heavier than the plates of food. The room was packed—a vibrant mix of the congregation and the crowd that had marched over from Lynn's City Hall flag raising—all brought together by organizer Billy Mulcahy Moser. Just three years prior, Perez had arrived in Lynn during the suffocating silence of the COVID-19 pandemic. It was a fragile time; the historic church wasn't just battling a virus, but also wrestling with its own identity, unsure if it was truly ready for an openly gay rector. But looking out at the room filled with fellowship, pride and laughter, Perez knew the answer was a resounding yes.

This moment of belonging was a long time coming. Ordained a Roman Catholic priest in 1986, Perez eventually left a church that had no room for his whole self. For years, he drifted until the Episcopal Church made history by electing Bishop Gene Robinson in New Hampshire. Seeing a gay man in a mitre signaled to Perez that there was a place for him at the altar, and he was received into the Episcopal priesthood in 2005.

> *Being gay is a gift that I weave in and use when necessary.*

Today, Perez's influence extends far beyond the walls of St. Stephen's. As a regional canon, he now shepherds 56 congregations across the North Shore and beyond, serving as a key advisor to the Bishop. In a remarkable testament to the Diocese of Massachusetts' commitment to inclusion, all three regional canons are queer, with Perez standing as the distinct Latino voice among them. From an outcast in one faith to a leader in another, Canon Perez has proved that the holiest ground is found in authenticity.

**Reverend Donna Spencer Collins** In the dim, smoke-choked light of a gritty Lynn bar, rival biker gangs were screaming threats, edging toward violence. Standing unexpectedly between them was Donna, terrified. When a biker threatened to punch her in the face, she didn't flinch. Instead, she felt a profound stillness wash over her—a peace unlike anything she had ever known. As she walked out of that bar, shaking but calm, a scripture echoed in her heart: "There is one who will stay closer to you than a brother."

This moment defined a lifetime of resilience. Born in Lynn and a graduate of Lynn Classical High School, Spencer Collins ' path to the pulpit was paved with broken glass. She extracted herself from a cult and battled a litany of medical crises, including cancer, severe arthritis and a broken knee. When her body failed her, her spirit didn't; she attended North Shore Community College in a wheelchair, determined to rise.

Her ministry began not in a cathedral, but in the trenches of nightlife. Running "Momma D's Karaoke," she realized that the "regulars" at the bar often cared for one another more deeply than congregants in the pews. She performed weddings and funerals amidst the neon signs, bringing the sacred into the secular and proving that God could be found in a karaoke line.

That grounding led her to found "Phoenix Rising" in Haverhill, a radically inclusive church that provided a safe


Reverend Donna Spencer Collins.

harbor for queer families rejected by traditional denominations. Though the pandemic eventually forced its doors to close, its impact endured. Since 2023, she has served as the Senior Pastor at Groveland Congregational Church, United Church of Christ. Whether facing down a biker gang or preaching inclusivity from the pulpit, Reverend Donna Spencer Collins remains a warrior for love, proving that the holiest ground is often found where people are most broken.

https://www.grovelanducc.org/

# Queer Groups

**North Shore LGBT Social Network** While North Shore municipalities focus on flag-raising during Pride Month in June, Michael Toby understands that queer people need community on the other 364 days of the year. When he realized that local events were vanishing into the void because no central organization was listing them, Toby stepped in to become the region's unofficial social architect. As the lead administrator of the North Shore LGBT Social Network, he has grown a modest meetup group into a powerhouse of connection with over 2,600 members.

Toby's work is the glue that holds the North Shore's diverse communities together. He tirelessly curates a calendar that highlights everything from drag brunches to queer movie screenings, ensuring that visibility is a year-round commitment. Beyond the online efforts, he creates physical spaces for belonging, organizing monthly dances, book clubs and the staple "Brodie's Social" mixers in

Michael Toby.

Salem. In doing so, he has proved that the strongest safety net is simply knowing where to find your people.

https://www.northshorelgbtsocialnetwork.com/

**North Shore LGBTQ Network** "For too long, finding LGBTQ+ support on the North Shore meant taking a train into Boston." This geographic disconnect drove the creation of the North Shore LGBTQ Resource Network. Founded by Lane Billings and now led by Devin Aronis Lawson, a 35-year-old trans non-binary activist, the organization operates with a simple but vital mission: to cultivate a localized ecosystem where queer people can find healthcare, social groups and support without leaving their own neighborhoods.

Board members: Devin Aronis Lawson - president (bottom center left, denim jacket), Triss Ingels - director of education (bottom right, wearing trans flag), Olivia Werth - treasurer (top right, light hair and light glasses), Corey Chapman - clerk (2nd in from the top right, next to Olivia - has a beard and is wearing a hat).

Devin's own journey mirrors this search for connection. Their transition reached a turning point only after discussing their experience with their partner and fellow trans person, Triss Ingels. That visibility changed everything. Fortified by the support of their partner, friends and family, Devin turned their energy outward to build the infrastructure they once needed.

Currently, the Network is working toward building a comprehensive online resource database. Unintentionally but powerfully, the board is entirely composed of trans individuals, a testament to the community's drive for self-determination. The ultimate goal is to establish a brick-and-mortar community center— a permanent physical home for the North Shore's queer population.

Yet, Devin's proudest achievement remains the grassroots gatherings that started it all. Before Devin was involved in the Network, they organized a monthly non-binary meetup called "Nonbinary North Shore" at Jaho in Salem. Drawing anywhere from six to twenty people, these casual coffee nights provided something rare: a space where non-binary people could simply exist, affirmed and happy. For Devin, witnessing that comfort is the fuel that powers the ambitious future of the Resource Network.

Over the Rainbow Social Club.

**Over the Rainbow Social Club** Aging is often described as a fading away, a slow retreat into invisibility. But for the seniors of the North Shore's queer community, silence was never an option—especially not if Deb Barber and Evan Dooley have anything to say about it. As dedicated board members of the Over the Rainbow Social Club, they have turned the "twilight years" into a time of neon-bright connection, proving that feeling part of a community doesn't have an expiration date.

What began fifteen years ago as a modest supper club under the leadership of Paul Lanzikos of North Shore Elder Services has blossomed into a vital lifeline for the generation that fought the first battles for queer rights. While younger folks had the nightlife, Barber and Dooley recognized that their peers needed a different

Over the Rainbow Social Club board members Deb Barber, left, and Evan Dooley.

kind of sanctuary—one built on shared history, safety and sustained friendship. Under their stewardship, the club has evolved from a simple meal program into a bustling hub of social life in Salem and beyond.

The calendar is now packed with joy: from lively monthly dinners where stories are swapped over hot meals, to film nights that celebrate queer cinema and high-stakes bingo games that get raucous enough to rival any bar scene. Then there is the beloved waterfront barbecue on the lawn of the House of the Seven Gables, a signature summer event that brings the community out into the sun. They don't just gather in private; they march, taking their place of honor in the North Shore Pride parade to remind the world that they are still here, still proud and still having the time of their lives. For Deb and Evan, Over the Rainbow isn't just a social club; it's a promise that no one in their chosen family has to grow old alone.

https://www.otrsocialclub.com/

**AgeSpan Senior Social Connection** For years, aging as a queer person in the Merrimack Valley often meant facing a brutal choice: travel over twenty-five miles to Boston for community or retreat into the closet. The isolation was palpable, a silence that Ron Bourque decided to break in 2013. Realizing that his neighbors were aging alone without the safety nets of partners or children, he launched a simple dinner program in Merrimac. His vision was to create a sanctuary where elders didn't just eat, but existed authentically.

**AgeSpan Senior Social Connection**

AgeSpan logo.

Today, Amelia DeStefano carries that torch as the driving force behind AgeSpan's Senior Social Connection, ensuring that what began as a single meal has blossomed into a vital regional network. Working in close collaboration with the local Councils on Aging, which host the meals, the program has expanded into thriving monthly gatherings in communities like Andover—now the largest group, welcoming allies—and the original, steadfast group in Merrimac. DeStefano and the Councils curate these events to be "more than just a meal," serving up connections alongside buffet dinners and activities ranging from estate planning workshops to spirited games of *Jeopardy*. This simple yet radical act of gathering gained national recognition with a 2018 Aging Achievement Award, proving that for queer seniors on the North Shore, the most powerful remedy for isolation is a place at the table.

https://agespan.org/solutions/health-equity/

AgeSpan Senior Social Connection meeting.

**Queer Gears** "We can't officially call it 'Queer Gears' because we have straight members," says endurance cyclist and trans activist Hannah Lister. She started the group to foster connection through movement, leading members on everything from the grueling Five Boro Bike Tour in New York City to casual rounds of mini-golf. But while her wheels still turn, her world has geographically narrowed; she no longer cycles in New Hampshire, where new laws banning her from public restrooms make the simple act of riding unsafe.

Hannah's journey began at age 50, when a therapist offered a life-changing insight: "You know, you can transition." Everything suddenly clicked. However, living authentically exacted a heavy toll. She lost her job, friends and half her family. When her medical insurance denied coverage, she didn't just fight back—she used her professional background to rewrite the company's discriminatory policies from the inside out. She now works at Habanero Cycles with Wendy Williams, a member of the North Shore Pride board.

Kris Lister, left, with her wife Hannah Lister.

As the only trans member of the North Shore Pride board, Lister is acutely aware she is operating in "scary times," citing the hundreds of anti-trans bills sweeping the country. She protects her mental health by ignoring social media "haters" and holding fast to a simple principle: "My choice to transition does not affect you." Yet, the fear of scrutiny is constant. In her first race as a woman in the NYC Grand Fondo, she deliberately slowed down for thirty minutes to ensure she wouldn't win, avoiding the inevitable backlash of a podium finish. For Lister, the priority is no longer just the finish line, but keeping the entire queer community moving forward together.

**Blush Bowling Beauties** People still talk about "The Hideaway." It wasn't a bar; it was a celebration. In 2012, Miriam Calixto looked at the North Shore and saw a void—women needed a place to dance and have fun. Taking initiative, she convinced the owner of Maddy's in Saugus to open his doors early for a monthly tea dance. She promised she could fill the room, but even she was surprised when nearly 400 people showed up.

The event was so successful that the owner of Anthony's in Malden drove past, saw the overflowing parking lot, and soon offered Miriam a venue. He provided a beautiful, private outdoor space that became affectionately known as The Hideaway. For three glorious years, it was a sanctuary for dancing under the stars, massive New Year's Eve galas and comedy nights. It was a golden era of inclusivity and connection.

While The Hideaway is now a cherished memory, Miriam's drive to create community hasn't faded. Today, that energy is channeled into a Monday night bowling league at Game Time Lanes & Entertainment at the North Shore Mall in Peabody. The group is called Blush Bowling Beauties, and the vibe is unmistakable. What started as a casual meetup has evolved into a tight-knit group of 32 women.

True to Miriam's style, it is about more than just the sport. There is food, laughter and a strictly curated playlist of R&B and Top 40 hits that often inspires the women to stop bowling and start dancing right in the lanes. The bond extends far beyond the alley, with the group organizing theater trips, house parties and excursions to Ogunquit, Maine. Whether hosting hundreds at a gala or thirty friends at the lanes, Miriam Calixto remains the North Shore's essential architect of joy.

Blush Bowling Beauties. Miriam Calixto, front, to the right of the white bowling ball.

**NALSEA** Launched in 2022, NALSEA (Newburyport Area Lesbian Social Events and Adventures) has quickly grown into a powerhouse of connection, with 1,000 women from across Massachusetts. Co-hosted by the dynamic duo of Amy LeJeune and Lori Towle, the group is driven by a desire to get women out of the house, into nature and into a supportive community.

True to the "Adventures" in its name, NALSEA goes far beyond the typical meetup. The calendar is packed with active experiences that range from rhythmic drumming circles and mystical full moon gatherings to spirited hikes and sunset boat cruises. Whether it's a high-energy dance or a laid-back social, LeJune and Towle have curated a space where friendship and fun take center stage, creating a vibrant network that keeps the North Shore connected.

https://www.facebook.com/groups/1235955283600124/

Amy LeJeune and Lori Towle of NALSEA.

**Queers & Beers** "Let's skip the hike and go straight to the brewery." That pragmatic decision by Sarah Dwyer's friends in Rhode Island shifted their social group from outdoor trekking to community building. When Dwyer moved to the North Shore for a teaching job, she found herself missing that specific joy—the freeing sensation of being in a room where she didn't have to mask her queerness or explain her identity. She missed the safety of being surrounded entirely by queer people.

Three years ago, Dwyer decided to recreate that magic, launching the North Shore chapter of Queers & Beers at Amesbury's Barewolf Brewing. It started small, but the hunger for connection was undeniable. Today, the group draws crowds of fifty for regular meetups and saw a massive 200 attendees at their "New Queers Eve" countdown to Pride Month. The events are as eclectic as the community itself, featuring everything from "Palentine's" mixers and gender-affirming bingo to craft nights involving potato printing on clothing.

Dwyer, who attended Emerson College—where she jokes the unofficial motto was "Gay by May or your money back"—knows the power of a welcoming environment. What makes her proudest isn't just the attendance numbers, but the depth of the bonds formed over beers. Members aren't just drinking buddies; they are attending

NALSEA at Joy Nest in Newburyport.

each other's weddings and building a chosen family. Now supported by a committee of three "amazing" members who help manage the expanding social calendar, Dwyer has turned a simple idea into a vital North Shore institution where the only requirement is to show up and be yourself.

https://www.instagram.com/queersandbeersnsma/

Rachel Green, left, Kaylynn Small, Lucia Mino, Sarah Dwyer.

# Rainbow Coalition

T NASH & HOPE WATT-BUCCI

"We don't want to reinvent the wheel." That simple realization—that organizers across the North Shore were often working in isolation rather than in connection—sparked a significant shift in how the region organized for justice. T Nash, working alongside the team from North Shore Pride, recognized that while individual groups were doing incredible work, they were often operating in silos. The issue wasn't that groups were competing for attention; it was that they were missing the chance to lean on one another. To bridge this gap, T and the team founded the "Rainbow Coalition" in 2023. The group meets regularly on Zoom from January to June, turning the long New England winter into a strategy session where established organizations can share institutional wisdom with emerging groups, and where peers coordinate calendars rather than struggle alone.

T Nash.

At a recent Rainbow Coalition Zoom meeting, scheduled and facilitated by Hope Watt-Bucci, each participant who asked for resources was met by another participant who said, "I can help with that."

Interview.

In the years before the coalition formed, Hope traveled around the North Shore, encouraging people to raise flags and plan festivals. Her advice on everything from non-profit status to insurance to working with City Hall was instrumental in forming many of the Pride groups that are active today.

T's instinct for connection stands in stark contrast to his beginnings on Alley Street in East Lynn. As a freshman at Lynn Tech, T idolized his tough older brother, Michael, and masked deep insecurities with aggression, getting expelled three times for being a "bully." But T eventually learned that fear isn't respect and pivoted toward a life of healing. This transformation culminated in T caring for his mother during her final days, an experience that inspired the book *Try Kindness*, a guide to patience and empathy that T had to learn to extend to themselves first.

*The strongest hands are the ones that help others up.*

Today, living authentically as a Black trans man who "loves who I am," T has turned that personal kindness into regional power. What began as a desire to share resources has exploded into a network of 23 municipalities and organizations. The coalition now knits together giants like NAGLY, North Shore Pride and United Lynn Pride with newer, hyper-local committees like the Hamilton-Wenham Human Rights Coalition and Cape Ann Pride. It embraces diverse interests, from the LGBTQ+ Social Network to "Queers & Beers" and the North Shore Health Project. By ensuring that resources flow freely between peers, T Nash has proven that the strongest thing a community can do is build a table where everyone—from the newest volunteer to the seasoned organizer—can sit together.

# Pride All Around

**Cape Ann Pride** Even over the music of the celebration that night at the Cut Live's pride dance, Mary Benard could hear the sobs as soon as she opened the door to the ladies' room. A young woman was crying, but when Mary offered help, she shook her head. "No, you don't understand," she said. "I grew up here. I moved away. I never thought I'd be going to a pride event in my hometown. This is everything!"

Those tears of joy confirmed exactly why Mary and her husband, George Grattan, both bisexual, had co-founded Cape Ann Pride along with Jai Fields, Stephen Hopkins and Matthew Murray. Inspired by Boston Pride for the People and various regional groups (especially North Shore Pride), the organization began not in a boardroom but at Pratty's C.A.V., a fishermen's bar in Gloucester, in May 2022. There, after asking the key question "Why *can't* Cape Ann have its own Pride?" five of them raised their glasses and – almost jokingly — toasted a new local pride into existence.

In just a few years, that toast has grown into a roar. A strategic partnership with the Greater Cape Ann Chamber of Commerce, facilitated by Colleen Murdock, who had been hearing the same key question from Chamber members, provided a bridge to the business community and sponsors. "They gave us legitimacy; we gave them authenticity," says Grattan. Now a registered non-profit with an active Facebook presence, the group has proven that the region was hungry for pride events and programming right on Cape Ann.

Today, the organization's year-round calendar is as vibrant as the community it serves. Far from just a single flag raising, Cape Ann Pride curates a diverse slate of events that reflects the local culture: annual kick-off parties at Drift, rooftop fundraisers at the Beauport Hotel, "Pride on the Pier" Tea Dances on Gloucester's harborfront, "Cape Ann Families and Friends Bowl with Pride" at Cape Ann Lanes that pack every lane, a "Queer Teens and Friends" private sail on the schooner *Adventure* and holiday potlucks for "Queer Families and Friends."

Looking ahead, Grattan insists there is "nowhere to go but to grow." The organization is actively recruiting new volunteers and board members, specifically seeking to diversify its leadership to ensure every voice in the rainbow is heard. What started with a toast made by five people in a bar and merged with parallel conversations

Cape Ann Pride.

happening among community business leaders has become a welcome demonstration that no one has to go far from home to find their pride.

https://www.capeannpride.org/

**Hamilton-Wenham Human Rights Coalition** "This is the first time our family has felt seen and safe in town." That tearful confession from a queer parent to Anna Siedzik, board president of the Hamilton-Wenham Human Rights Coalition (HWHRC), encapsulates the profound impact of the annual Pride Picnic. The event was born from the seismic energy of June 2020, when over 700 neighbors marched through Hamilton to protest racial violence. Realizing that the momentum needed a permanent home, a group of local activists formed the coalition to transition from reactive protest to proactive, hyperlocal everyday activism.

In June 2021, they launched the first Pride event in the town's history. It was driven by a collective desire to make a purposeful, outward statement: that everyone is welcome here, and that the

Hamilton-Wenham Human Rights Coalition.

queer community in Hamilton and Wenham is strong, proud and vibrant.

Far from a quiet gathering, the Pride Picnic now explodes with color and life at the Patton Homestead. It is a full-blown festival, featuring local food trucks, live bands and a marketplace showcasing queer-owned businesses and artists. Children run between lawn games, kite flying and face-painting stations while families lounge on blankets, soaking in the supportive atmosphere.

Siedzik recalls a high school student who was out to their mother but not the rest of their family. The student chose the Pride Picnic as the moment to come out to their grandparents and extended relatives. Gesturing to the vibrant celebration around them, they were able to say, "This is who I am. This is my community." Surrounded by joy and acceptance, the picnic provided the safety they needed to finally share their full self with the people they loved.

https://www.hwhumanrights.org/

**Haverhill Pride** Shock. Awe. Disbelief. Nathan Phillips almost stopped dead in his tracks. It was June 2025, the day of Haverhill's inaugural Pride Parade, and the sky had opened up. Rain was pouring down, and Phillips, a marketing professional turned activist, feared the weather would wash away months of planning. But as he turned the corner onto Main Street, the gloom vanished. Lining the streets were 1,200 people, cheering, waving flags and refusing to let the rain dampen the historic moment.

The road to that moment was paved with obstacles. Just weeks prior, the event almost didn't happen. In a tense meeting, the police chief—who was later replaced—claimed he thought the event was a simple "walk," not a parade, and argued he lacked the staff to secure the route. He even tried to ban them from downtown, citing safety.

That was when Michael Oster, a retired psychotherapist on the advisory board, drew a line in the sand: "We want this to be a parade. But if it has to be, it will be a protest." With the backing of Tom Sullivan, the city council president and an openly gay man, the mayor intervened, and the streets were cleared.

*We want this to be a parade. But if it has to be, it will be a protest.*

The result was a triumph. It wasn't just a march; it was a full-scale takeover of the city's culture. The day included a flag-raising, a resource fair, a Drag King Story Hour, and a vibrant drag festival spread across downtown venues.

Haverhill Pride Sponsor, left, Nathan Phillips, Emilio Viscio, Madam Zapple, Sarah Viscio, Erin Padilla, Kristina Ploof.

Haverhill Pride began as a project of "Creative Haverhill." Still, under the leadership of Phillips, Emilio Viscio, Catherine Chandler, Patrick Sainato and Chelsea Lopes-Daigle, it quickly evolved into a sophisticated, independent powerhouse. Drawing on Phillips' business background, they run the group as an "agile organization," rejecting slow, bureaucratic processes in favor of small, specialized teams. This structure allows them to "fail quickly," learning immediately what works and iterating on their programming in real-time.

This data-driven approach has turned a one-off event into a permanent institution. Under the banner "Queer All Year," the group now organizes quarterly fundraisers and monthly meetups to ensure the community remains connected long after June. Phillips came to Haverhill asking where the queer people hung out; when he didn't find an answer, he built the venue himself.

https://www.haverhillpride.org/

Haverhill Pride Flag Raising 2023.

**Marblehead Pride** "What's happening in Marblehead?" Hope Watt-Bucci asked Sherry Gagne, a new member of the North Shore Pride board.

"Nothing yet," came the reply.

That silence wasn't an answer; it was a challenge. Gagne didn't just ask for a flag; she engineered a movement. Knowing that change in a traditional town required consensus, she worked the back channels, mobilizing the town's clergy to write letters of moral support to the selectboard and aligning with the "No Place for Hate" committee. Her strategy worked. The flag went up at Abbot Hall, transforming a quiet town center into a beacon of visibility.

Sherry wanted more than a moment; she wanted a legacy. After the third year, realizing the event needed to outlast her own tenure, she convened a Zoom call to form a permanent committee. Her proudest moment wasn't just the applause of the crowd, but seeing Pride institutionalized—marked by an official annual proclamation and a community plaque permanently displayed on the town's wall.

Hope Watt-Bucci, Rev. Wendy von Courter, Holly Aloha Jaynes, and Sherry Gagne at 2019 Marblehead flag raising.

Holly Aloha Jaynes stepped forward on this new committee. As a member of the Marblehead Cultural Council, she commissioned a local Danish artist to paint a Progress Flag adorned with hearts outside the Marblehead Visitor Center. It was a stubborn battle for visibility. Though local prejudice left its mark—kids defaced the art with skid marks, and the vibrant path was eventually removed—the message endured. Because of Sherry's foundational strategy and Holly's persistent advocacy, Marblehead's Pride is no longer a solitary act, but a permanent, public celebration.

https://www.facebook.com/profile.php?
id=100094006961900&sk=about

**Newburyport Pride** Tarah Luciano hid behind her sunglasses, but they couldn't conceal the tears of joy streaming down her face. It was pouring rain during Newburyport's inaugural Pride parade in 2023, yet 500 people lined the streets, cheering as 150 marchers splashed through the puddles. For Tarah, this wet, wonderful celebration was the defiant answer to a frustration she had felt for years: "I don't want to go to Boston or Salem for a Pride parade. We can do it here."

The road to that parade began in 2022, not with fanfare, but with a defensive line. When a youth dance at the Mason's Hall featuring a drag-queen DJ was targeted by protesters, the town didn't buckle. Instead, hundreds of neighbors turned out to form a human "Welcome Wall," physically shielding over 100

Sweet Paws Dog Rescue.

queer youth from the hate outside so they could dance in peace. That profound act of protection proved the city was ready for more.

The city's momentum built through local businesses holding their own celebrations beginning in the early 2020s. Riverwalk Brewing's Chuck Barbados hosted Sweet Paws Dog Rescue Pride events, led by Cynthia Sweet and her team. These early efforts ran parallel to Sarah Lord's launch of the "Pride in the Port" Pride dance at Bar 25, along with a Pride sunset boat cruise. These gatherings inspired Lori Towle to found Newburyport Area Lesbian Social Events and Adventures (NALSEA) in March of 2022. What started small quickly grew into a vibrant community hub, co-led by Amy LeJeune, hosting outings, hikes, blood drives, and meetups.

While the city's first flag-raising in 2022 drew only 9 people, the tide was turning. Luciano joined Towle and Marianne Vesey that summer to form a single, powerful coalition: Newburyport Pride Board. With the backing of Mayor Reardon and Board members like Holly Cashman and Paul Goldberg—who tirelessly made the parade his full-time job—Pride exploded in scale. What began as siloed events has transformed into a four-day Pride festival featuring 60 parade groups, family-friendly events, art galleries, a dedicated youth space and a contest that turns the city's storefronts into rainbows. Lord continues to offer the annual Pride Cruise through Pride In The Port, and Towle and LeJeune host annual NALSEA events to support queer youth scholarships. All of this was inspired

The 2022 Newburyport "Welcome Wall."

by pioneers like Shelly Cullen, who has offered lesbian DJ dances in Newburyport since the 1980s.

For Tarah, the ultimate validation came during the 2023 flag raising. Standing shoulder-to-shoulder with Massachusetts Governor Maura Healey, the nation's first openly lesbian governor, she realized that Newburyport wasn't just hosting a party; it was making history.

https://www.newburyportpride.com/

**Rowley Pride** Small but fiercely proud, Rowley Pride proves you don't need a massive crowd to make a statement. Founded in 2023 by Denzil Rice and Anya Ciarametaro, the group marches behind a reclaimed banner—hand-painted by Anya—transforming a discarded object into a symbol of resilience. Though just a half-dozen strong, this group of friends and neighbors brings undeniable joy to the Newburyport and Tri-Town parades. Now, they are looking to the future, eager to pass the torch and involve the next generation of local youth.

Rowley Pride group at the 2025 Tri-Town Pride Parade.

**Tri-Town Pride** "Let's throw the loudest, proudest pride parade this town has ever seen!"

It wasn't a corporate strategy session; it was a challenge issued over coffee. Sitting in Zumi's Espresso & Ice Cream, openly queer founders Janelle Pescatore and Grayson Cohen looked around at a small core group of friends and neighbors and decided it was time to make some noise. That bold proposal, however, immediately turned into a race against the calendar. It was June 2022, and with only three weeks left in the month, the ambition to launch a full-scale parade collided with the reality of logistics.

They didn't quit; they pivoted. Encouraged by neighbor and then-Select Board Chair Marshall Hook, Pescatore met with town officials and realized that while the runway for a parade was too short, they could start with a picnic. The goal was simple: plant a flag and see who saluted. They hoped for a handful of friends. Instead, over 100 people showed up. That afternoon, supported by local stalwarts like Zumi's owners Umesh and Zillie Bhuju, the Congregational Church of Topsfield, Creative Co-Op and businesses like The Perfectly Imperfect Gift Shoppe and Rosie Realtor, the seed was planted.

Janelle Pescatore.

From that frantic, joyful start, Tri-Town Pride—uniting Topsfield, Boxford and Middleton—has exploded. Cohen helped build the structure and continuity that allowed the group to scale. With mentorship from the Hamilton-Wenham Human Rights Coalition, the group formalized as a non-profit in 2024. By 2025, the growth was undeniable. The organizers set an optimistic goal of 500 attendees for their parade and festival. They were wrong. In a town with only about 5,000 registered voters, 1,000 people turned out. It remains Pescatore's proudest moment: looking out at a town common packed with 40 vendors, food trucks and a sea of rainbows in a place often assumed to be quiet suburbia.

What makes Tri-Town Pride distinct is its heartbeat: the children. This focus is deeply influenced by Pescatore's role as the owner of Ms. Janelle's Neighbor School, an explicit safe space for queer families. Her students are not just spectators; they are the VIPs. They rode the six-seat "Bunch Bike" in the 2024 and 2025 parades, symbolizing a family-first approach. The event eschews corporate sterility for deep intention, highlighted by "Story Time" sessions where performers like nonbinary drag king Darren Tashine read books like *Calvin* to uplift transgender youth.

Today, Pescatore serves as chair, supported by her life partner and board member Talisa Rafferty, along with a dedicated board including Jackie Jansky, Marissa Hathaway, Roger Bourgeois and

Tri-Town Pride Parade.

Sara Tollerud. Together they have proven a powerful truth: in the quiet corners of the North Shore, love doesn't just win—it grows.

https://tritownhrc.org/

**United Lynn Pride** When world-renowned salsa dancer Ana Tinajero swapped the bustling rhythm of Boston for a quiet home by the Lynn waterfront in 2018, she found peace, but she missed the pulse of a connected community. She knew the queer population in Lynn was vibrant and diverse, yet the network remained invisible to newcomers. In 2020, Tinajero launched Queer Lynn Scene to bring those connections to the surface. She originally envisioned a history exhibition at a local café to celebrate her new neighbors, but when the pandemic locked the world down, she pivoted to the digital realm, launching a city-wide survey and video project to weave a virtual tapestry of Lynn's queer voices.

Ana Tinajero.

That digital beacon caught the attention of Cristian Recinos, a lifelong resident who had navigated Lynn's schools and neighborhoods with quiet resilience. Cristian saw the project as a vital step for his hometown and joined Ana not just as a participant, but as a partner, helping to turn raw survey data into a roadmap for action.

By 2022, the city's energy was undeniable. Various groups were hosting independent Pride events, but the efforts felt scattered. Guided by City Councilor Coco Alinsug's mentorship, Tinajero and Recinos spearheaded a coalition to weave these threads together. They united the city's disparate organizations under a single banner: United Lynn Pride. It was this expansive vision that fully captured Recinos's imagination. "I wanted to be part of it," he recalled. "You know, it aligned with my interests and things I've done in the past, and it was in my own community, so it all just sort of lined up."

What began as a week-long celebration quickly became a permanent shift in the city's DNA. With the community's blessing, the initiative evolved from a coalition into a standalone non-profit, with Recinos stepping up to serve as its executive director.

Today, under Cristian's leadership, United Lynn Pride has grown from a digital spark into a roaring engine of advocacy and celebration. The organization now coordinates over a dozen signature events during Pride Week alone, transforming the city into a canvas of visibility. From the celebratory cheers at the flag raising to the spectacle of lighting High Rock Tower and the Rainbow Bridge, the city shines. The schedule is packed with connections: Paint Nights, Youth Pride, the "Rainbows on the River" kayak flotilla, historical walking tours, community meals, art shows and even Queer Zumba. What began as one woman's search for neighbors has become an institution, ensuring that future generations of Lynners won't have to leave home to find their pride.

unitedlynnpride.com

Cristian Recinos.

**Flag Raisings** Half of the municipalities on the North Shore raise a Pride Flag at some point in June.

United Lynn Pride flag raising.

# A Sea of Visibility

Driven by a fierce belief that education and advocacy were the only antidotes to hate, Hope Watt -Bucci gathered like-minded people in her living room to fight back against anti-LGBTQ+ sentiment, and North Shore Pride was born. They scraped together the application fee for non-profit status by literally pulling cash and loose change from their pockets.

2025 North Shore Pride Parade.

From those humble, scrappy beginnings in 2012, North Shore Pride has grown into a massive cultural phenomenon. This year, 2026, the organization celebrates 15 years of transforming the region. The inaugural parade was a bold declaration that queer people belonged in the historic center of Salem, not just in the shadows. Under Watt-Bucci's tenure as president, the event has exploded from grassroots events into a parade and festival drawing over 40,000 attendees annually.

Yet, the organization is far more than just a party; it is a lifeline. While the festival features a staggering 95 vendors, the board enforces a strict mandate that prioritizes substance over commerce: "More than 50% of our vendors have to be some sort of service provider to our community," says Watt-Bucci. This ensures that, amidst the celebration, attendees find the healthcare, legal and social support they desperately need.

Volunteers and members of the North Shore Pride board rest after the 2025 parade and festival.

The organization's commitment to education and advocacy happens year-round, far from the parade route. When Gordon College faced controversy regarding its LGBTQ+ Alliance, North Shore Pride went in to facilitate difficult conversations. They maintain a presence at the Lawrence Trial Court for cultural appreciation days and table at every "Out Night" performance at the North Shore Music Theatre to provide resources. During the pandemic, they launched virtual community forums covering critical topics like transgender violence and how to protest safely.

Punctuating the afternoon of festival entertainment is a presentation honoring those who fight for the community, with past recipients including NAGLY, RAW Arts, Steve Buckley, Bill Hanney, Rev. Joe Amico, Pat Gozemba, Nancy Nangeroni, Chelsea Page Moses, Marilyn Humphries, and the Sisters of Perpetual Indulgence, among others. Grand Marshals have included prominent figures such as TV personality Randy Price, Glee star Alex Newell and Sabrina the Teenage Witch star actor and comedian Caroline Rhea.

ITM ( In The Mak'n ) perform at the 2025 North Shore Pride festival.

Crucially, Hope understood that a single parade in Salem wasn't enough to change the daily reality for someone living in a neighboring suburb. Along with T Nash, she championed the "Rainbow Coalition," an initiative designed to mentor other towns in creating their own celebrations. Their work planted seeds in town halls across the county, empowering communities to hoist the rainbow flag on their own official poles. Today, the work of the all-volunteer board of North Shore Pride has rippled outward, inspiring official events in Amesbury, Danvers, Gloucester, Haverhill, Lynn, Marblehead, Newburyport, and Tri-Town (Topsfield, Middleton and Boxford).

The current members of the board are Hope Watt-Bucci, Rachel Pelley, Libby McSwiney, Daniel Collins, T Nash, John Paul Ryan, Hannah Lister, Matt Chilliak, Colby Bomberowitz, Ingrid Farelli, Patti Gillis, Charles Mendes, Savannah Hopkins and Elene Karlberg

"In today's political climate, North Shore Pride is needed now more than ever," Watt-Bucci asserts. "We will be here as long as we need to." She proved that when you are brave enough to be the first to march, an entire region will gratefully fall in step beside you.

https://northshorepride.org/

# A Rainbow Lens

JIM MOSER, DREW DARIEN, CRISTIAN RECINOS & PAT GOZEMBA

It began, as so many modern revolutions do, with a casual remark during a Zoom call. In the midst of a planning session for United Lynn Pride, community stalwarts Kirsten Freni and Coco Alinsug dropped a comment that would spark a movement: "Somebody should write the LGBT history of Lynn. We had like five bars." That simple observation—that a city known for its industrial grit also held a secret geography of queer sanctuaries—ignited a curiosity that could not be extinguished. It was the seed of *Through a Rainbow Lens*, a project that would uncover a hidden century of

The *Through a Rainbow Lens* team; Jim Moser, left, Pat Gozemba, Cristian Recinos, rear, and Drew Darien.

struggle and celebration on the North Shore and document 19 queer bars.

360° Virtual Museum.

To bring this history to light, Jim Moser and Cristian Recinos reached out to the history department at Salem State University, hoping to recruit a student intern to help with the legwork. Instead of an undergraduate seeking credit, they wound up with Professor Andrew Darien, an experienced oral historian who recognized the project's profound value and signed on himself. But the team needed someone who had lived the history, a guide to the nuances of the movement. Jim turned to Facebook to recruit Pat Gozemba, a legendary local activist and historian. The digital courtship was rocky at first; Gozemba initially ignored the messages, convinced Jim was just a college student trying to trick her into writing his term paper. Persistence paid off; however, once she realized the scope of their ambition, she joined what would become a powerhouse coalition.

Opening night at the *Throught a Rainbow Lens* exhibit at the Lynn Museum, June 5, 2024.

Website.

Fueling their efforts was a pivotal $20,000 grant from Mass Humanities, part of the "Expand Massachusetts Stories" initiative. With funding secured and a team assembled, the work began in earnest. They tracked down narrators and artifacts, eventually recording 32 video oral histories and collecting over 1,400 images. The narrators included native and foreign-born Americans whose families came from the Philippines, Ireland, El Salvador, Italy, Panama, India and Zimbabwe. They unearthed stories of resilience that had been whispered in bars but never written in books—tales of Fran's Place, the oldest queer bar in Massachusetts, and the courageous couples who were the first to marry in 2004.

The resulting exhibit at the Lynn Museum was not just a collection of objects; it was a reclamation of space. It featured timelines, maps of long-gone bars and the faces of those who built the community. The exhibit and live events were viewed by 4,460 people. It challenged the narrative of Lynn as merely a hard-scrabble city,

Billy Mulcahy Moser, James Ferrante and Tony The Tiger Lecondino at the exhibit opening.

revealing it as a vibrant hub of queer life. The impact was national. The project was honored with the 2025 Albert B. Corey Award from the American Association for State and Local History, a prestigious accolade given to only one volunteer-operated organization in the country each year for displaying "vigor, scholarship, and imagination."

Documentary.

*Through a Rainbow Lens* proved that history is not just what is written in textbooks, but what people who lived it remember. It transformed a "hidden past" into a source of public pride, ensuring that the stories of the "five bars" and the thousands of lives they touched would never again be lost to silence.

*Through a Rainbow Lens*

Website: www.UnitedLynnPride.com/lgbtqhistory

360° Virtual Museum: https://througharainbowlens.vrticalmedia.digital/

Oral History Highlights: https://youtu.be/r4QI-3WGyHY

*Finding Refuge, Demanding Equality: A Century of LGBTQ+ Lynn*

Full Documentary : https://youtu.be/pCbIpu4LI5M

Trailer:  https://www.unitedlynnpride.com/documentary

# Be a Queer Hero!

Your Name Here

We have traveled a long, hard and joyful road together in these pages. We started in the frozen silence of the Puritan colonies, where love was a hanging offense, and authenticity was a death sentence. We walked the marble halls of "Dabsville," peering through the glass closets of 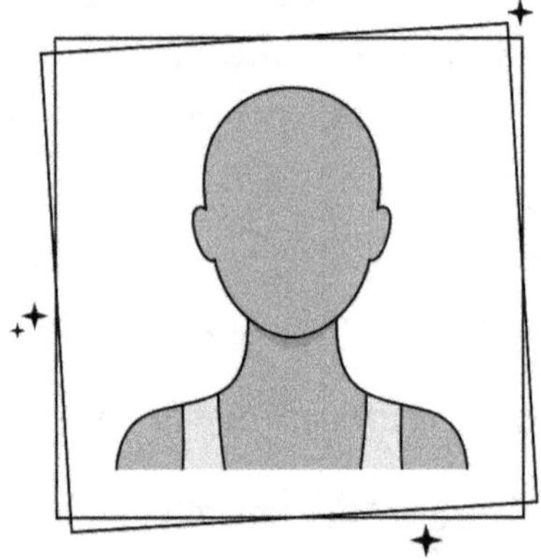 the wealthy who bought their privacy with fortunes. We stood on the sticky floors of Fran's Place as bricks shattered the windows, and we watched a generation rise from the ashes of the AIDS crisis to build a world where marriage was possible, and Pride was a visible parade, not a covert gathering in a darkened bar.

For a brief, shining moment at the turn of this century, it felt as though the war was won. We lulled ourselves into believing the arc of the moral universe had finally bent toward justice and was locked permanently in place.

We were wrong.

Look around you. The sky is darkening again. The very existence of queer people—our stories, our healthcare, our right to be mentioned in a classroom—is under a coordinated and ferocious attack. Books like this one are being challenged. Laws are being drafted to push us back into the shadows, to silence the Tony the Tigers, T Nashes, Coco Alinsugs and Marcia Hams of the future before they even find their voices. The closet is being rebuilt, plank by plank, by those who fear what we represent: the unstoppable power of authenticity.

But history is not a straight line; it is a tide. It goes out, but it also comes crashing back in. The stories in this book prove that we have survived worse than this. We survived when the law called us criminals. We survived when medicine called us sick. We survived when the world watched us die and looked away. The heroes of the North Shore did not wait for permission to exist. They understood that freedom is not a gift you are given; it is a territory you must occupy and defend every single day.

Now, the watch has passed to you. The forces of erasure are counting on your silence. They are banking on your fear. Do not give it to them. Instead, look to the toolkit left behind by those who came before us.

It begins with *Visibility*, the simple, radical power of "Hello." The opposition relies on us remaining abstract stereotypes. You must break that illusion. Introduce yourself to your neighbors. Put the sticker on your car. It is much harder to hate a person than a concept.

You must create *Space*. If the bars are closing, we must build new sanctuaries in our living rooms, our churches and our libraries. Be the person who forms the "Welcome Wall" to shield the vulnerable from the hate outside. Ensure that wherever you stand is a place where others can drop their armor.

We must mobilize *Care*. When the government failed us during the plague years, we survived because we became each other's safety net. Look for the gaps where people are falling through—the youth kicked out of their homes, the elders aging in isolation—and fill them with mercy.

Use your *Voice* to speak truth to power. Silence is the oxygen of oppression. Whether it is at a school board meeting, in a letter to the editor, or at the ballot box, you must refuse to let bigotry go unchallenged.

Seek *Connection*. It is easy to retreat into our silos, but we must do the hard work of finding common ground. Build bridges where others build walls. Win the friendship of someone who disagrees with you. We outnumber the haters, but only if we are willing to engage.

Practice *Resilience* by celebrating joy. Do not let the struggle consume you. The bowling leagues, the drag shows and the dances are not distractions; they are the fuel of our resistance. To be happy in the face of those who want you miserable is the ultimate victory.

Finally, honor your *Legacy* by learning and sharing this history. You stand on the shoulders of giants—from the lesbians at the Light House Café to the marchers in Newburyport—but you cannot inherit what you do not know. Learn these stories. Share them with the next generation so they understand they are part of a powerful lineage of survival, not a mistake to be erased.

Register to vote as if your life depends on it, because it does. Run for office. Support your local library. Stand between a bully and their target. Be the person who refuses to leave the building when the heat rises.

We have weathered 400 years of storms on this rocky coast, and we are not going back. The tide is rising again, and you are the wave.

You don't need to be a mayor or a movie star to be a hero. You just need to show up, speak out and take care of your people. The North Shore is full of everyday heroes. Will you be next?

# Acknowledgements

I am humbled by the number of people who contributed to this book and the depth of their efforts. This book would not be possible without the amazing support of the North Shore queer community.

I deeply appreciate the endless support of my husband, Billy,  the encouragement from my queer history muse, Pat Gozemba, and the advice of my careful readers and editors,  Jack Armitage, Tom Dalton, Kirsten Freni, Pat Gozemba, George Gratten, Karen Kahn, Peter Konrad, Mark MacKay, Gordene MacKenzie, Tiffany Magnolia, Caleb McMurphy, Connie Moser, Nancy Nangeroni, Leo Peiken, Baikyo Wendy Pirsig, Rev. Donna Spencer Collins, Ruthanne Switzer, Ellie Tamplin, Keja Valens and Olivia Werth.

I thank photographers Marilyn Humphries, Ferns Francois and Jay Salois for their generosity and beautiful photographs. I thank my main informants, Jack Armitage, Lemaris Bell, Dr. Holly Cashman, Greg Cook, Sebastian Crane, R. Tripp Evans, 3rian King, Caleb McMurphy, Janelle Pescatore, Elisa Rolle, Michael Tobey, Lori Towle and Hope Watt-Bucci. I thank many amazing librarians and archivists and their institutions, Nikki Lebenson Angulo of AFS Intercultural Programs, Molly Brown of The Northeastern University Archives and Special Collections, Leon Doucette of Cape Ann Museum, Dee Duarte of The Isabella Stewart Gardner Museum, Donna E. Russo of Historic New England, Ashley Serveiss of Museum of Old Newbury, Sarah Tripp of Cape Ann Museum, Beth Welin of Hammond Castle Museum, William Whiting of Topsfield Historical Society, Caroline Picard of City Lights Booksellers and Publishers, The Lynn Public Library and Ted Grant of The Daily Item of Lynn.

I thank my design advisors, Sarah Bennet, Mark MacKay, Rev. Donna Spencer Collins and my advisors on "your first book", Ana Tinajero and Rev. Donna Spencer Collins. I thank the 80+ people I interviewed. I thank all the truly wonderful authors in my bibliography.

I thank my Zen teacher, Myozen Joan Amaral, for helping me to work with nothing forced. I thank composer Stephen Thelen for great music for writing and relaxing. I thank Mass Humanities for funding the *Through A Rainbow Lens* project, and thank Drew Darien, Christian Recinos, and Pat Gozemba for their amazing work on that project. I thank the American Association for State and Local History for honoring the project with the 2025 Albert B. Corey award.

Finally, I thank my research and writing partners, coffee, my computer named "Rainbow", Jazz, Inter-Library Loan, Gemini AI, breaks, snacks, naps, flowers, sunshine and our cats., Tiger and Masa.

# Image Credits

"Public Domain" is abbreviated as "PD."
"Courtesy of" is abbreviated as "c."

Creeative Commons License links
CC BY-SA 4.0
https://creativecommons.org/licenses/by-sa/4.0/
CC BY-SA 3.0
https://creativecommons.org/licenses/by-sa/3.0/
CC BY 2.0
https://creativecommons.org/licenses/by/2.0/
CC0 1.0
https://creativecommons.org/publicdomain/zero/1.0/deed.en

Front cover, Jim Moser, Rev. Donna Spencer Collins and Gemini AI .
Back cover, Jim Moser
Title page top. photo Patricia A. Gozemba.
Title page bottom. photo Marilyn Humphries.
Section introductions 1-9, Gemini AI.
Chapter flourish, freepik.
Hero Collage c. Jim Moser, credits as below.
Author photo c. Jim Moser
Page 3, Samuel…, c. The Cape Ann Museum.
Page 6, Jesse…, c. Holly Aloha Jaynes.
Page 8, John…, PD.
Page 10, John…, Gemini AI.
Page 13, Witches…, c. Marilyn Humphries
Page 14, Matelotage…, Gemini AI.
Page 16, Fanny…, PD.
Page 18, Dorothie…, Bing AI.
Page 20, Sammy…, Digital Commonwealth, unrestricted.
Page 21, Rev., PD.
Page 26, Ralph…, Sketch by Samuel Worcester Rowse, PD.
Page 27, Nathaniel…, Nathaniel Hawthorne by Brady, 1860-64, PD.
Page 29, Herman…, Herman Melville by Joseph O Eaton, PD.
Page 30, Illustration…, PD.
Page 32, Charles…, by Gardner, Alexander, PD.

Page 34, Samuel…, PD
Page 35, Statue…, CC BY-SA 3.0.
Page 37, Henry…, by Janice Corkin Rudolt. p. Jack Armitage.
Page 38, John…, at age 29 in 1898. PD.
Page 39, The…, CC BY-SA 3.0.
Page 40, Lucy…, Wikimedia, No known copyright restrictions.
Page 41, Mills…, "View of Boott Cotton Mills At Lowell, Massachusetts." The engraving is from "Gleason's Pictorial" (Boston: 1852), PD.
Page 43, Louisa…, Louisa May Alcott, c. 1870 - Warren's Portraits, PD.
Page 44, Illustration…, Louisa May Alcott Little Women 1880 Frank T Merrill, PD.
Page 46, Mary…, Gail Hamilton's Life and Letters frontispiece, 1866, PD.
Page 47, Woman's…, 1868, PD.
Page 48, Sarah…, 1894, PD.
Page 48, Annie…, by John Singer Sargent, 1890, PD.
Page 49, Annie…, 1922, No known copyright restrictions.
Page 50, Eaglehead…, 2015, CC BY-SA 4.0
Page 51, Louisa…, 1861, PD.
Page 52, Louisa…, PD.
Page 54, Women…, Hester Trott and four friends, Junction City, Kansas, 1899. PD.
Page 55, A…, CC BY-SA 3.0
Page 57, Alice…, PD.

Page 122, Robert..., Gay Community
News, 1973-11-17, c. Northeastern
University Archives and Special
Collections.
Page 123, Advertisement..., Gay
Community News,1973-07-12, c.
Northeastern University Archives and
Special Collections.
Page 124, Advertisement..., Gay
Community News, 1974-06-01, c.
Northeastern University Archives and
Special Collections.
Page 125, Postcard..., Tichnor Bros.
Inc., Boston, Mass., PD.
Page 126, Grace..., c. Grace Schrafft.
Page 127, Grace..., c. Grace Schrafft.
Page 129, Frances..., c. Museum of Old
Newbury Archives.
Page 129, Frank..., photo Bill Lane, c.
Bill Lane.
Page 130, Frank..., c. Museum of Old
Newbury Archives.
Page 131, The..., c. Museum of Old
Newbury Archives.
Page 131, Photograph..., c. Museum of
Old Newbury Archives.
Page 132, Jim..., 1991, c. Roberta
Seymour.
Page 136, Interview., QRC.
Page 134, Advertisement..., Gay
Community News,1981-01-24, c.
Northeastern University Archives and
Special Collections.
Page 137, Kathy..., photo Patricia A.
Gozemba.
Page 138, The..., Gay Community
News,1974-04-20, c. Northeastern
University Archives and Special
Collections.
Page 139, Interview., QRC.
Page 140, Joanne..., photo Patricia A.
Gozemba.
Page 139, Interview., QRC.
Page 143, Tisha..., photos Dave
Granese.
Page 144, Outside..., photo Marilyn
Humphries.
Page 146, Tisha..., photo Ferns
Francois.
Page 147, Wendy..., photo Marilyn
Humphries.

Page 148, Patrons..., photo Patricia A.
Gozemba.
Page 149, Paper., QRC.
Page 150, Interview, QRC.
Page 151, The..., 1981-11-28, c. The
Daily Item of Lynn, MA.
Page 153, Tony,..., c. Tony Lecondino.
Page 154, Interview., QRC.
Page 156, The..., 1986-11, The Guide to
Gay New England, c. Northeastern
University Archives and Special
Collections.
Page 157, Gary..., c. Tony Lecondino.
Page 159, Mr., 1986-09-25, page 8, c.
The Daily Item of Lynn, MA.
Page 160, Hat..., photo Jay Salois.
Page 161, Joseph's..., photo Tim
Deegan.
Page 163, Nelio..., 2007-07-11 c. The
Daily Item of Lynn, MA.
Page 164, Interview., QRC.
Page 164, 47..., photo Amy L. Munoz
Page 165, Lunch..., photo Jay Salois.
Page 166, Shauna..., c. Shaun Watson.
Page 167, Shauna..., c. Shaun Watson.
Page 168, Jay..., 1979-12-18, c. The
Daily Item of Lynn, MA.
Page 169, Protest..., 1985-11-23, Gay
Community News, c. Northeastern
University Archives and Special
Collections.
Page 170, Jay..., 1979-12-04, c. The
Daily Item of Lynn, MA.
Page 173, Article..., 1981-04-04, c. The
Daily Item of Lynn, MA.
Page 174, Bluiston..., photo Bluiston
DeYoung.
Page 175, Interview., QRC.
Page 177, Pat..., photo Marilyn
Humphries.
Page 178, An..., c. Peter Abate.
Page 179, Interview., QRC.
Page 179, Pat..., photo Marilyn
Humphries.
Page 181, Bill..., photo Marilyn
Humphries.
Page 183, Thomas..., c. THomas
MacDonald.
Page 186, Lemaris..., c. Lemaris Bell.
Page 188, Interviews., QRC.
Page 190, Peter..., c. Jack Armitage.

# Selected Bibliography


Atkins, C.J. "Remembering Gary Dotterman: Anti-Racist Oklahoman, Vietnam Vet for Peace, and Irrepressible Gay Communist." People's World, 26 June 2023.

Baker, Emerson W. A Storm of Witchcraft: The Salem Trials and the American Experience. Oxford University Press, 2015.

Bedell, Madelon. The Alcotts: Biography of a Family. C.N. Potter: Distributed by Crown Publishers, 1980.

Bell, Lemaris. "The Salem Rainbow Stroll 2022." Unpublished, Lemaris Bell, 2022.

Bernstein, Leonard, and Nigel Simeone. The Leonard Bernstein Letters Leonard Bernstein. Yale University Press, 2020.

Bierfelt, Kristin. The North Shore Literary Trail: From Bradstreet's Andover to Hawthorne's Salem. History Press, 2009.

Bronski, Michael. A Queer History of the United States. 2011.

Burg, B. R. Sodomy and the Pirate Tradition: English Sea Rovers in the Seventeenth-Century Caribbean. New York University Press, 1995.

Calhoun, Charles C. Longfellow: A Rediscovered Life. Beacon Press, 2016.

Collins, Donna J. S. Thus Says the Lord: NOT THIS: A Faithful Rebuke of Christian Nationalism and Justice for All. Independently Published, 2025.

Connolly, Robin. "Everyone Knows Your Name Here." The Daily Item.

Cook, Greg. "Midcentury Gay Haven In Gloucester Revealed In Long Lost Ellsworth Kelly Drawing." Wonderland, 8 June 2024, https://gregcookland.com/wonderland/2024/06/08/hammond-castle/.

Cook, Greg. "Remembering Poet Gerrit Lansing: The Bridge To A Much Larger World." Wonderland, 2 Mar. 2018, https://gregcookland.com/wonderland/2018/03/02/gerrit-lansing-3/.

Coultrap-McQuin, Susan Margaret. Doing Literary Business: American Women Writers in the Nineteenth Century. The University of North Carolina Press, 2025.

Crain, Caleb. American Sympathy: Men, Friendship, and Literature in the New Nation. Yale University Press, 2001.

Demos, John. Entertaining Satan: Witchcraft and the Culture of Early New England. Oxford University Press, 2004.

Dewhurst, Robert. ORAL HISTORY INITIATIVE On John Wieners Woodberry Poetry Room, 21 Oct. 2015, https://www.youtube.com/watch?v=KNg0iJkasEc.

Evans, R. Tripp. The Importance of Being Furnished: Four Bachelors at Home. Rowman & Littlefield, 2024.

Faderman, Lillian. Surpassing the Love of Men: Romantic Friendship and Love between Women from the Renaissance to the Present. Magnus Books, 2012.

Fisher, Paul. The Grand Affair: John Singer Sargent in His World. Picador, 2023.

"Focus On Robert Dow." Gay Community News, 17 Nov. 1973, p. 3.

Forest, Christopher. Lost History of the North Shore: Little Known Tales from Massachusetts. Schiffer Publishing Ltd, 2010.

Garland, Joseph E. Eastern Point: A Nautical, Rustical, and More or Less Sociable Chronicle of Gloucester's Outer Shield and Inner Sanctum, 1606-1990.

Commonwealth Editions, 1999.

"A Gay Man's Search for Peace." North Shore Sunday, 18 Dec. 1983.

"Gemini AI." Google, Google, gemini.google.com/.

Gertner, Nancy. "Thoughts on Comparable Worth Litigation and Organizational Strategies." University of Michigan Journal of Law Reform, vol. 20, no. 1, 1986. Fall 1986.

Godbeer, Richard. The Overflowing of Friendship: Love between Men and the Creation of the American Republic. Johns Hopkins University Press, 2014.

Graham. "Robert Culliford." World Queerstory, 3 Oct. 2020, https://worldqueerstory. wordpress.com/2020/10/03/robert-culliford/.

Greven, David. Men beyond Desire: Male Sexuality in Nineteenth-Century America. Springer Nature Switzerland Palgrave Macmillan, 2024.

Greven, David. Men beyond Desire: Manhood, Sex, and Violation in American Literature. Palgrave Macmillan, 2005.

Grundy, David. Never by Itself Alone: Queer Poetry, Queer Communities in Boston and the Bay Area, 1944-Present. Oxford University Press, 2024.

Guerra, Lya, director. The Love Part of This. Centaur Entertainment.

Guilfoy, Christine. "Lynn Woman Dyke-Bashed." Gay Community News, 12 Nov. 1985.

Hamilton, Gail. Gail Hamilton: Selected Writings. Edited by Susan Margaret Coultrap-McQuin, Rutgers University Press, 1992.

Harding, Walter. "Thoreau's Sexuality." Journal of Homosexuality, vol. 21, no. 3, p. 23. 1991.

Hartley, Marsden, and Susan Elizabeth Ryan. Somehow a Past: The Autobiography of Marsden Hartley. MIT Press, 1998.

Hastings, Patricia. "Growing up Gay." The Daily Item, 4 Nov. 1979.

Herbert, Rosemary. "Fran Dalton Retrospective Documents Beauty and Grandeur of Newburyport." WickedLocal.Com, 8 June 2012, https://www.wickedlocal.com/

History Project, and Barney Frank. Improper Bostonians: Lesbian and Gay History from the Puritans to Playland. Beacon Press (MA), 1999.

Jacobs, Sue-Ellen, editor. Two-Spirit People: Native American Gender Identity, Sexuality, and Spirituality. University of Illinois Press, 2005.

Jonas, Stephen, et al. Arcana: A Stephen Jonas Reader. City Lights Books, 2019.

Kahn, Janet, and Patricia A. Gozemba. "In and around the Lighthouse: Working-Class Lesbian Bar Culture in the 1950s and 1960s." Gendered Domains: Rethinking Public and Private in Women's History, De Gruyter Brill, 1987, pp. 90–106.

Kahn, Karen, and Patricia A. Gozemba with photographs by Marilyn Humphries. Courting Equality: A Documentary History of America's First Legal Same-Sex Marriages. Beacon Press (MA), 2009.

Katz, Jonathan Ned. Love Stories: Sex between Men before Homosexuality. University of Chicago Press, 2013.

Katz, Jonathan. Gay American History: Lesbians and Gay Men in the U.S.A.: A Documentary History. Meridian, 1992.

Kinross, Patrick Balfour. The Innocents at Home. Readers Union : John Murray, 1961.

Kiristy, Laura. "A Bittersweet Victory At Last." Bay Windows, 30 Aug. 2001, pp. 1–5.

LARCOM, LUCY. New England Girlhood. ANSON STREET PRESS, 2025.

Lopez, Russ. The Hub of the Gay Universe: An LGBTQ History of Boston,

Provincetown, and Beyond. Shawmut Peninsula Press, 2019.

"Main Page." Wikipedia, Wikimedia Foundation, 6 Feb. 2026, en.wikipedia.org/wiki/Main_Page.

Matteson, John. Eden's Outcasts: The Story of Louisa May Alcott and Her Father. W.W. Norton, 2009.

McMurphy, Caleb. "Poetry Night Slides." Caleb McMurphy, June 2024.

McMurphy, Caleb. "Pride Copy for Mary." Caleb McMurphy, June 2024.

Mellow, James R. Nathaniel Hawthorne in His Times. Houghton Mifflin Co, 1980.

Moore, Honor. The White Blackbird a Life of the Painter Margarett Sargent by Her Granddaughter. W. W. Norton & Company, 2012.

Morris, David. "Women Charge Police Abuse." Gay Community News, 4 Apr. 1981.

Moser, James R, et al. "Through a Rainbow Lens." Through a Rainbow Lens, A Reflection on Lynn's LGBTQ+ History, United Lynn Pride, www.UnitedLynnPride.com/lgbtqhistory. Accessed 2026.

Moser, James R. "Queer Heroes of the North Shore Interviews." 2026.

Muise, Peter. "John Godfrey: Witch and Troublemaker." New England Folklore, 2017, https://newenglandfolklore.blogspot.com/2017/11/john-godfrey-witch-and-troublemaker.html.

Muise, Peter. Legends and Lore of the North Shore. The History Press, 2014.

Muise, Peter. Witches and Warlocks of Massachusetts: Legends, Victims, and Sinister Spellcasters. Globe Pequot, 2021.

National Park Service, Department of the Interior. LGBTQ America, A Theme Study of Lesbian, Gay, Bisexual, Transgender and Queer History, 2016, https://npshistory.com/publications/nhl/theme-studies/lgbtq-america.pdf.

Nissen, Axel. The Romantic Friendship Reader: Love Stories between Men in Victorian America. Northeastern University Press, 2003.

Paley, Amit R. "The Secret Court of 1920." The Crimson, Harvard University, 21 Nov. 2002, https://www.thecrimson.com/article/2002/11/21/the-secret-court-of-1920-at/.

PARSONS, KITTY. Dogtown Common. LITERARY LICENSING, LLC, 2013.

Performance by R. Tripp Evans, et al., Pride in the Archives Virtual Lecture - 6.2.2021, Cape Ann Museum, 2 June 2021, https://vimeo.com/558669799?fl=pl&fe=sh.

"REEL TIME: On Stephen Jonas (with Joseph Torra) | Woodberry Poetry Room." Performance by Joseph Torra, Woodberry Poetry Room, 18 Nov. 2016, https://www.youtube.com/watch?v=qH5ZKlE8OcA.

Robinson, Esther B., director. A Walk Into the Sea: Danny Williams and the Warhol Factory. Arthouse Films, 2007.

Rolle, Elisa. "Articles." Personal Blog, Queerspaces, reviews-and-ramblings.elisarolle.com/articles.

Rolle, Elisa. Days of Love: Celebrating LGBT History One Story at a Time. Elisa Rolle, 2014.

Rosswood, Eric. The Book of Awesome Queer Heroes: How the Lgbtq+ Community Changed the World for the Better. Mango Publishing, 2024.

Sargent, William. "Rev. Bentley's Man of Curious Habits." G&LR, The Gay and Lesbian Review, July 2019, https://glreview.org/article/rev-bentleys-man-of-curious-habits/.

Shand-Tucci, Douglass. The Art of Scandal: The Life and Times of Isabella Stewart Gardner. HarperCollins World; Hi Marketing, 1999.

Shand-Tucci, Douglass. The Crimson Letter: Harvard, Homosexuality, and the Shaping of American Culture. St. Martin's Press, 2024.

Sleeper, Henry Davis, et al. Beauport Chronicle: The Intimate Letters of Henry Davis Sleeper to Abram Piatt Andrew, Jr., 1906-1915. Society for the Preservation of New England Antiquities, 1991.

"Spinsters' Party." The Daily Evening Item, 5 June 1896, p. 4.

STIRITI, FRANK. Images of Life, Change & Beauty: Photographs, Poetry & Art - Selections from the Works of... Fran Dalton, Newburyport, Massachusetts. JETTY HOUSE, 2023.

Strobel, Christoph. Native Americans of New England. Praeger.

Strouse, Jean. Alice James: A Biography. Houghton Mifflin, 1984.

"Suspicious Fires Rip Lynn Nightclub, Home; Inquiries Under Way." The Daily Item, 24 Apr. 1971, p. 1.

Tameez, Zaakir, and David Lee Garver. Charles Sumner: Conscience of a Nation. Tantor Media, 2025.

Weinberg, Jonathan. Speaking for Vice: Homosexuality in the Art of Charles Demuth, Marsden Hartley, and the First American Avant-Garde. Yale University Press, 1995.

West, Bill. "THE CASE OF DOROTHY HOYT." West in New England, 7 July 2009, https://westinnewengland.blogspot.com/2009/07/case-of-dorothy-hoyt.html.

Westheimer, Kim. "Lesbians Demonstrate at 'Dyke-Bashing' Hearing." Gay Community News, 23 Nov. 1985, p. 2.

Wieners, John, and Michael Seth Stewart. Stars Seen in Person: Selected Journals of John Wieners. City Lights, 2015.

Wind, L. "Who's the Monster? (Hint: It's not the whale.)." English Journal, vol. 110, no. 1, 2020, pp. 114–116.

Wright, William. Harvard's Secret Court: The Savage 1920 Purge of Campus Homosexuals. St. Martin's Press, 2013.

# Laws

Massachusetts' legal treatment of queer people has evolved from colonial criminalization to pioneering civil rights. In the 17th century, laws in Plymouth and Massachusetts Bay classified sodomy and "buggery" as capital offenses. The legal code also enforced gender norms, including a 1695 statute prohibiting crossdressing. By 1805, the state replaced the death penalty for sodomy with hard labor and solitary confinement , though restrictions expanded in 1887 to criminalize "unnatural and lascivious acts".

The legal landscape shifted significantly in the late 20th century. In 1972, the State Supreme Judicial Court ruled that "unnatural acts" statutes could not apply to private, consensual adult conduct , and same-sex sexual activity was fully decriminalized by 1974. By 1989, Massachusetts became the second state to prohibit discrimination based on sexual orientation in housing and employment.

In the 21st century, the state secured historic protections. Following the "Goodridge" decision, Massachusetts became the first U.S. state to grant same-sex marriage licenses in 2004. Subsequent laws banned transgender discrimination in state employment and public accommodations , and in 2019, the state banned conversion therapy for minors.

# Resources

https://historicipswich.net/native-americans-of-the-massachusetts-north-shore/

https://www.queerhistoryboston.org/

https://www.historicnewengland.org/property/beauport-sleeper-mccann-house/

https://hammondcastle.org/

https://www.hostcatholic.org/

https://healthq.org/

https://healthproject.org/index.html

https://www.nagly.org/

https://www.facebook.com/groups/992320235869986/

https://www.grovelanducc.org/

https://lynnmuseum.org/

https://www.speakoutboston.org/

https://www.centerboard.org/frc

https://tbabeverly.org/

https://tabernaclechurch.org/

https://www.zionbaptistlynnma.org/

https://www.gloucesteruu.org/

https://www.fbcbeverly.org/

https://www.thebostonsisters.org/

https://www.zencenternorthshore.org/

https://www.ststephenslynn.org/

https://www.grovelanducc.org/

https://www.northshorelgbtsocialnetwork.com/

https://www.otrsocialclub.com/

https://agespan.org/solutions/health-equity/

https://www.facebook.com/groups/1235955283600124/

https://www.instagram.com/queersandbeersnsma/

https://northshorepride.org/

https://www.capeannpride.org/

https://www.hwhumanrights.org/

https://www.haverhillpride.org/

https://www.facebook.com/profile.php?
   id=100094006961900&sk=about

https://www.newburyportpride.com/

https://tritownhrc.org/

https://www.unitedlynnpride.com/

https://www.unitedlynnpride.com/trl-about

## O



## P

# Heroes Collage

# About this Book

They told you that you didn't belong, didn't exist. For too long, history books have been written in silence, leaving young queer people to feel like glitches in a Puritan machine—rootless, isolated, and erased. But that silence is a lie. You are the heir to a rebellious, vibrant dynasty that has thrived on this rocky coast for 400 years. ***Queer Heroes of the North Shore*** is your story of belonging, shattering the myth that you are alone. From the granite cliffs of Gloucester to the concrete seawalls of Lynn, this ground was paved by a family you never knew you had—everyday rebels who defied convention, and groundbreaking artists who built the future. Discover your roots. Claim your power.

Jim Moser, the filmmaker and historian behind the award-winning *Through a Rainbow Lens* project, doesn't just chronicle the past; he uncovers a lineage of resistance. He reveals how our heroes used raw courage and stubborn integrity to live authentically when the world demanded their invisibility. This book is a torch passed from their hands to yours, illuminating our path toward liberation. But knowing their names is only the beginning. The true power of this legacy is a challenge left just for you. Open these pages to find your map to understanding your present by learning about our past. You'll discover why the most important chapter of North Shore queer history is the one you are about to write.

This book profiles over 150 queer people and groups, including historical figures, present-day community leaders and everyday queer people, and includes over 275 color and black and white images.

# About the Author

Jim Moser circa 1985.

Jim Moser (he/him) is a filmmaker and award-winning historian dedicated to preserving the queer experience. He produced the documentary *Finding Refuge, Demanding Equality: A Century of LGBTQ+ Lynn* and served as Project Director for *Through a Rainbow Lens: A Reflection on Lynn's LGBTQ+ History*. This groundbreaking archive, which curates 35 oral histories and over a thousand images of local queer life, was honored with the 2025 Albert B. Corey Award from the American Association for State and Local History.

Before his work in public history, Jim was a user interface designer. He originally arrived in Massachusetts on a National Science Foundation fellowship to MIT, where he earned an M.S. in Perception and Brain Science. He currently lives in Lynn with his husband, Billy, two cats, and a backyard full of flowers.

# Praise

## for *Queer Heroes of the North Shore*

"Jim Moser preserves the courage, suffering, and resilience of LGBTQ+ people on the North Shore—those who loved in hiding, endured slander, and paved the way for today's freedoms. That struggle has allowed me to serve openly as an ordained gay Christian minister. One generation calls to the next to continue the work of justice and freedom." *Rev. Donna Spencer Collins MDiv. Groveland Congregational Church*

"The sheer ambition of tackling the North Shore's Queer history on this scale deserves acknowledgement. Some of the figures included are household names worldwide, with many volumes devoted to their lives; others are remembered only in the memory of the community in which they lived and loved. The legacy of the North Shore's Queer heroes is long, complicated—and can even be intimidating—but as the author reminds us: "the alternative is silence." Moser invites the reader not only to learn about and celebrate Queer history but also to become part of a living legacy of Queer culture and to embrace the mantle of a Queer hero. " *Caleb McMurphy, Director of Visitor Services and Education, Hammond Castle Museum*

"Queer Heroes of the North Shore begins with a radical reimagining of queerness in historical context and catapults the reader through this history. We can see how the erasure and innuendo lead to pride and presence. This is a history for the beginner to learn how to read between the lines as real lives are examined in their glorious possibility, in a thread unbroken to this present moment." *Tiffany Magnolia, Ph.D. Professor of English, North Shore Community College*

# Praise

## for *Queer Heroes of the North Shore*

"I loved your book, and once I started reading it, I couldn't put it down. Your lively writing vividly captured the North Shore's queer ancestors. Thank you. You made them come to life for me." *Gordene MacKensie, co-producer of Gender Talk*

"A compelling and sensitive recounting of the North Shore's hidden queer history. Entertaining stories that will make you laugh, cry, and feel proud." *Pat Gozemba, Co-founder of The History Project*

"Queer Heroes of the North Shore is both a mirror and a megaphone, reflecting lives too often erased while amplifying stories that demand to be honored. This book matters now because visibility is not a luxury; it is a lifeline!" *Rev. Dr. Andre K. Bennett, Zion Baptist Church*

"At a terrifying moment when hard-won rights are being legislatively dismantled, and queer narratives are being scrubbed from our schools, this book stands as a defiant, necessary act of preservation. By amplifying the voices of the North Shore's past, it proves that while laws may be repealed, the truth of our resilience—once witnessed and written—cannot be erased." *Sherry Smiling Otter Gagne*

"To win internationally was a dream realized for myself; to be etched into the history of the North Shore is a promise kept to those who come after me. I stand here as proof that Black Trans joy is not just a moment—it is a legacy." *Love Miss Trans Global Diamond Chelsea Page Moses*

"This book is a brave chronicling of the stories of courageous individuals." *Elise Tamplin, history buff*

www.ingramcontent.com/pod-product-compliance
Lightning Source LLC
Chambersburg PA
CBHW051458150726
47997CB00001B/27